PETER PORTER

Collected Poems

VOLUME 2

1984–1999

Oxford   Melbourne

OXFORD UNIVERSITY PRESS

1999

Oxford University Press, Great Clarendon Street, Oxford OX2 6DP

Oxford New York

Athens Auckland Bangkok Bogotá Buenos Aires Calcutta
Cape Town Chennai Dar es Salaam Delhi Florence Hong Kong Istanbul
Karachi Kuala Lumpur Madrid Melbourne Mexico City Mumbai
Nairobi Paris São Paulo Singapore Taipei Tokyo Toronto Warsaw

and associated companies in Berlin Ibadan

Oxford is a registered trade mark of Oxford University Press

Collected Poems first published in Oxford Poets
as an Oxford University Press paperback (two volumes) 1999
Volume 2 (1984–1999)

British Library Cataloguing in Publication Data
Data available

Library of Congress Cataloging in Publication Data
ISBN 0-19-288098-5

1 3 5 7 9 10 8 6 4 2

Typeset by
GCS, Leighton Buzzard, Bedfordshire
Printed in Great Britain by
Cox & Wyman Ltd, Reading, Berks

PREFACE

This two-volume *Collected Poems* includes the work of about forty years. The first volume contains my nine books from 1961 until 1981, plus a group of poems of 1962/63 first published in *Penguin Modern Poets*, No. 2 (1962) or in *A Group Anthology* (1963), before they were included in an earlier *Collected Poems* (Oxford University Press, 1983). My thanks are due once again to Scorpion Press, the original publisher of my first three books: *Once Bitten, Twice Bitten, Poems Ancient & Modern*, and *A Porter Folio*. Since then, Oxford University Press has published all my poetry titles, other than collaborations with the painter, Arthur Boyd.

The second volume begins in 1984, and includes the six books published by Oxford up until 1997. It also includes a new collection, now published entire for the first time: *Both Ends Against the Middle* (1999).

In the Preface to my first *Collected Poems* I said that I had been reluctant to reject or rewrite earlier poems, believing that, in Louis MacNeice's words, the poet, faced with collecting his past utterance, is well advised to 'leave even not-so-well alone'. However, in this larger collection I have been a little more exigent and left out a few poems that now seem to me otiose, particularly from my more recent books.

Each book retains its original dedication.

P.P.

CONTENTS

Fast Forward (1984)

The Automatic Oracle (1987)

Possible Worlds (1989)

The Chair of Babel (1992)

Millennial Fables (1994)

I

Both Ends Against the Middle (1999)

FAST FORWARD

For Clive James

AT THE PORTA HUMANA

We, the intelligent,
who print ourselves with words,
dream of a race as natural as snails
who talk by walking on footpaths
and whose clatter shines through
clambering of customs.

There, behind the words,
those artful façades for which
so many sacrifices are demanded,
even to the agony that hardens,
sits Stuffy, old signaller
of sickness, always wanting things.

*To be loved, to be lovable,
and to print 'not negotiable'
on moments of high illumination—*
that's his uncreating touch,
turning perfection back
into personal dots and quavers.

Naturally, real truth
in its comely self-protection
shuns this guardian of drabs:
it takes holidays
among tragic brochures,
even to the pliant madhouse.

The galleries, the gardens
fill with its humanist harvest,
its belvederes are impaled on beauty.
Stuffy sits sharpening pencils,
writing explanatory letters
about love to the psychiatrists.

And the great gong sounds,
ordering, '*forget your fear of faces,
of the inexplicable, men in the lift
with too much loathing—
populate the prose-world,
inseminate the versicles.*'

But can there be a time
for plainness in this jazzle?
Can the plates and arms of fear and love
keep the species talking? Which words
will come through air unbent,
saying, so to say, only what they mean?

THE DECLINE OF THE NORTH

Round the house, among the ruined cars
And pick-ups, where the armoured lizards
Shelter in a tyre, five dogs are chained,
Five kelpies on a statutory watch.
Decibels of silence fill the day
When belling dogs and creek are tired at heart:
A kingdom comes with dust, a slaughtered sheep
Hangs from a river oak, the text of life.

Your heresy is in new starts, that wheels
And economics travel latitudes
Across the bays of hope. Home might be anywhere,
As otherwise perhaps as in a Jute Town's
Darkened warehouses abutting water
And the smell of sugar burning—that or glass
Receiving seafood pizza, hands at love
And novels with the rigor of the hour.

THE FLOCK AND THE STAR

They stepped through the gate of life,
They moved by emergency
To the exact place of delight
There by the instinct tree.

Palmer stood them in gold
And Blake invented truth
To supplement their world,
A prison without a roof.

They are the people we know
We have been or will become:
To see them best you draw
Night and a star from the sun.

They huddle because they have no
Purpose and yet are alive.
Perhaps the beauty they see
Is why they are a tribe.

Take to this picture, God,
Consider the thing you are—
The unguideable flock,
The painstaking star.

THE MISSIONARY POSITION

Since those first days it has been like this with Tellus,
That the stiff sky is always on the point of breaking
And intervention, above the roof of a shearer's hut
Or in a shower of gold, is what we may expect
Of such pent-up presences. Then there comes that
Augustinian fairness which gives us metaphors

Appropriate to our condition. Upon the roads
After a drenching resurrection, or eating in darkness,
The abandoned followers are shown a sign so
Comforting it sets as a star upon their flag,
A dog recognizes its master by a tone of tail,
The pools fill up with abstractions of the Spring.
The Little Soul itself, natured and then flung upon
The world, revisits cabins of its gloom, kiosks
Where marvellous things matured. Among the queueing gods
Long Service Veterans sigh for ordinariness,
To bring the brilliant seed of the future down
To an average hearth, there among the rugs and rules
Of generations, removed from graphs of passion,
Serve their chosen companionship face to face,
The decency and boredom of diurnal love.

ANALOGUE OF HELEN

All ladies should have one,
an eidolon for days
they kicked over the traces
so they can say
'I was here all the time in spirit
which makes the presence
of my physical body in that other place
of little consequence.'

Euripides puts it the other way round,
all Paris got was a light show,
but we are more practical
and believe in equality.
Let it be herself she disposes
not just for adultery
or interesting changeableness
but to reinforce her

exquisite readiness
to meet each moment as absolutely
alive: then she will bring
to long-postponed quarrels
some of that wide-ranging
understanding her husband displays.

And let there be signs
that the usefulness of lies
is fully understood
by civilized persons.
What you write down in love
is never untrue; the paper
grows old around the words
and any truth-loving ego
would fight a ten-years' war
in the family house to keep it so.

Eyes look at the world as emperors,
even their soft return at evening
is feudal. Where they cannot enter,
touch too is kept out.
Perhaps oddity alone will tame
baffled possessiveness—the boy
Auden and his mother
singing and playing the *Liebestod* together.
When the neurons in the brain
are tucked-up for the night
a man may have Helen to himself.

JUMPING TO CONCLUSIONS

The most unexpected things,
the way girls in the street suddenly
come to resemble Pontormo's women
and behind a frond at the pizza palace
Arethusa's fountain frothing,
the map of the sexual republic spread.
Let them race to surf or tennis,
the true corona is in books:
later, at a party, tell a blonde
how the castello was built
to terrorize the subjects of the Duke,
and when first light fizzes in your bed
console yourself that nothing but bad
literature ever happens in real life.
Nor is this a corseting or structuring,
writing essays and not poems.
Rather it's divine displacement,
the world not having any fairness
our urge to perfectibility
seeks quality in randomness.
Going backwards can be good,
Pope never again attained the maturity
he had at twenty-one: we have to know
more than we can feel, we have
to make heartless aphorisms
out of misery, even our own despair.
Such charming vistas, the river banks
approaching death, the postures of the gods,
Illyrian survival! Doomed to claim
all that we envisage, we startle
watchers on peninsulas
with feats of simply seeming,
the form is in the summoning.
Those monkeys typing encyclopaedias
seem devotional, even tactful,
they could be working on

a New Book of the Dead. Then to borrow
sweetness for a second from the species,
irritable dreams, jumping to conclusions,
among the delegates with cardboard badges,
greet the future at a soapstone villa,
the history of the world upon your tongue.

CLEANING THE PICTURE AT THE EDGES

At the Retrospective, they were full of
transferred clarity, voices explaining
that elegance is how the lecturer keeps
ahead of his bright students—his rust chimneys,
cyanide sky, Sickert taxi skidding
seen blooming alongside portraits
judged novelistic, a bend in the colon
of time/space/taste. A reviewer added
this damaging gloss: Rembrandt's grandeur
is made the subject of the caution
of a pale contemporary, thus it dies
in neatness. But he didn't ask
whether R's greatness wasn't a seeking-out
of peace, its exhaustion of itself
a quest for perfection, tidy in its way
as the neatest poem. Tomorrow Rembrandt
would have to start again, there is no end
to *terribilità* (let us for once take
Michelangelo off duty). So it is with us,
we are sure that Bach has more in common
with Shakespeare than with Gödel
but we should be careful of the books we read.
Was there not a dream where someone
rather like a poet introduced himself
as 'Anon Sequitur'? Dreams admit no jokes,
it was a warning. Then the quavers
pushed the Jordan through its banks again

and calmness separated from the dark.
Where I am sitting I have put the whole past
into a room although I know the papers
at my feet are no more than the rubbish
which floats at night to corners of the Baths.
A page from a memorandum pad
supplied by a pharmaceutical firm,
Sadlers Wells in 1957, a hopeful letter
bringing Leeds to London—I must start
to file it all away. Pain will set me on,
it wants its peace as well. Those parts of my brain
which have escaped the claws of alcohol
are setting up a federation: what
have you done to make our future certain?
Cleaned the picture at the edges, whispered
to the queue of frightened memories,
'It doesn't matter where the semen goes'—
Now I shall look into detail
for a census of good style, assigning
images to their stations on the Overground.

POEM EMPLOYING WORDS FROM AN
ARTICLE ON COMBAT STRATEGY

In the garden of our first Summer's day,
the suspension of disbelief is shown
as something to do with taking the strain,
metaphor solidifying itself
in persons once again, and here comes
the purest attrition mind-set
concluding with a slim girl in tailored jeans
asking for *Disque Bleu* in a Dumfries accent.
About her buffets the wind's body-count,
more than whole numbers of the sun,
evolution proved on deck. But she must die,
worse, must age. The General Staff cannot agree

what would fit her for a high tech. fate,
what little and expensive love
might get her flying. Sex and bewilderment
allay the afternoon, gold-plating
for the mind's most complex model.
A pity we cannot use the phrase 'come out'
of her, since that is what she's done
in emblems of the Summer, no more
a hangar-queen, with all her polished parts
stripped down, but manifest in service,
a butterfly upon the wing.
                The deterministic crowd
parts for her as she slips sideways
into Cowgate, back to its beer,
her truck-kills garnered in the gloom
of ever-open *post meridiem*.
                Another little gismo
on reality, says the poet, accessory
before the fact of helplessness.

CLIPBOARD

Just this from a life and house of plenty,
The racks of records, the books unread and read,
(Buy them and they cannot persecute you)
Cats dead, one living, wife a sheet of contacts,
Children flighting of their own volition,
Television filtering among wine glasses,
The horrible telephone biting its tongue,
A few out-of-place tropical plants—
Only this to offer the dungareed gateman,
A clipboard of papers, roster of reality,
Off-prints of dreams, the documents of an end.

The bottom ones so curly yellow and the type
Old-fashioned. They go with gardens in the heat,
A university of touch under the house
And fields of strangers circling on a lawn.
The middle ones official, stamped with what
Might be insignia of failure or success,
So interchangeable their world. The ones on top have splashes
You might use to authenticate
A legacy to libraries—coffee, wine or semen.
Whatever their value or significance
These have been gathered to present you here.

They are your hieroglyphs, your flying signs
That wing the soul under the roofs of heaven.
How much more glowing in the dying light
Might seem those towering and objective works
You never saw or mastered, that way of truth
Opaque to all biography. The sonatas, genre scenes,
Odes to Demeter are not included. Paper betrayal,
Words unredeemed by anything but death,
Such to be handed to the unattentive porter
At the gates. You lived on these poor promises,
Now they must be your friends and witnesses.

THE ARBITRARY ABROLHOS

After indifference,
a survey of vulnerability—
a liftdriver with Liszt's keyboard
in his smile, the Festival of Open Desks,
the arbitrary abrolhos!
                        What evidence
will I file against her?
Love is a fluke you might make
evolutionary by faith. Till then
dreams and logic. The grass beneath your feet

is a station of fond tombs,
the bees are fed on memory.
                    'I have not worn
my wedding ring since meeting you,
absolutely not a coincidence.'
Which of her many faces will
the sea-shouldered goddess wear
when she summons me for judgement?
                    Shadows breed shadows,
corners for dead fears, her picture,
reclining on the royal balustrade
or sharing a gin-and-tonic
with a sculpted harpy. Now to retire
like Diocletian from the mess
of a mad empire, an end to naming—
                    She is the image
silently controlling valency.

DOLL'S HOUSE

Against the haunting of our cats,
Shy raids by children visiting, it stays
As truthful as the willow flats
        Which blocked her days.

Its owner slammed the door and fled
Like Nora to the liberal hinterland.
What could resite that jostled bed?
        No grown-up hand.

The miniature hoover lies
Brim-full of dust, the chest-of-drawers gapes;
On holidays a sobbing tries
        To fluff the drapes.

And now to play at house you need
Another sort of house inside your head
 Where duty states you soothe and feed
  The plastic dead.

 Her children have outgrown it too,
But do they hear the twisting of the key,
 Entail their ruined space in lieu
  Of charity?

 Love, orderer of dolls and towns,
Has Lilliputianized the scale of pain,
 So the wide adult eye looks down,
  Bereaved again

 Of esperance, the childhood flush,
And has no passage into afternoons
 But through diminished doors and hush
  Of darkened rooms.

COMEDY LIES

Thinking of the different sorts of loneliness—

Adolescence and not to be a student
amid the glaring competence of youth—

Marriage and wheels turning in the clock-
bound passages of kith and kitchen—

Holidays with lines at midnight
playing back from hours on crumbling beaches—

Knowledge that however serious the world
its terrible moments return as jokes—

Wonderful for those poets who keep away
from meaning, living somewhere better—

Forgive me, my love, but I can remember
the poor things I wrote when I was trying—

That our private language should look cold
when all that's left of it is public

Is not surprising. Every answered dream
is merely editorial in sunlight—

Thus Hardy's point: 'Tragedy is true guise',
feelings never appearing out of uniform—

But how could we, such amateurs,
afford a panoply? We were laughing unto death—

So I pile beside my hand those books
which hold my lies and I hope you'll say your lies—

All I hear are heavy lines of diphthongs,
they tell of two people (you and I) in touch—

All sorts of loneliness become the same—

VENETIAN INCIDENT

I take for my sermon a Sunday
in Venice, walking from the dazed hotel
along the shortest way
to the Salute, and then, as so often, propelled
by my Britannic bowels, forced to take
a red-white-and-blue trip back
to our room, and you, rather than make
a fuss, said you'd meet me at the Anglican Church

on Campo San Vio (I found
the name in the Pisan pages of Pound
and it moved me more than I guessed
such a glossing reference could)—
My intestines are a species' research,
but soon enough I entered, a guest
of the Low Church sort, in the House of God
and saw you cheerfully raising and lowering,
along with some seven people and a dog,
in a ritual just short of Rome
and the priest, camply flowering
through the familiar words. You were home,
a devoted unbeliever but English and real:
I a frightened sceptic
ever willing to make a coward's deal
but till then too stiff and quick
to be at ease in High Church mysteries.
'I know my way through Holy Communion
by heart, ever since that awful Father John
taught us at Elmhirst.' Your words,
your dispensation. But God was pleased.
How do I know? Because, even if he doesn't exist,
he likes us to try to belong,
and though you were not relaxed in his world
and needed by lunch to be pissed
your lightness at living and dying expressed
Creation's plain tenure, the warrant of birds.
I saw then that those who cling to their life
are death's real retainers, that the Mass
mumbled and bobbed through is counted a pass—
I could outlive my wife
but never be natured into the space
which she proprietored.
It will never be sufficient to speak of
the peace following after;
some text must be found to remove
the permanent discord
which flesh sets on flesh. Whence comes the need

for punishment, as native to liberal souls
as to Savonarolas? Our minds breed
a cancer of starting—from God or Black Holes
we surge into certainty and thence
to eternity, dying and dying and dying
and always the wrong side of the fence.
It was joy then to pause on the path
at things coming round once more,
some words and some gestures, familiar and hollow,
a welcoming door,
the voice of our language and our sort of dogs,
expatriate ladies that cats learn to follow,
a chance of forgiving
with Venice behind us, like us exhausted
by life, and pleased to be living.

ELEGY AND FANFARE

When that cry which broke the heavens
intervened in the poet's rage,
the shape of Creation showed itself.
Think of God's large work, for which
armchairs were set out by prophets
and by elders; think this relived
by each new mind encroaching on to life—
Thus the Rilkean spatter of angels,
a glass shaking at sea; and thus
the business of invention,
dispersing feeling's clamour,
our duty to rein melancholy.
      Where in my damaged words
will you surface now to me,
bright with separation
as if eight years' passing
had washed away all pain,
language once more the twisted path

to knowledge? Standing by the headstone
in that neatly fenced new cemetery
in Cambridgeshire, I was fanned
by all your absence, wings intending
degrees of nothing, a pleasant void
one tear would rupture—and no tear came
to swing the afternoon up to my face
or as a postulant to ancient trees
alter the pace of selfishness,
my expedition to Newmarket Races.
      The cry Rilke heard
was never stilled among our fallen gods:
I listened for it through the midday hush
accommodating bees upon the little blooms
of this scarcely half-filled graveyard.
I could not fancy what his angels made,
carved out of air; indeed both past and present
murmured on. 'Whither thou goest
I shall go, thy people shall be my people
and thy God my God.' Leaded windows
enclosing panelled glass the colour
of sucked sweets, the passion of Ruth
for daily loyalty, and myself
a boy already conscious of being born
out of his time. This connected with sunny
suffering, and spurred by cowardice,
I imagined a welcome from the speaking stone,
words of Popean sylphs, the humid nymphs
of memory, '*In deinem Grab
will ich mit dir begraben sein.*'
      This is an elegy,
so forgive my German and the words I put
into your mouth. I need this distance
to proclaim the truth, and I'm the one
not yet secure in perfect night.
      No tocsin of towns
will resurrect you from the alphabet,
there is only refrigeration of remembrance,

that rhetoric the poet heard booming
and blooming in himself, most precious
of his properties, as, starred with vigilance,
he looked down the unrecurring light
to death. In his hell his heaven blazed.
        Those angels fanfared
once above the Adriatic, then again
in salons of his Middle Europe.
For me they were the English ends of hope
from which I now reluctantly retreat
recalling insolence of a young man's doom,
destined to outlive the only truth
he ever met. In Cambridgeshire
the singing will not stop until the book
of everlasting infancy is closed.
        The urn below the soil,
meridian of Meldreth,
is for geographers of finished love.

WHERE WE CAME IN

I collected my father's possessions,
a half-sovereign case, a gold watch,
fourteen carat only, my mother's rings,
and walked into the breathing sun,
                Another heat shield gone.

Fine powder of selfishness along
my upper lip, the time of jacaranda falling,
here where I was born, the cycle
not yet complete but estrangement
                Made absolute by time.

I tacked to the car as if I were drunk.
Indeed, I had lost my common sense
of ownership: when inheritance shrinks
to memory and thirty cents in cash,
                    Who's then the family man?

Yet soon in the bar above the cricket field
I rallied, due to timely punishment.
At last I was alone with incandescence
and did not question the mystery,
                    The son was now the father.

DEJECTION: AN ODE

The oven door being opened is the start of
the last movement of Rachmaninov's Second Symphony—
the bathroom window pushed up
is the orchestra in the recitative
of the Countess's big aria in *Figaro*, Act Three.
Catch the conspiracy, when mundane action
borrows heart from happenings. We are surrounded
by such leaking categories the only consequence
is melancholy. Hear the tramp of trochees
as the poet, filming his own university,
gets everything right since Plato. What faith in
paper and the marks we make with stencils
when a great assurance settles into cantos.
The Dark Lady was no more than the blackness of his ink
say those whose girl friends are readier than Shakespeare's.
Just turn the mind off for a moment
to let the inner silence flow into itself—
this is the beauty of dejection, as if our unimaginable death
were free of the collapse of heart and liver,
its faultless shape some sort of architecture,
an aphorism fleeing its own words.
Betrayal goes so far back there's no point in

putting it in poems. I see beyond the pyramid
of faces to strong monosyllables—faith, hope and love—
charitable in halcyon's memory, fine days
upon the water and weed round the propeller.
Now all the theses out of dehydration
swarm upon my lids: I was never brave
yet half an empire comes into my room
to settle honey on my mind. Last night
I quarrelled with some friends on politics,
sillier than seeing ghosts, and now this neuro-pad
is dirging for Armenia. Despair's the one
with the chewy centre, you can take your pick.
I listened to misanthropy and had
the record straight. The woman in white,
the lady with the special presents of mind,
may now be on the phone from out of town
just to keep in touch. Think, she usually tells me,
of Coleridge and days in record shops
and all those 'likes' that love is like,
a settlement to put our world in place.
What has the truth done to our children's room?
The toys are scattered, the pillow damp with crying,
chiefly the light is poor and no one comes
all afternoon: *Meermädchen* of the swamp of mind.
I kept my father waiting, he will know
that the disc, long-playing for however, ends
in sounds of surface, of the hinge and wind,
an average door, a tree against the pane.

MATUTINAL

This is ramshackle occasional,
the soft centre of a city dweller
watching swinging surgeons
at pedicure upon the plane trees.

It is a sermon of white on blueness
and a blundering at meaning
where we sat outside the restaurant
of dreams. Cover more paper
till my eyes are bright for the dark,
travelling to the mind of flame.
And for those whose flavour
is really afternoon, let light
give them this sinecure of morning,
the quiet flat, new leaves on
the imprisoned plant, a frog-like green,
the restfulness of starting.
I said I was a Puritan
but did not know myself,
disdainful of the cause of living.
I have been rescued momentarily
from all connections,
love perhaps, truth most certainly,
by this substantial missingness
beyond my window: by the 'the'
of itself, the moon-corrected air.

STUDENT CANTEEN

An arsenal of tilting flesh
Around me with its trays and shine,
Its absolutes of yours and mine,
Impatience's cute micromesh
That keeps the oldest envy fresh—
Is anything more ordinary,
More just the thing you're expecting,
Decent students one weekday?

And yet to license girls with such
Lethal weapons as their own
Faces, voices, tilt of bone,
Characteristic stance, is much
As if the upper goddess touched
Down on earth Endymion-wards,
Not for the sake of beauty's ache
But to ring sex about with swords.

The dream which keeps us comatose
However haggard we become
Is that the moon will think us young,
Go down on us where we repose,
An open excellence like a rose,
And show that hope is truly love—
What we have done concerns no one
Since value is confessed above.

You cannot hold such fancies here
Where youth is massing for the kill
(It doesn't know this is its skill).
The creamy tension of this fear
Lights the coffee, dulls the beer,
Sets constellations in the hair
Of sultry teens of average means,
Their novels unread on a chair.

I come here almost every day
As if I walked from heavy dreams
Into some light supporting scenes,
Metalogue to a Satyr Play.
Discontent won't go away,
It marches miles from class to quad
To parody humourlessly
The chauvinism of a god.

THE BIOGRAPHER PROMENADES

Consider the terraced living of these cows,
Devoid of soul but denizens of fields
From the Ringback Hills to Divagation Brook—
Pondered at depth, their biographies
Have all the lucid exaggeration of Jesus
From passivity of clover to a Via Dolorosa
Of slatted trucks. Best of all, they typify
My huge good fortune; their lives need me
To make importance—for once the publisher
Will say, 'I am almost in a position
To put nothing but your name upon the jacket.'

This sort of symbolism pleases me.
I am at one with scholars in their freezing texts.
Our exhibits are worthy only because we
Are their custodians. I might stage a search
In one of the better picture libraries
For a shot of a specially scabrous sort
(Like Nietzsche and Rée in the cart at Zürich),
But I would not even hope for more revealing
Information. More means worse. The Devil
Puts his arm round each of us and whispers
'Your secret life is absolutely riveting.'

O but I have seen them! My quintets, sextets, octets,
As I put them in the shafts! On good days,
I drink a narrow glass of water, laced
With lemon, and set out for the Archive
Knowing that the evening brings the raw stuff
Closer, a raffish party at which I act
Pecksniff, and we know, yes we all appreciate,
I'm just kidding—getting in on the ground floor—
But that is where I venture naturally
(The good biographer is part of what he tells),
Upstaging subjects for the public's sake.

Ever since Tacitus it's been like this,
Or perhaps the man who followed Gilgamesh
With pad and pencil. Sorting the plankton, bandar-log
Of followers, girl-friends, pimps, hand-holders,
Mothers, vicars, fellow-undergraduates,
Colluders in the cold. Art can look after
Its own, but men's frail putrid lives
Need advocates. I need a space myself
If not upon Parnassus then on that slope
Appropriate to late democracy
Where words, not bones or faces, are laid down.

MARIANNE NORTH'S SUBMISSION

We are born to whiteness,
And must mark it with those graphic miles,
Creaturely or vegetable,
Scribbled on the gums of New South Wales,
Firmly sententious lines
Though not of God. Such squiggles may seem
Appropriate roads on maps in Heaven. If there is a Heaven
It's because there must be something
We have moved away from. It's hardly heavy,
Only a smoke to emerge from
As if above an orchid-flooded valley,
With a dry sketching-pad, a day ahead of me
And nerves for once indicative.
I cannot remember when I consented
To be born. It was many years after
My entrance on this earth. I was poised
High enough, though what our flesh must do
To be naturally patrician I leave to those
To calculate who find our planet habitable.
So many do, and oh my heart and more my eyes
Go out to unreflective strugglers,
Vines, stamens, steamed-open lilies,

Voluptuous catechizers of the death camp
We call jungle—or the reticulated root,
Shading a scorpion, which knows the hour
To lift leaf systems to the sanded air.
I can bore even myself, working at
My natural wonders. I know as well as you
That this is complex only to the pen
And to my difficult purveyance. I could pack
A camera and put my life's work
Out of business. All my laborious
And loving pictures sometimes seem
Like women's dress materials laid out
In a mercer's pattern-room. I like
All complexities to be of shape
And observation, of pure distinctive essence.
The Higher Creature has simplicities of action
And arrangements called philosophy,
The which they tell me our spirited country
Has brought to their apogee. I put away galoshes
And take out my deepest waders. To any watcher,
Including God, I am a middle-aged lady
Of the dauntless British sort feeling not
Very well in a Burmese swamp—there she goes,
You say, escaping the Victorian Sick Room
But not evading fear. Do you know
My farthest journey has been away from suicide?
Let this lizard fern I'm sketching
Speak for me: 'she serves that filigree
Along the air my svelte and dappled self
Keeps pennanting above our high monsoon,
A single real beyond imagining.'

THE CATS OF CAMPAGNATICO

Since a harebrained Devil has changed the world
To scenes from a Nature Documentary,
There are those of us who will forever seek
Rational landscapes, dotted with walled cemeteries,
Unquestioned rivers of familiar fords
And an efficient bus from which adulteresses
Alight before the ascent to the neighbour village.
Not that His blocked thumb is absent: those
English families tooting along the scatty road
(Our fifteen-year-old crunching the clutch
Of the little Fiat) are outside the cemetery
Before anyone notices the just-widowed blob
At the armorial gates—the regret, the shame,
The silence—she at the gardens of death which need
A constant tending, and us hurrying
To lunch at the hydrophilic villa—
The Oldest Presence of All will be well pleased.
Not just a vignette, we reflect, this shadowless day
In Southern Tuscany, more a looking for shades
Which match the petrified intelligence of time:
One sees the small bends which history makes
In the lanes of scarcely-visited villages.
True, this one is in Dante, and that oleander-screened wall
You take for the headquarters of the Carabinieri
Might be an out-station of the Piccolomini,
If only you could remember which is which
Among the towers that mark the lesions of the sky.
Siena is as far away as London; life as far away
As last night's dream whose every promontory
Is in the present. Now, coming through the gate,
The view is a pastoral benediction for those
Who have never lived in Arcadia. *Thank God,*
Grace à Dieu, Gott sei dank—we are
As international as an opera festival,
We who love Italy. We have no home
And come from nowhere, a marvellous patrimony.

Then before the laying of the table in the arbour,
The helpful barefoot girls from good schools,
The gossip and the wine, a sudden vision
Of belonging. The cats of Campagnatico,
Which are never fully grown and have never
Been kittens, will not move for the honking motorist
But expect to be gone round. Thin and cared-for,
Fat and neglected, watchful and hardly seen awake,
Cool-haired in the sun and warm in shadow,
Embodying Nature's own perversity,
They lie on this man-made floor, the dialectic
Of survival. O God, we cry, help us through
Your school of adaptation—between the fur of the cat
And the cement of extinction, there are only
Cypress moments lingering and the long tray of the sky.

A GUIDE TO THE GODS

You must recall that here they are intense,
Our gods. Each corner shop may need oblations
So the genius rests content. Kick a dog turd
Leftways to the gutter, but only if it be
Dry and crumbling. Every third display of okra
On the footpath must be stolen from—one finger
Will suffice. Touch your collar points when
Passing electricity showrooms, for there
The ghost of light supports a goddess
Veiled in wrath. Parades of the holy mad
Transferring parcels should be followed
(But judiciously). Bag women and drunks
Have been identified as Furies, but I
Do not wholly credit this. Hurry home before
The postman if you see him near your door:
That letter threatening a visit will not come.
Parse the shorter sentences in Health Food Stores,
Their higher prices are most magical.

Believe me, burst water mains may be
Oracular, but every man of sense resists
Coercion. When they wish to speak to us
The Gods behave with plainness and with modesty.
Next time I'll tell you about Zeus
Haephestos, Artemis and other probabilities,
But that is fiction and not upon our scale.

SANTA CECILIA IN TRASTEVERE

I found here only the music of exclusion,
gates locked upon flowers and fountain,
a *hortus conclusus* of organized sound
for its mother to rest in when the birds
and children blanched her silence. I had wanted
this best of picture-postcard saints to be at home
when I called, bringing her I thought
greetings from the contrapuntal North,
territories where ears hear differently.

How hard they had to work to kill her—
nearly snuffed out in the calidarium,
hacked in the neck by a swordsman and singing
to the end. But lucky after all to have
this architectural palimpsest for home,
far from those grim and anal catacombs,
the Christian labyrinth. The sun blazed on gates
which kept me out and the garden shone with dust,
a fleck for everything put here to dance.

With Christ and his radiant eschatology
she can have little to do. A cardinal might weep
to behold her bones in golden wrappings, but we
will hear her in the lift of blood as, joyful
for the world she sets before us, patroness,

we trek the dry Janiculum. Her thunder
is the face of beasts, apotheosis of
a natural sweetness, death at the end
sounding a miracle, tempering transcendence.

One of her adepts pronounced that art
posing as religion is the worst vulgarity,
yet what more baffling for the tired pilgrim
than to find himself excluded from a shrine
hallowed by a working saint? Rome and Florence
it seems are always closed to us
but fond Cecilia leaves her door ajar. 'This not
unpleasing Eighteenth Century church' (I quote)
enfolds a darkness round our lightest step.

UNFINISHED REQUIEMS

How could they come to an end,
With the grateful creator completing
His blots and boredom and writing his
Laus Deo, as he has done so often
And as he knows his Father in Heaven
Would had He someone to look up to?

Symphonies are different, abandoned
Perhaps, essentially themselves
Whatever the state of the manuscript
Or ambivalence of the critic. We'll prove this
By asking you to point to one
Where the long-lost scherzo isn't dull.

That is why there are only two ways out:
Either you plan your requiem for
A hero of the state, and write it all
If your collaborators are sluggish,
Or you welcome The Stranger in Grey
Never doubting who or what he is.

You can escape the danger perhaps
By writing two or more requiems
(If C Minor first, then D Minor later).
Which is the one for yourself? Silly to ask,
They both are, and the liturgy
Is a long letter from you to nowhere.

So even if your fever shouts at you
Halfway through the *lacrymosa*
And your pet canary seems a soul
On Charon's bark, your work
Is no less finished than that of
The shy man bowing towards the Royal Box.

Life is left in middle manuscript
And widows, critics and descendants
Can get it ready for performance
And those warming royalties. Predecessors
Enjoying eternal rest will tell you
The unfinished theme is always bitterness.

LITTLE HARMONIC LABYRINTH

Come stars and beg of the one star
a progress through the laughing fields
beyond our pink-walled town.
The little monkey on its cushion
brings the priceless gift
of sexual desire. Without this rubbing
luxury there'd be no chasseresse
of envy, nothing but our getting staler
on the avenues of evening.
How dare they share this gift,
these best of lucky solipsists—
'On this soft anvil all mankind was made.'
And the tyrant will,

unrepentant of its mediocrity,
is governor of created things.
The flight from meaning is our magic:
overhead a perfect line of birds
pegged out to dry—the picture shows
where dreams have passed,
trooping to a reborn god.
O captains of your consciences,
the world's a middle sea
washing tearful stories to the shore—
Tell of blushing Psyches
in little breasts and sneakers
bringing serfdom to tomorrow,
reflate the fluffy trees, the cobalt sky,
in allegories of sin
with all our ages snickering in bushes.
Even the guaranteed untalented
have style of their own, our God
has given us immunity
from everything except ourselves.
No wonder I have dreamed
the living and the dead are one,
that out of their congestion
a planet rises which has sounds for air
whose syntax may be synthesized.
O eyes I cannot meet,
yours, preppy teenage gods,
show me something serious
beyond imagination. When sex dries
all that's left is abstract,
completed outlines without presences.
Find me a star to shine
through the whiteness of the mind.

TO HIMSELF

A Working from Leopardi

My exhausted heart
It is time for you to rest.
The final deceit is over, the one
I thought would last for ever.
It is dead, this love is dead
and I am content that with it
dies all hope of fond illusions
and any real desire to harbour them.
Rest now forever, heart,
you have worked too hard,
your every movement comes to nothing
and the earth which moves beneath you
is not worth sighing for.
Bitterness and emptiness compose our world,
there is nothing else; our life is made of mud.
Heart, be quietened now,
you have found your last despair.
To human kind fate has allocated
only dying: scorn Nature then,
the brutal power which rules for misery,
and the vanity of everything that is.

DIS MANIBUS

In Memory of Claudius, died August 1980

Here before me is a space
which should contain you.
I still live in it, ridiculous
this definition of happiness.
You were a cat and humans are designed
to love other special humans.

When they do they try a little.
We never tried with you,
we didn't have to.
We must be decent people
to have been given you for company.

You deserve a very formal poem
in a complex stanza shape
and a cat-flap-banging metre
(but we had no cat flap
and you had to sneak out and play
jokes on us upon the stairs)—
Let's see you take again our teasing love
as you took your narrow world above the street
and pain beside the piano's icy pedals.

God forgive this helplessness of friends.
You died in a box in a car
and love could not get you out.
The theory is that what we write
mimics what we feel
and that's worth a prisoner's laugh.
Sleep, Claudie, where you are.
God's rule-makers will not give
you a soul, but, believe me,
you are no worse off without one.
Winter is upon us, the tree of life
is withering. To settle into death
with your tail at a comfortable curve,
that's style. Short views, few words
and empty evenings now. They are coming
to take me to a marvellous party
and whom do I expect to see? My host—
a big black dazzling ambulatory cat.

A VEIN OF RACINE'S

In this vain valley of ambition pleas cannot be bargained.
As in the spent Renaissance, life turns to the ideal,
And thus, distrustful of its place, its plage, the hotting-up
Domain of Demos, it sets its transcendental cooker for
An hour beyond all frenzy to call us to that noble feast,
Interior satori, a dish to put before Self-Emperors.
Sitting in the nylon static of motels, what alexandrines
Have we to repel the public day? Form is a lazy witness
Seeing whatever it finds easiest to see. The classics are brought
  down
To courses on comparative belief. This is not the fault
Of idle teachers; rather such consummate victories were bought
At high rates once by calm custodians in rooms so
Humanistically exact for sunlight and approved debate
That when the trays were cleared and once the mercenaries had
  swarmed
Past tapestry that muffled Tasso, only blows by brutes
Had style. Everything and everyone was clangorous for honesty,
The world became one Salon des Refusées. But do not look
Just at our telemetric world and its refined abstainers:
Consider in its place academies at one of several palaces
Where feudal waters sink into evening gold—what did
Those princes and those poets promise defenestrated Man?
Only to confuse his single fate with that of species,
Blood and the burden of our winsome natures he
Might find a phantom for. Always there was elsewhere,
The Golden Age, the Innocentest Isthmus, a land on
Stalks beyond the eyes of youth. When the Prince had raged
Through statues, tempios and the scrolls of his Isotta
He grafted Nature; he could think of welfare, care for
The nameless many casting his shadow on the square.
They took the hint; love alone will tell all shades of creatures
They are one. Thus came the Proverbs of Democracy—
You will get the broad apotheosis you are waiting for,
You will put the gods inside you and make death their king,

You will know your nervous system a bland oracle—
And yet the gathering storm approaches, it seems that Man,
Tamed by his tapestries to play Actaeon on the plain,
Cannot be redeemed. The youth his girl friend, the warrior
His tall challenge, the poet his obsession in the head,
A programme vulgar as the planet is unveiled:
Power and response, the Myth of Circumstance,
Great men impaled on history—nothing comes between
The goddess and her darkness when she loves, disturbance
Of the common decencies of lust, that moment when she sees
Her prey, about to inherit the innocence of the world.

GOING TO PARTIES

for Philip Larkin

Truth to experience, to the sombre facts,
    We all believe in;
That men get overtaken by their acts,
That the randy and highminded both inherit
Space enough for morals to conceive in
    And prove the pitch of merit;
Such insight hangs upon the scraping pen
Of the deep-browed author writing after ten.

But there behind him, if he chose to look,
    The ranks of those
Whose sheerest now is always in a book
Are closing; yes, he's broken up some ground;
It lies about in other people's prose,
    Great graces that abound—
Meanwhile, incorrigibly, people seem
To write their own existence from a dream.

Perhaps it makes him think of earlier days
    When parties beckoned,
Quartz studs glittering in a bank of clays,
And he'd set out, though apprehensive,
Hoping this time to come in first, not second,
    Ready to really live,
Only to find that life which offers chances
Ignores the sitters-out and picks the dancers.

Yet he got something there. How to enjoy
    Expansive moments,
How it must stun the gods to be a boy
Who will not bear the cup, how unasked
Guests act prosecution and defence
    (Who was the man in the mask?)
And how exhilarating when alone
To know those dandies walk on stilts of bone.

Tributes then; the party isn't over,
    A few guests linger.
From heartland England on to distant Dover
People are shutting doors they know too well
And following their feet to hope, the bringer
    Of several shapes of Hell,
Of time, experience, and all we use
To make art of a life we didn't choose.

THE HEDONISTS
REHEARSE THE UPRISING

In two hours it will be Fasching
and our watches will tell us
we are having a good time.
Misery, say those returning from
the temple where the scanner
reads the lump, is as palpable
as sunshine.

The countrymen of God
are setting out the sails, the oars,
the sandwiches, or to some,
who like to place their bets both ways,
the stomach pumps.
Slaves to duty,
as much at fifty as fifteen,
the hedonists are still in service
lest Saturday night and holidays
be their accusers. But what of work,
a drug beyond addiction?
'I continue to compose because
it fatigues me less than resting.'
Who could face meeting such a God
in abstract dark?
Grave lines of souls
are pressing to the waterside,
the boys like Botticelli angels
in the tinted air, the girls immaculate
in skinshine. How art nouveau
the very leaves of longitude
and berries of contentment!
A spider might swing from this
encampment of bold staves
in search of morning succulence.
The play-power oxymoron
has us in its thrall. We shall
never know how dense time was
in Paradise, nor what it is
to put things simply.
Meanwhile, the One
we nominate looks up from joy
of being here: he has not forgotten
what he wrote so many years ago
upon his pencil box:
John Everyman,
Home Villas, 1, Fabled Prospect,
Good Town, La Patria, This Hemisphere,
The Earth, The Solar System,
The Milky Way, The Universe.

FAST FORWARD

The view from Patmos, the ghost inside
the module! Living neither long enough
nor so curtly brings us nominative snakes,
time turned to blood upon the hour,
fours and sevens when the Lamb lies down
with Fury. And then Sir Headlong tells us
he has tripped and toiled along a donkey path,
the scala of so many angels, with a guide
who features in the brochures: old white hopes
that flavour an apocalypse, aunties
of the terrible abstractions, all made decent
when the fire has crept into a governed switch.

Now it is remaindered into visions,
into the history of the race, fast-forward,
the tape so stretched it might at any second
snap to oblivion. And they understood,
those heavy visionaries on poles
or sorting through the dung of lions,
that the countenance of state,
rock-featured and as bright as Caesar's eyes,
floats on insane shoulders. The boat for Patmos
is never late and though the island's rainfall's
doubtful its climate is compact despair,
angels in uniform identified on land.

Sitting with a little health-food lunch
among the flowers of a military estate,
we have to calm ourselves by crooning
death songs to the mush of midday heat.
Left to itself, the brain, circuiting the world,
becomes a rapid deployment force
and blasts ashore on any troubled sand.
Where will the end be staged, and whose hand,
held against the light, shall glow, brighter
than a thousand suns? Helicoptering
in lightning numbers, the god of prose
hears his own voice prophesying peace.

THE AUTOMATIC ORACLE

For Christine

A SOUR DECADE

These are the years which furnish no repentance
       Though seamed with sore regret:
       So much would selflessly be done and yet
Print no true sentence.

That grief sits down in books but is no writer
       Must be the just rebuke,
       And every lightless evening proves a fluke
The one grown brighter.

A careless management of things, they call it
       Who pose for God or Fate
       The purpose of the Infinite and Great
And here install it.

These decades, all the decimals of feeling,
       Are pressing on our schemes.
       On childhood walls, on corridors of dreams,
The paint is peeling.

CLUTCHING AT CULTURE

That same purr-voiced disc jockey
has been too long among the toast today—
we've had them all,
a rave from the grave,
a rumble in the tumbril,
a suture on the future—
And breakfast used to be sanctuary
after the draught of dreams
and before the shop-front terror.
My daughter has gone out to work
and left me with the cat.
I look above my head
to the hardboard pinned with family snaps.

There she is, dressed in a tabard
with braided edges, holding tight the hand
of someone safe. A seraph
of the dangerous world, it seems
she's one step only from omnipotence,
as if she said with her unfailing smile,
Now is the ending of the world
and now goes on forever.

RURITANIAN RESIDUALS

There, in the re-grown jungle,
a crashed Dakota or a Zero
and skeletons in khaki shorts
to be chanced upon by mineralogists—

Fathoms down, outside Murmansk,
after the acetylene intrusion
on the door-stopped ingots,
putty, cod-soft corpses in the dark—

Metaphors of human hope,
something we should not disturb
when we try the archaeology
of reminiscence—

At the Durbar of a thousand curry houses
the British Empire seems the greatest
piece of theatre the world has ever seen,
the gatling stuttering, the battleships in circles—

Thinking of love and duty, trying to hear
imagination's voice, the noise-floor
is too high, the Hooghly jammed with bodies,
a death-tide in the blood—

And drifting over, a cloud
of radioactive history presaging
cancer when? The spooks were always there
in Ruritanian redoubts—

If we executed one in seven
of our economists, the financial pages
would look rosier: but the curtain rises
on actors at an empty matinée—

Terrorists cannot stop material flow
or new Prep Schools appearing.
Listen in the Pleasure Gardens, that's
the Ghost Train running into Dachau—

The life of dividends, residuals
of the world's colossal comedies,
grosse Kleinkunst versus kleine Grosskunst,
nightmares of conviction—

And where to place the verbs in this?
Life has turned to pictures of us
as we were, and the Great Exhibition
plays host again to staring mendicants—

THE PRINCE OF ANACHRONISMS

Adolescents smelling frangipanni
Watch with healthy hopelessness the girl
Next door whose breasts jog past the paling fence.
A Virgin by Matteo di Giovanni
Nets a million for a Seventh Earl:
Everything is in the present tense.

Screw those experts who insist they know
Tuscan economics or what Haydn
Heard when his french horns played B in alt.
Winds that live inside the mind may blow
Quarter on to quarter, they collide in
Safe Sargassos of imagined salt.

Friends, I love you but I will not buy
Transcendental global sophistry—
Nature's what it is, no shibboleth,
History's perspective is a lie.
Art is the same age eternally,
Births are anniversaries of death.

STICKING TO THE TEXT

In the Great Book of Beginning we read
That the word was God and was with God,
And are betrayed by the tiniest seed
Of all the world's beginnings, to thrash
Like sprats in a bucket, caught in deed
As in essence by shapes of ourselves,
Our sounds the only bargains we may plead.

So starts this solipsistic essay about words,
Its first stanza chasing its own tail,
Since no word will betray another word
In this sodality, self-repressing and male,
And we discover, hardly believing our eyes
And ears, a sort of chromatic scale,
That whatever lives and feels is logos.

Tell us then, vanity, what is truth
And how does it differ from honesty?
Ecclesiastics and analysts play sleuth
To that slippery murderer, but they require
The rack and the couch, tell the story of Ruth
Out of her country, such cheats of championship
As the Noble Savage or General Booth.

We can know only what words may say
Though we may say what we know is untrue.
Honesty lines up its troops—Thersites,
Iago, Tartuffe, The Abbess of Crewe—
The confessional rolls, the lottery pays
Timely prizes to me and to you,
Truly honest people, tied to the wheel.

And when love announces it is here
Either with a lily and spasm of light
Or rising from a childhood bed of fear
To assume its pilgrimage of grace,
It brings its style wars and its gear,
The triolets of touch, the ribboned letters,
Pictures of Annus Mirabilis or just last year.

Keeping ahead of death and Deconstruction
We have the text we need to play the game,
But what should we do to make it personal—
Your text, my text—are they the same?
The rules are on the inside of the lid
As fate appoints its contestants and fame
Picks one from the Great House and one from the Pale.

Too many fortunes are made by the Absurd:
It's better to run in the linear race
Where everything connects which has occurred,
Better to suffer the nightmares natural to
The body and tell what you have heard
Among your fellow-sufferers and hope
The story's end won't choke you on a word.

THROW THE BOOK AT THEM

Where do we go to live? We're born ticking
on the page and from the first disclosure on
we sense that time is useless without fear.
So here must gather all those claques of fact
we make good use of—and what are they
but words? Imagine the tight nucleus we know
is true inheritance: we find nothing more
to do with it than turn it back to chaos.
Proust could get ten thousand lines from
one night at a party and Robert Browning
knew he was in love only when he found he'd
said so on the page. How Elizabeth
loved his profile when it hovered over her
in trochees. Personification's special dangers
outweighed Daddy's growlings and the bladder
weakness of poor Flush. Rochefoucauld
spoiled things with his fully-frontal maxim:
it's all much cooler really, exile under cypresses
and chatting at the well, but never far
from the cherished self-immersing diaries—
no matter how fast they fill, white paper presses
on the eyes of nightmare and the black dog
barks defensively. There are mornings
in the bathroom when a wonky razor seems
pons asinorum of responsibility,
but don't despair, a brush with life's not final
till it's found a way to do the rope-trick
with dependent clauses. Dying's a book
with uncut pages; the pentel scurries and the tea
grows cold, and back in London a publisher
announces a burnished tome on Tuscany.
To get through life, just join the dots up, they
may prove a subcutaneous punctuation.
Today in Rouen there is an Avenue
Gustave Flaubert, but nothing spoils the stillness

at his desk. The DPP has all he needs
to start the trial—the boys in blue, the talkative
punk witnesses slurping from chipped cups.
The rules remain: you are the books you write.

THE ACHING CATALYST

Flaking in a private room
All he has of fifty years
Hired from his mother's gloom
Seems a patronage of fears,
Balustrade and harbour-boom
More than gallows or death-bed,
Foolish gold not chosen lead.

Comfort finds a way to say
Greyness is a gloating light,
Abstract of the burning day
Changed to pictures in the night,
But the process slips away—
Here's the chair and he's here too
Guessing what the world might do.

World's the aching catalyst
Actions cannot do without.
Feelings think they can exist
Here and now and never doubt
Skill of eye and tongue and wrist,
But they camouflage the act,
Accessories before the fact.

the last Muse is waiting on the corner
in the coldest weather. There have been
arts and achievements piled as high
as ziggurats in a National Geographic
artist's impression of Babylon,
but real desire is a smaller thing
and bolder—it is to possess a body
just long enough for a part of ecstasy
to detach itself from the mainspring of the world
and come to you. You'll have time left over
to consider the Hanging Gardens . . .

ready to run after the public when
they've got ahead, saying 'Wait for me,
I renounce all my old obscurity'.
Temperament trips you up, you're left
with difficult books among the weekend shopping,
and still no grant. This is an old art
with too many new faces and the jargon
is always changing. 'Video killed the radio star'
as clouds drift down the valley, changing
green to grey to blue, assaults on misery
which must be hidden from your notebooks . . .

if those clouds went blue to green to grey
you would know the world had gifts, rain
upon a reservoir, the first drops speckling
its surface like the skin of trout and you'd say
grace for a blessing: the trouble is your shock,
too much talent in the world, it can't absorb
its own creation; there are queues in Heaven
as the million dreams fight to be born
and troop before the face of vindication—
these tribunes of themselves are pleased and helpless,
kissing a cheek held up in practised sorrow . . .

under this sign you will conquer,
go on and over the page to new worlds
and new movements. Run now down the hill
to a coast of high-cliffed islands
with a valance of bright picnic-grounds,
be reunited where they sell fresh chances
with a slimness long since squandered—
here must be forgiveness for existing,
'muddled and disappointing', and then she's *there*
your laconic Muse, bow-legged, in her wedding-suit,
instantly recognizable, coming up and saying . . .

THE REST ON THE FLIGHT

The painted pale projectile moves and seems
Hardly to move to those inside its tide
Of twilight, as the close alliterative
Miles are ticked off charts of cloud and ocean
And still the pilgrim's face is held to sun
And still his stomach turns. A comb of words
Runs through his strands of thought continually,
Reminding him of God and lunch, of dust
At the end of day discountenancing shoes,
Of mango trees and winds in March. These props
Are human, more so than the glittering sprays
Of alcohol, the swimming-pools of in-
flight movies, or reminiscences of men
Returning to the Gulf. Packed into fear
With splendidly unlikely comrades, he
Out-herods Herod in this great escape
And relishes the massacre. Calling
The stewardess and asking for another
Miniature, he relaxes momentarily,
Is able even to risk formal scansion,
Seeming in this nowhere to stand up
Alone for seriousness, and yet frivol

In uncertainty—caparisoned
In blank verse in the blanker sky, his wings
Take him on to no place just to make
It plain to rulers of nativity
That godhead starts at home. Bring another
Whisky to the caravanserai—
At thirty thousand feet all solemn words
Are juggled out of sentence by the air,
What bubbles up is terror in its handy shape,
Heard through the headset as the ghost of hope—
Now you can write the history of the world,
Soon the little plates of Pentecost
Will be brought round accompanied by a tray
Of heated napkins, and the nose will dip
Towards the phosphor of a city; you're
Back once more to merchandising truth
Under wings of excellence, a miracle
Which Boeings make from immanence of sky.

TO LACEDAEMON DID
MY LAND EXTEND

The heavy spirit of ambition
tells you to write first this way,
then the next, to station envy
at the door of Nature's clubmates,
circulate among Time's franchise-takers,
simply to make the most of being here—
there is no coming back, don't sourpuss
the talent-network which is all you have.
　　　　　　Good advice, right feeling,
though it's well to think of standing
on a wood verandah, with the gale
flapping briefly through the canvas booms
and know just as the house lizards know
that legs of self are made for running

          Once life can sense its end,
the grinding ghost inside is what
the ego-soul most wants to let go of—
departed now the tenant who would suck his soup,
the housekeeper who moulded soap-ends
into parti-coloured balls,
fled with the breakfast post
the cashiered colonel who let you test
his regimental sword—
                    If these are fiction's butts
it makes no odds: life's particulars
are interchangeable at the end,
our memories written by the blood
in uproar. Judgement Day will be a raffle
or the spirit's hankerings
noted by the watchful staff—
the 'good' Russian table and the 'bad'.
                    Inside the egg
first stirrings are fatigued already:
Creation must create itself once more
to find the fire. When I was young
I drugged myself with opportunity
and so lay speechless on my bed all day
unplaiting shadows. Words which spoke to me
I locked in amber. Now I am by the water,
under vines and stars, waiting for nothing,
another glass of wine to hand, a page
cooled by turning: the inventory is short—
the ants, the kitchen light, a bat re-crossing,
a drying shirt, Doreen the Dog.

A TRIBUTE TO MY ENEMIES

Apart from God I suppose I have none.
It takes some nerve to scale the heights
Of another person's privatest decorum,
I mean his hate. Better locate them,
Such hired riparians of straight reportage,
Jaundiced judges of a bootleg happiness,
In the sad intestines, losing out through age,
Opacity and alcohol.
          But they would be useful,
Those enemies, to give my life a kind
Of focus. Not just besieging horrors
Scanned and sulked at in some North of England
Editorial, or subsidized experimenters
Glowering in grey-faced halls of education,
Hastening with terracotta folders to a class
Of willing Sufis—not even the towering
Yea-preachers whose laser scorn could track
Me down through all my dark of triteness
With the cry, 'You, especially you, don't matter.'
          No, I must play creator
And make them up, these hierophants.
Invention is the mother of necessity
In the dreaming mind: fear abhors
A vacuum. Since God's on holiday
These are my shadows of impatience,
My nutrients of the future. Chiefs of Capability
Who can hold the corners of the world down,
Frogmen of the sexual swamp who have title
To all treasure, realtors, Realpolitikers,
Plainsmen with blue eyes come into town
Clutching translations of Catullus—
Would they be myself had I the courage?
          I have dreamed them back so far
They are sexless, legless appetite in a mouth
Beneath a leaf waiting for the tell-tale shine
Of presence. This pad of words is just

My camouflage. I am the prototype
Of elderly animosity whose extenuation
Is to eat the words of love. I await them here,
My enemies in a thousand colours,
They will know me, I'm listening
To Bellini in the frosty dusk, the same
Performance once we heard at the Fenice
Vespering death. Music will last until
The brain has massacred its ambient creatures.

HOME AND HOSED

To whom it may concern,
the matter of disposal of my body at my death.

I shall get the jokes over early.
My cat Flora is not likely to outlive me,
otherwise I would will her my feet and guts
and, of course, my genitals,
(about the weight of a small tin of Whiskas),
but we are still within the Unitary State
and may not feed our cats
on the riddling remnants of our lives.

No, consign it to the fire.
Take it to the undenominational ghats
set down drives of sycamores
beyond the golfing suburbs;
there the parsons are all locums,
prayers are culled from instances
of Anglican good taste and Presbyterian surprise,
the wreaths alone baroque,
and Bach without belief washes our formal faces.
Keep this shell in which I hermited
from the black and invoice-laden men
who cleanse our world of death.

The priggish Baron who told Mozart's widow
not to waste her cash on coffins
wasn't wrong—'eine schöne Leich'
fits out the Viennese for festival
but Mozart's unmarked resting place
is inspiration to us all. I summon up
the silly cardboard castles and ideal lodges
of Australian Undertakers,
their presidencies of Rotary Clubs,
their Sunday programmes of soft music.
Surely the dead are livid at the living.
Hunter and hunted must come home.
Heaven which listened with ears of flesh
still sits insipid in the eaves of time:
Hell the forthright can't hold its own
against the newest movies; only blood,
blocked from tending to far-off oedemas,
races up-river to replete apocalypse.

I have limped far from high seriousness.
Assessors with my card in hand
will raise not a smile—'this flesh you were lent
is due for replacement, but yours is a case
without special merit. You made little sense
with your cries, bent no tonality
out of its rictus; you seem to us like
a sheep on an A road burst through a fence,
all tangle and terror. But, as proprietor
of some of our maker's immaculate filament,
you may call on the guarantee. Love,
great star of the terrified heavens,
shines on your head. It is time, true time
to give back your body. Know that the creek
keeps on flowing, the swallow skims to the wire,
someone is starting to climb up Saddleback.'

Soul's straightforwardness is crimped in the fire.

PARADIS ARTIFICIEL

Barbel-cheeked and hammer-toed,
I'm scrambling up a river bank
in a landscape by Claude.

I'm not bothered by that group
of humid Muses, or Apollo's
booming cattle, his frogs with croup.

I am myself a metaphor
the painter didn't think of. I'm
the monster the readers are waiting for.

The countryside's classic,
stuffed with temples and nymphs,
glazed like boracic.

And into Arcadia, bump,
comes me. As Terry Southern said,
girls go for ghouls, hump! hump!

The music I make them hear
is genital intarsia,
kinaesthesia, or sex in the ear.

How did Europe get like this?
Look at the boring planning,
crepuscular taking the piss.

Out on a verandah the gods
are having a sundowner.
They live forever, poor sods.

Unlike the sharp-eyed fellow
who dreamed this picture up,
wetting his death-bed's pillow.

I'm off then, truffling through grass
like Nebuchadnezzar, all knees—
the artist can kiss my arse.

His world's not a pretty sight,
he and his nymphs need me
to guide them through the night.

PARADISE PARK

It is a time of the distancing of friends,
Of quarrels between the possible and impossible,
Of a face thrust at yours calling itself honest,
Of complex words outfacing polysyllables
Shouting through darkness to grey Menschenhass—
Now the sun is setting on the Great Divide
And there is nothing to do and nowhere to hide.

The New has been made and the afterwork sparkles
On barbicans of tenderized cement;
First Worlds and Third Worlds are equally fatigued
Importing and exporting barely describable butterflies
And alloys of the perfect miracle: trade goes on
Beyond Apocalypse and the dying and the hopeless,
Hurdles of misrule leapt lightly by the Press.

It is also a time of renunciation, of the artist
That master of paradox, becoming invaluable
By giving up hope, of his escaping his egotism
By abandoning his art. And who will notice,
Among the lengthening queues for Retrospectives,
A sacrifice so slight it moves no pivot's sliver
On warning systems in the nocturnal silver?

For, despite Doomwatch and its calibrated fright,
The human creature is forever coming into
Its inheritance, and out of little towns making
Famous hats and from stevedoring fastnesses
On unsavoury rivers, provincial hopefuls
Arrive at the capital, saving for the Weekend Ark,
The Violent Prater, the sails of Paradise Park.

You may sit at glass-topped tables with white wine
Or play the board games with commanding titles—
Conspiracy Theory, Life Support, The Pursuit of the
                                    Millennium—
But nobody gives up early, there is always a smile
Just behind the carousel's blind horse which hints
That being born is coming into pleasure and so who
Is waiting out there for you to be unfaithful to?

CLEARING THE DESK

All night I rode his back, claws well in,
The cat of God endearing myself to
A crazed omnipotent, tearing his skin
And biting until his liver showed through—
       This is a dream, he said,
       It's only in my head.

It's come about through too much drink,
That and the acid rain of sleep.
Like eyeless Gloucester at the brink,
The Unconscious will not look, but leap.
       He kids himself, of course,
       A side-effect of remorse.

I get these assignments from time to time,
Self-accusers, all the self-regarding fools;
I am punishment, they must be crime
And dreams the multiple choice of schools—
        He is, no doubt, a liberal,
        But the age is mostly feral.

Astounding arbitrariness! I said in his ear,
'You must post the Holy Egg to my London Club.'
Explain that one, Dr Jung. In practice, fear
Is the pedal of evolutionary hubbub.
        What a song we all sing
        Going to meet the Demon King.

And now it's like a serial on the box,
Control has got wind of something big,
Our hero's sent to check certain stocks
And to bury the Egg beneath a Tuscan fig—
        No such luck, this is death,
        The real meaning underneath.

I've done my work for him. His desk is clear,
Letters willed to a National Library,
Manuscripts in folders, one for each year,
Incunabula collected. 'Stay with me,'
        He moans, 'the night is long.'
        And the cat's claws and the song.

TIPP-EX FOR THE OSCAR

Coming down from the high riparian park
whose municipal trees among the statued
victors of sad forts bear names of poets,
our this year's laureate finds some gristle
between two teeth and as he probes it free
he's struck by what will be preliminary
to the great excursion he is planning—

ah, now he has interior resources
for his invective; this Thalassotherapy
has worked. Among the salt-flecked palms he's found
his task laid out: an Ode to Western Ocean,
to that embarking which is a returning,
a nightpiece of the European soul.

Unpacking his Anglo-Teuton portmanteaux,
setting a timeloss on its true grief base,
he hears the grumpy oarstrokes round Odysseus
and Henry the Navigator's humpbacked ocean groan.
A child, he'd wondered at the starfish wheeling,
the men'o'war like lampshades, blue-bags
for his mother's washday—in fact the thousand 'likes'
expected by the listening crowd, and yet more subtle
metaphors, cartouches for those whose jaded
ears lack words and morbid eyes seek paraphrases;
he knew it would prove useful for the doors
of childhood to stand open in his lines
to observation, his seeming of the act.

But how to keep his poem in the fast lane?
Literature which feasts on poisoned tears
lies dead in libraries till the wind of fashion
bears it up: where will a living writer find
explicators who will say these tropes of sea
have led our estuarial history back
to our diurnal selves; we're made to mirror
islands in our allegories? You must have noticed
Kipling is rated in the University
Departments of English and that Shaw is not—
both famous in their time. O guide me God
and make me choose the words which flatter best
the passeggiata of the relevant.

The light stays on till 3 a.m. He's in
his room and fastened to his Ode. Downstairs
the smell of ham and cloves has not abated
its seaside boarding-house authentication,
but he can lock it out from here, his cave
of making. Sunk in his speluncan world
of Cabot, Camoes and even Kingsley,
the tempest acres of a great migration
surround his pen, tall fleets of hubris charge
across the Tropics, twilight men disturb
the Noble Savage and the *Monitor*
confronts the *Merrimac*. A thousand years
of history fill less than ninety lines.

Some faults (perhaps not faults but merely tics
of style) look out at him from what he's written—
tell-tale gruppetti in his adjectives
and clauses running into sand. But worse,
the pattern is not sticking, he can hear
more nervous coughs than claps inside the hall
of his imagination. Desperate for sleep
he seizes Tipp-Ex for those finished sheets
he'd loved to look on, and in fear he prays
the God of White-Outs to resolve his fate—
'O grant me those most blessed similitudes
which make from poets' words good novel titles.
The Ceremony of Immanence is gowned.'

LEGS ON WHEELS

Behold the Master Species
which haruspicates its faeces
and builds amazing churches
where an invisible God has perches,
a sort of playful demon
that christens itself human,

the top of the great tree
of evolutionary
existence. It lays out gardens,
uses up hydrocarbons,
has forgotten how to walk
but stuffs itself with talk,
jumps into the car
if it has to go a yard
to get the cigarettes
and hoards like nuts regrets.
A challenge to the seasons,
it has its special reasons
for poisoning itself
with recipes for health,
but though it screws the planet
from Andaman to Thanet
it dreams a Green Revival
and sponsors the survival
of all attractive creatures
(O hide your ugly features,
you vultures, snakes and rats
and purr you pussy cats!)
This arbitrary biped
invents a far-off Sky-Bed
where lies a scolding Father
working himself in a lather,
and having stripped the jungles
our very Prince of Mongrels
likes to settle down
in some well-hemstitched town
dotted with aforementioned churches
and rook-inviting birches:
there its family chariot
will so succinctly carry it
the sure suburban round
it hardly touches ground.
Light verse's inclination
is not to indignation

but yet its rhymes and rhythms
may choose the noble Houyhnhnms
above the Yahoos' shouting
on any public outing,
and then the doggerel canon
finds moral tales to hang on,
looks at stumpy legs
and foreheads tall as eggs,
applauds the Life Force which
inhabits touch and itch
and spurs us to the station
of superior adaptation.
May we avoid disaster,
escaping ever faster
from all the patent deaths
(Aids, cancer, madness, meths),
rejoice we swirl on wheels
instead of our bare heels
and changing down for climbing
perfect our human timing,
unnatural in our daring,
quite naturally despairing
of just our own devices
but clever in a crisis
show evolution that
we are the where it's at.

THE AUTOMATIC ORACLE

The nation knew that it was winning
By the applause of its diseases
And from application forms for brute longevity
Stuffed into every burgher's letter-box.
Many now took the Panglossian Grand Tour
On narrow-gauge circuitries past
Morganatic lakes, the landscape curiously like

A tamed Shantung, a province great
With cormorants and round-legged women washing.
Civil Servants changed to Public Servants
When the annual examinations grew
More and more parodic. Fancy coming from
A breakfast room of dogs-beneath-your-feet
To answer Question Ten: 'Complicate
The issues raised by Arms Control
Using only language of an Agatha Christie
Novel set in the Fertile Crescent.' Word changes
Were the windmills of our trade
And auguries of platitude. Why did everyone,
So long anterior to the Age of Steam,
Have such violent public cramps,
Exaggerate the anger of occasion,
For all the world like Cobbett on his horse
Dredging the public's whiskers for assent?
That time of prior seriousness was a dream,
A precise description of a nothing—
Travellers knew without enlightenment
That brothels backed up to cathedrals,
And the fields of rape were raised
For bored geographers. Colour me love,
A tone of weekends braving wading birds,
And in that hue I'll show a universe
Relaxed from taking thought. It did think once,
In a freshly furnished interregnum
Before fatigue invaded syllables,
But do not let such recollection spoil
Today's obsessive emptiness. It's our duty
To inspire our critics, high on history,
To new feats of rodent disapproval,
Reading, as they do, for decadent invention.
See how the tenses snaggle up the scene
In Modern Poetry: not making kingdoms
Of the murder in our minds we miss
An opulent and Tennysonian calm.
The world still hurts as much: it is the loss

Of register which boils the brains of each
Ambitious legislator. What was it,
Say pilgrims on the beach at Lerici
Trailing white toes through liver-coloured mud,
Gave that great pain its shape? Oh ask again
When the very trees have voices and the clocks
Drip death-watch on a home divinity.
Our age has its appropriateness, a playful
Sort of sepsis, and each of us is offered
Sponsorship of his own bookish end.
Meanwhile, mean temperature of elegance,
The state and its white sheets shall be
An oracle, one doing magic on
A minor scale. Walled by the sun
And burnished by the moon, our planet
Seems a garden from a catalogue.
Four feet, five feet from the mask of God
A veil is lifted and the sweet environment
Flowers like Easter Day. A world of innocence
Is back, but do not look too closely at
Its rich empleachment. Eden filters through
The public parks, the weekend wilderness,
As stiff as astroturf with fallen blood.

WHO NEEDS IT?

Sitting the bad summer through
Above the Square's leaf-thickened view,
    A writer might take heart
    From all that mars his art.

Though this is Nineteen Eighty-five
With Mankind strangely still alive,
    Selfishness asserts
    That more than his deserts

Shall be his luck, as word by word,
He battens on what has occurred,
       And makes some flimsy things
       Out of his happenings.

Thus, fours and threes, in Marvell's way,
May help him dangerously essay
       Horatian persiflage
       In a Martian Age.

For all the Caves of Making are
Solitary Confinement in a star
       And as for relevance,
       That's a mask of chance.

We can't write well unless we think
Of something unapproached by ink
       And yet we're caught in rules
       Of Writing/Reading schools.

It happens here, at the fibre's end,
The blood-sharp surge of words that send
       Codes of memory
       To the cortex-tree.

It shakes the branch of life, the leaves
Are strewn, and there between two thieves
       God is crucified—
       What if the story lied?

When the truth is known and told
The writer's face looks blandly bold
       But not one Jew is saved
       And Mankind's still enslaved.

Tremendous Art! But that's the real
Whirlwind which the people feel:
       In notes and paper, it
       Loses life a bit.

The poets, like the gods at lunch,
Are such a greedy fumbling bunch—
        Was beauty massacred here?
        They saw mascara smeared.

Things not for changing still cry out
And truth may even pack some clout,
        But artistic glory
        Is another story.

Our human genius—who feeds it?
And professorial art—who needs it?
        Stravinsky works all night,
        The others shouldn't write.

Our vanity may save us yet,
Dogs *do* get better—ask the Vet.
        Milton was sent to bat in
        Poor light, and *he* knew Latin.

No reprimand will stop the writers
Proving fops and clowns and biters,
        But when they've gone, a line
        May fill with light and shine.

A toast then! Old Equivocators,
Envious friends, resourceful haters,
        All the way from Blimps
        To sub-suburban wimps.

Now praise the publishers, our kin,
Who do such good and don't get thin—
        Endure tautologies
        In famed anthologies.

The Pen is mightier than the Sword.
The Sword and Pen are in accord.
        Their power leaves the hand
        And decimates the land.

Thus each connives in dying light
To freeze the human heart in spite
       Of centuries of hope
         And Shakespeare, Donne and Pope.

NEVERTHELESS

Heretofore

you could use words like heretofore
without embarrassment, and catch the tail
of lyricism in some suburban garden
where words were still silver
and stoically inventive verse stayed new
through all the limits of recurring sound,
being at once proconsular
and steeped in sadness. This was a time
when needles, once a shining store,
clicked in the dusk of cottage madness
under a maidenly predestined order
like the village poplars: a sad connective
linked complicity and fate,
Calvinism and the empty grate.

Moreover

what was more emphatic tipped over
into rhetoric, itself a form from which
the cooler mind could distance its approval
if the sought exaggeration seemed
too smug: viz. the walls of oak round England
and bloodless the untrodden snow.
Words went in carriages and knew
which world was which and who was who.

Notwithstanding

such non-literary facts as one may note
with understanding when the scientists
of history and language point to verse
as the least apposite of checks on how
the language went in any chosen past:
look to the lawyers and the letter-writers,
the estate agents in their coaches,
ironfounders and top-hatted railway men.
Now all the practical romantics
called from high-walled gardens
to God in a lunette: retreat was sounded
in that melancholy long withdrawing roar.
Circumlocution for these times
was the shape of Empire and an office
where words were banked or shovelled into coffers.

Nevertheless

we never move too far from Presbyterian
small print—wireless becomes the radio,
the word processor is a crutch for brains,
glossy paper takes the images of famine.
Poetry goes on being made from sounds
and syntax though even its friends confess
the sad old thing is superannuated.
Watch, though, its spritely gait as
like a bent mosquito in it walks
on the arms of three tall women in black
to mutter envious obscenities at large—
its task is still to point incredulously
at death, a child who won't be silenced,
among the shattered images to hear
what the salt hay whispers to tide's change,
dull in the dark, to climb to bed
with all the dross of time inside its head

ALAS, FLEETING

Oh, the Old Roman,
churning up the mud of our hearts
(What do you mean, old?—
he was a brisk young placemaker
when he crammed his nose into his odes)—
Oh, the man we'd like to be,
choosing badly and recovering,
finding friends among the Villa Men,
those parvenus who are the only lords
to share the artist's sense of jeopardy,
the man who mixed regret and duty
in the spiciest yet blackest numbers,
who consoled untidy schoolboys
once they had become good District Officers,
talking all the time of how time passes,
how youth becomes cold useless age
and beauty drops away from limbs
like hoar frost on the apple trees
of Daddy's witless orchard—talking indeed
of passions gone which truth admits
were never there at all: Suave Moderate,
the wonder-working craftsmen trusting only
language and its un-pin-downableness,
patron saint of everyone born old
or timid. And the glimpsing sensuality,
a flicker of white lust, or like one horn
of a snail's reconnaissance,
the morning boys still sleepy in the showers,
a girl's arm trailed along the water's edge,
punting out of lilies. Wonderfully exploitable,
the human race! Not just time's erosion
but the spirit of all awfulness in the past
which willingly we won't remember, so that
hope comes round again and we are tricked.
My old headmaster, whose phrase this was,
following his entrance like a Disney dinosaur,

would purge the class: 'Eheu, fugaces,
can this be indeed the erudite Sixth?'
Horace would have hated him but known
how to placate him. At the end,
placating doesn't work, and yet he had
some odes stuffed in his pocket when he got there
and the bees of the underworld were singing,
'Welcome, poet, to our half-mast world,
Who'll do, does;
Who can, cans.'

AND NO HELP CAME

Where would you look for blessing who are caught
In published acres of millennia
By ravishments of salt and raucous saints
Or janissaries drilling a Big Bang?
The parish of the poor you'd seek, far from
The high grandstands of words and notes and paints:

And when you drove your flagged and honking jeep
Among the huts of starving, brutalized
Dependants, you might chance to hear them playing
Sentimental songs of flowers and moons
Chiefly to keep them safe from art, whose gods
Build palaces adorned with scenes of flaying.

ESSAY ON CLOUDS

A complacent Gulliver, I lie
in silent dripping Norfolk
watching these flying islands
with selfish unconcern—
here are planetary worlds
of silvered science
but I care only that they
block the sun from signing my dull skin.

So far down, this temperate garden
and such reefs above!
Oceans floating over us
and still we breathe the neophyte
scent of disengaging pollen.
The rug, my books, the cruising cat
are drowned with me,
we do not even seem to sleep
in our afternoon pavilion.

The clouds address me:
'you will never see us after this,
though our obliging cousins
will bring continuity,
but we have marked you, flying over,
the last one of the dynasty of self.'
I can calmly wait
for such archaeologists to find me.

Why is the sea in the air?
It's only books which say it is the sea,
the clouds abhor redundancy.
Now a black stripe and then
a pall of grey bring in
tormenting voices.

They are the sensitive ones
whose ears can hear the million cries
of animals in abattoirs.
The garden is sticky with their blood.

The sun comes out
to purge exaggeration.
The sun enjoys short sentences
but clouds prefer
a shifting Jamesian syntax.

Tea is brought out on the terrace.
Once more the clouds reproach me:
'because you are so incomplete
you cannot think of us without
dragging in yourself. You are fit
for nothing better than for prophecy.'

I watch one cloud come visiting.
In half an hour it disappears
to keep an appointment in the Wash.
I wave goodbye knowing I shall miss it
less than the passing cyclist on the road.

Night awaits the upper wind.
I decide I should not like to live
in a universe kept up by love
yet unequipped to tell a joke
or contemplate the sources of its fear.

ESSAY ON DREAMS

To set the impossible as homework!
The only thing more boring than
someone else's dream is being told
the plots of films. So, to be arbitrary,
dreams are like Italian landscapes.

The known and felt and the surprising
brought together on a patterned plain
approached through car lots and untidy vines,
the Val di Chiana with a fattoria in sight
and irrigation jets spasmic in the grain.
You could be a caterpillar on a stalk
or Totila down on one knee
among the frescoes. A country you know is yours
but totally indifferent to you
where you cannot speak the language
and frogs leap into your hands,
sand underfoot like saintliness,
the modern and the ruined perfectly combined
until you're purged of every scent of home,
a true adventurer with the aegis,
warts appearing on your flying hands.

Gods cannot hide themselves. You see the spear
and brow of white Athena and you say,
What is the meaning of this masquerade,
you are not my mother. But others hide.
Training for death is what we do:
such ponderous mixtures, classic shrubbery
and a red poinsettia climbing to a door
of whitewashed lattice, heavyweight hubris
in two hemispheres . . . but try to make report
to any ghostly father and the dream will laugh
and settle in the curtains like a scream.

Look to the island where the herd of goats
is from a shipwreck and every dangerous
bird is widowed: seek to explain to the whole
houseparty that you'll reveal the murderer
tonight at cocktail time; find the faces
you were sure of sweaty now and snarling
as some tourists burst into the kitchen
accusing you of being Anti-American.

Arbitrary is arbitration
as the light inside the mind reveals
each dusty truth on its collapse,
and dreams are no one's coded messages,
merely the second life our flesh is fed.

Daylight drags itself through windows.
They are coming round collecting papers,
you must hand yours in. You have covered it
with nonsense, or left it white with fear.
The great poems you could write
are all assigned to Dickinson and Donne.
Peculiar to hear 'a person so obtuse
he could not even dream us a straight line'.

Round the promontory, bursting like a cake,
the ferry comes and soon its wave runs up
the slimy ramp. Perhaps this is the spot
where everything began; it could be we
can leave the toys out on the lawn and start
for home. Why not repeat yourself, the noisy
insects in the trees assert—all good is
habit that invades the homeless mind.
And dreams have never heard of history
or style, but like our childhood games
they knock us into love with present fear.

A BAG OF PRESSMINTS

In the middle of a difficult book,
called I see 'The Allegy of Love',
I ask through a cloud of interference
or is it the Claud of Unknowing
why the spectral voice of truth
is fiddling with my chosen words.

It's not that these are simple messages,
God getting in touch with Pharaoh
or the Dog of Death mooching with the Furies,
rather it's the sky unscrambling
in its joy of chaos: everything in place
but huge disorder in our view of it.
The world was misprinted its first day.
In the beginning was the lord;
Coercion or Correction was His name;
He hungered in the Book of Genocide
and the great beast, the Adversary,
was Grauniad, the ever-eating mother,
appearing soon afterwards at the breakfast table
as reason's voice, The Guardian.

This is to snatch significance
from decadence of purpose. Language,
though it says it knows its place,
will always try to be subversive,
telling the eight a.m. analysand
that jokes or tumblersful of sherry
won't blunten Grandma's teeth one bit
and little girls will never get out of the wood
even if they do know how to spell.

Here it comes again, like an ellipse
of the sun. I'm correcting proofs
in a dream and find I've written
'Patriots always stand for the
National Anathema.' And two lines later,
'Seven Hypes of Ambiguity'—
I'm quite relieved my misprints
make such sense. A pity my books
are kept so plain by too much meaning.

Help yourself to a strong mint from my bag,
it will take responsibility off your breath.

RADIO CALIBAN

This is Imagination's nuclear-free zone,
so answer, airwaves, answer!
And hello to the girl
who asked for Ariel's new single.

Personally I'd take Wallace Stevens
to Prospero any day, and here's
that smouldering oldie, 'The Bermudas'—
Andy Marvell in the English Boat.

Time now for our popular feature
'My Most Wimpish Moment',
but first let's join Trink and Steff
singing 'I Cried to Dream Again.'

Our Studio Doctor says
women who eat meat grow more body hair—
Remember you heard it first on Radio Caliban,
the voice from the middle of the sandwich.

I saw God in an oleander bush,
writes Mrs Sycorax of Alfred Avenue
and, yes, Miss Mandeville, by starlight
a word may seem a planet. Hang on in.

Don Alonso of Bellosguardo
wants to know what became of
'The Thousand Twangling Instruments'—
same group, Don, I've got them on the brain.

If you don't want worms, lay off the cheese.
When the big wedding's on—Miranda
and Ferdy coming down the aisle—
all eyes are on the bridesmaids' boobs.

Watch an ant drag ten times its weight,
that's your blood holding back your death.
What you write makes sense or else words
would curl up in your palm like a paper fish.

Not much rhythm, not much art—
all right, but it's got feelings, listeners!
So let a lady wrangle with the blues,
'They flee from me that sometime did me seek.'

Absolute Milan where wise savers go.
A great video, those cloud-capped towers,
and Giorgione storming on the shelf—
a coral island ringed by sun and surf.

TRY A TRIOLET

I

There are no seasons in this flat,
though out of doors the sun shines bright.

The open window tempts the cat.
There are no seasons in this flat.

Heat steps inside, the night comes pat.
Our dreams are black as anthracite.

There are no seasons in this flat,
though out of doors the sun shines bright.

2

Hell is other people, Sartre thought,
good companions for eternity.

The gaping O of self becomes a nought,
yet Hell is other people, Sartre thought.

We make mistakes however well we're taught
to conjugate the restless verb 'to be'.

The Hell of other people, Sartre thought,
gives good companions to eternity.

3
Heaney, Hughes and Hill and Harrison—
top poets' names begin with H.

A team beyond comparison,
Heaney, Hughes and Hill and Harrison.

They're so grown up, we're in the crèche;
they're generals, we're garrison.

Heaney, Hughes and Hill and Harrison—
top poets' names begin with H.

4
The nearly mindless triolet
is the one form that Auden shirked.

With Wilde it turned quite violet,
the nearly mindless triolet.

And drops of Baby Bio let
potted plants seem overworked.

The nearly mindless triolet,
the only form that Auden shirked.

SUSANNAH AND THE ELDERS

If you knew that this was Mrs Cartwright
just home from Santorini
with a truly super tan, you could be
halfway to justification as a peeping-tom,
the repairs to the building having
exposed the bathroom in a positively
Versalian manner, the light brickdust
talcing her terracotta feet beneath the towel
as she decides it is time to shave her legs again
for the last party of the summer. Such are
the practicalities of living,
skin superbly intense as a location of light,
mirror misted over until one arced swipe
restores its two-way voyeurism
and your disappointment at being separate
less intense than your relief that attractive creatures
are their own dilemma, or presumably
the special traffic of distinct personae
cluttered up with memories of meals and money.

Once they painted things this way
and they insisted on virtuosity
of technique. Researchers ask
how many children did the painter have
or when did he become a Catholic?
What sort of provenance would you provide
the experts with if you told them that
you often encountered Mrs Cartwright
at get-togethers in the Square?
Will the mind as readily as the wrist
limn the surfaces of lust? Tomorrow
we shall pour ourselves into the street
to bring such worries to the barricades.
Tomorrow or next Tuesday. We get only
the poorer Arabs in this quarter,
servants of the ones in darkened cars

and often with glaucoma. What joy
to see the risen flesh as separate
from the soul and independent of
continuous late-night colloquy.

THE WORLD'S WEDDING

The most dangerous people are those
for whom the present is the only reality.
There is no mystery appropriate to them,
no season of loneliness for disappointment.
Now cut the carousel of slides to show
a round-towered church with pheasants
up to the door, an expedition of content
when all you'll hear is cheeky hopefulness
at this, the noisiest of betrayals—
there are those who'll go down unmade roads
or leap the shuddering pay-train just
to keep their RSVPs true,
hurrying in heat and high-heels to
the prophetical weddings of the world.

Pictures painted stand for ends beyond
ourselves, while photographs are pinned
by truth to be the epilogues of life.
Shun then the snaps that tumble from
the airmail letter (Cousin Circe's wedding)—
look above the chimney-piece—in browns
and dew-flecked mauves a river scene with cows
is half the history of the boarding house
and half the plains of hell. We have to make
accommodation of the separate oracles—
don't go down to the woods today or what
shall we do to be saved? Nobody quarrels
with banks and barristers, but the reckoning
to be frightened of is a dusty scene in oils.

You've followed me so far. Of course you know
it's dreams I'm talking of, of which all pictures
from the quattrocento to the ROI
are nothing more than shorthand reveries.
Thus, when we get the chance, we crowd into
the topless tents of Camberley to sip the fizz
and glimpse the bride changed for the journey south.
Changed she will be, but be less deployed,
her head upon Italian pillows, than when once
she sought a wedding every day, response
to being brimfully alive and hating life,
uncoupling what her feet felt from the hope
of arms, making from her mother at the ironing
a massacre of golds and mortal tints.

Speed is eloquence, rushing on to judgement;
Nature the bardic never blots a line.
See how these worriers, neater by a franchise,
settle a grid of surface treachery
on everything; tracing the referent
is basting St Lawrence. We need such nuptials
of world and world if only to catch up
with dismalest relations, glass in hand.
Didn't I meet you in that dream, the one
of tip-truck and tricycle? Who said
the silver-wattled pheasant had to die?
The honeymoon car's a nimbus when sunlight stripes
the headstones. Imagine them now, keepers and carvers,
generations marrying in death.

DISC HORSE

'Hi, folks, this is the high season for forks,
for getting out the Esky and the Ute,
packing beer and wine and eggs,
us waddling and well-fed urbanites

setting out to trap the sun
where the river picnics on its raft of lilies
and pelicans dock beside the swans.
What horrors our ancestors must have known,
German names, obscure cemeteries,
a hierarchy of the various hopes.'
          That's it, my voice!
You recognize it now, the tape of language
trying to sound like thought: a riderless phantom,
haunter of a million articles and host
to ego at the conference. Round and round
go galaxies of talk and everyone knows
not to intrude on anyone else's space
for fear that no one then will have the power
to recuperate the narrative.
          Old friends, new antitheses!
What if instead we go on automatic pilot?
          Zgtfpxxlrjkdxrhgggkk . . . ooof
          Sound poetry . . .
'What a work of peace is a man,
how golden in season,
how fond of the infinitive,
in porn and loving how depressed and animal,
in faction at all angles
and apprehensive of the gods,
the futility of the world,
the marathon of cannibals.'
          Something has gone wrong.
All afternoon we zapped the ether
like Mazeppa strapped to history
with every famous name agog
and buzzing in the Junior Common Room—
'Go down with floppy discs on every side,
          Inscribe! Inscribe!'
These texts mean nothing, even Shakespeare's,
it's the shape the theory makes that counts.

Lost in the dark
an old lyricism keeps coming back
through breathless new lacunae: antiphons
of ageless matriarchy tell the son
he has to pay the price of discourse.
Enter a hot room, past the potted plants
and whispers of Vienna; listen to the Big Bad Wolf
of Parsifal Road—the jockeys of our joylessness
are liberators really. What if we are born
in the colours of compulsion, seeking on the moon
our pale lost wits, sfumato of the sun.
Pack all the artbursts there have been into a box—
they would not tip an inch against
 a single phrase of truth. Unless you find
your misery you will rage retardless
up among the fox-furs, furioso of N8.
          No, apocalyptic steed,
canter closer from your turning world
and bring us voices mandevilled
upon the trees of night. After the blaze of music
and the tang of immortality
prepare to listen to those other sounds,
that heartbeat which has given us syntax,
the trope of nerves we say is sweet
erasure, proving that displacement
makes divinity—the god of itself talking
in shape of its most favoured deputy,
a much too loquacious poet
hanging in his participles,
denying everything, including death.

THE MELBOURNE GENERAL
CEMETERY

This is a territory strange
To me, not the dead's embankment
But this southern city's range
Across a watered sky, the scent
Of burning, gravity's exchange.

My kept-neat city friends, the dead
I'll never meet, seem quite at one
With me. They are, no doubt, well-read,
Their stones and mounds dry in the sun
Following rain. They read in bed

Good news which goes on being news,
Old letters held before their eyes.
What we above must sift for clues
To them is fact and no surmise,
The loss of all there is to lose

Is not a loss at all. They're back
Where heavy Nothing weighs an ounce,
Where Truth is in some distant stack
And all the clawing notions pounce
On shadows in their dawn attack.

Behold amid the left-behinds
A cautious man-amphibian:
Once groping on to shore, he finds
He breathes both elements and can
Take his chance of creeds and kinds.

Almost able now to live
In life or death, this stalker looks
At those he loves, appreciative,
And knows them pictures and the books
Of Thanatation his to give.

SOUTHSEA BUBBLES

The box tree in the garden
helped navigators guide
ships to New Farm Wharf,
or else Grandfather lied.

He might have done, he had
a beard like Bernard Shaw
and nothing much beside—
that was in '94.

We came from nowhere, a knock
on a wooden citadel,
we had a family tree
sited in hell.

It was Adam's house
our forebears left
and all our felonies
were for his theft.

The past a clear sky
and we the nimbus grouping
but the rain brings
grasshoppers looping.

Thick among the eucalypts,
paspalum and lantana
and Moreton Bay figs
dropping manna.

Boys in serge and parakeets,
alike the sun's darlings,
share watered grass
with strolling starlings.

Prep Schools and private griefs
take sprays and wreaths
to honey fields of death
where hot bees feast.

Not theirs history's bubbles
chained along the beach,
bright convicts of deportment,
each by each.

Days improve, new sons
go sooling a dull nerve,
South Coast Hi-Fi tracks
an azimuth curve.

The honeymoon river runs
past a rotting wharf,
the children of light
are in the surf.

Play history for melody
and not for truth,
possums and sparrows
waltz the roof.

And I must hear before I die
this oracled South
speak true love
from a lying mouth.

SPIDERWISE

To Clive James

Trapdoor

The origin of metaphor is strange.
As boys we used (but don't let me forget
I only watched, I wasn't very brave)
To put two spiders in a bottle, wave
It over flame, which usually made them fight,
Or flood them from their deep holes for a change.

These were the deadly Trapdoors whose one bite
Sent an inclusive poison racing through
Your veins: I think we thought the risk absolved
Us from all guilt, our cruelty dissolved
In danger. I used my fear of football to
Ward off death fears in the dorm at night.

And then I thought of dying on the field
When someone passed the ball to me. I say,
When challenged to declare what virtue I'd
Like most to have, 'It's too late now to hide
From balls and tackles, you can't get away;
If I'd had courage, I'd at least have squealed.'

We are shut out of our own universe.
Perhaps the spiders in the bottle howled
Or cursed those lumpen schoolboy gods of theirs
Or practised spider jests upon the stairs
Where tyrants crack because one wit has scowled.
We fume and Rupert Murdoch's none the worse.

And writing in this corset-stanza may
Be nothing more than flying in the face
Of new technology. And now they're topping
Up the latest tank of history at Wapping—
A metaphor is when you have one space
To fill and all of life to file away.

Most metaphor, as Kipling guessed when he
Made Shakespeare witness as a child the end
Of kittens at a sister's hand, is home-
produced. The tribal creature is alone
With only tribal words to help him blend
His uncloned self with all humanity.

But metaphor is often out of date.
I find a powerful trope: 'the straitjacket
Of all our childhoods', but I've never seen
A straitjacket—drugged, behind a screen,
The madman of today can raise a racket
And none of it will reach the ears of state.

We live on dead skin of the mind. To write
Is to commit oneself to the past tense
Within the present act of mixing words
Whose immanences settle as occurreds:
And so we pay with pence these bills in cents
And stoke a microchip with anthracite.

The language will not move except to laugh
At Big and Little Enders, Old v. New—
Thus pedantry is publishing a stricture
While TV Gnomes are 'massaging a picture',
The dictionary hasn't got a clue,
The wind blows out the door both wheat and chaff.

The long relays of childhood can provide a
Range of wrongs to stake a moral claim.
The lie of words (O ambiguity!),
The rust of rhyme, short-cut of simile,
Make yours and mine and Swift's desire the same—
The angry soul is quite a bottled spider.

Redback

My next portmanteau-spider is a cert
To raise Australian hackles (and bare bums
Off dunny seats): the Redback scuttles out
From underneath your fallen strides to scout
The scene. You always wonder what becomes
Of him when brooms and Lysol lay the dirt.

But let the Redback be my image of
The naturally malevolent activist,
The dried-blood cross upon his back be rubric
Of the Unsettled Terrorist, his Kubrick
Horror-sequence of a bite de-mist
The mirror of normality at Sydney Cove.

Unlike the Trapdoor he is quite at home
In human homes. Communications architecture
Suits his way of feeding on the grid
Of everyday existence. He stays hid
In myriad corners, happily the vector
Of challenges from brushed velour to chrome.

I'd like to think that he was waiting there
When that initial cargo of strong rum
And human refuse hit Australia's shore.
To flog, to dream, to endlessly explore
Might make Arcadia of a rural slum:
The Redback gave the hedonists a scare.

'Simply the thing I am shall make me live.'
Bravo, the Redback! But he stands for more.
That some shall live, some others have to die,
What my will urges, your will must supply—
The Crowded Ark's the spider's metaphor:
He has to eat, and then he will forgive.

And he survives the change of gear which
Pulls Australia from remote back number
To Brave New World of Opportunity.
His atavism's there for all to see,
Devoid of any Panglossian lumber,
A backyard warning to the newly rich.

Especially as we've tamed the whole wide land
To seem Pelagian peninsula
Where terrors have a user-friendly feel.
The bush looks Art Nouveau, the wattles steal
Their hazy shapes from Mucha; in the car
The Esky waits the barbecue's command.

No doubt the mainframe's large enough to cope
With sharks and bushfires, droughts and mining rights.
The people have been told they're legatees
Of freedom lovers from five centuries:
They've made stigmata of their appetites
And trust in God and in their horoscope.

The Redback understands. He's his own priest
And has an Opus Dei in each leg
To race him to the necessary prey.
Perhaps he likes to keep Australia Day
Among the stacks of stubbies and the keg,
And wave the Southern Cross above the feast.

He has no need of words, a true numbskull.
He will evolve no further, like the shark,
But at cohabitation is a whizz.
How subtle this philosophy of his,
To warn us, as we fumble in the dark.
Relieving Nature won't be comfortable.

THE DULL MAY WAKEN TO A
HUMMING-BIRD

Now it is neither dark nor light,
swimming off Liverpool, coming ashore
on a shingle beach to valiant figures saying
'Entertain me, take the printed wrapper
off conjecture.' Surprising it is not surprising
later in those pea-fields with fast friends
along a brushwood track, then to watch
a flower exploding like a sneeze, 'something
to do with its way of reproduction'
says the voice of explanation,
reductive but obliging, and beside the flower
a bird which closes up into itself,
sublimest sphincter acting out a joke
but nicer than that paid-up omphalos
where time is tucked away. A Royal
Commission is sitting all the daylight hours
investigating the word 'when', a hundred lawyers
lounging in the court and all the parts-of-speech
on call: Justice is known to be a case
of polyester versus cotton and no decision
yet expected. Three friends are watching
as a four-engined jet comes in
for emergency landing on a playing field.
From the perfect crash we pull out screamers
as the fire spreads along a wing, each one
inside his harness, and still the dead
are thought to be spectators at the last
gymkhana of the season. Threatened by burns
which you could feel through sleep, creeping
up behind the murdered rainmaker, a murmur
giving warning of resolve and all the feet
of relatives piled in the poring dark,
the self is hailed—'I know you, you are he
whose shadow fills the hemisphere,
a vision twice as wide as chaos.'

93

A second voice is singing in the leaves,
vessel of the insubstantiality of love:
'You are none other than that unpronounceable
Bohemian whose quartet was adapted
by Franz Schubert; you are a tone of talent
lost in the splendour of the universe.'
Greyness spreads like sand through fingers
as they untie the boat beneath the little wharf
and leave this coast of fearful breakfasting.

Interior waking that the moon draws up
or slavish constancy of blood
breeds thus the contiguity of words
and feeling. Tell the sons of Freud
there are no templates and no temples,
only the ancient harness of grey thought
which dresses us for true extinction,
merely the wished-for continuity
of age and enzyme. Remarkable under the sun
this everything of memory,
the first goodbye of coming to the world,
the final entry in the book of gold.

THE EMPEROR HADRIAN

Animula vagula blandula . . .

Little soul, like a cloud, like a feather,
my body's small ghost and companion,
where now must you go, to what region?
Pale little, cold little, naked little soul
who will you play with, what will you laugh at now?

THE PANTOUM OF THE OPERA

Life has thrown its acid in his face
and so he haunts the decks and tiers of light.
Susannahs he has watched cannot replace
the mother-love which ran from him in fright.

The booking clerk observed him: yes, he thought,
life has thrown its acid in his face,
and he'll recall each amoroso note
Susannahs he has watched cannot replace.

Tonight the trucker from Emilia sings.
The booking clerk observed him: yes, he thought,
ten years from now heart failure in the wings
and he'll recall each amoroso note.

They've queued for this, they've paid three times the rate.
Tonight the trucker from Emilia sings.
Domingo-fanciers in the slips debate
ten years from now heart failure in the wings.

Sometimes a new-found friend will take him home.
They've queued for this, they've paid three times the rate.
You might get killed, you might just wake alone,
Domingo-fanciers in the slips debate.

Swart Papageno practises his bells,
sometimes a new-found friend will take him home,
and Don Giovanni has a choice of hells:
you might get killed, you might just wake alone.

Our phantom selves dance wildly when they hear
swart Papageno practising his bells.
Say No to Heavenly Takeaway; it's clear
that Don Giovanni has a choice of hells.

Say No to Heavenly Takeaway; it's clear
Susannahs he has watched cannot replace
the mother-love that fled from him in fear.
Life has thrown its acid in his face.

DOES A RAKE GO TO A
BROTHEL TO SING?

(*In memory of the creators of* The Rake's Progress)

We have been deceived by our idealists—
Tom Rakewell acts the audible
and not the consequent: for something to be real
it must be possible to sing it.

And we can sing the starting of the world,
a balancing of love, the games of touching teeth,
the desert dreams of conquerors,
yet wake beside the innocentest teacher
in real time, kept shadowless
beneath the cuckoo clock's retard.

Dreams are the grandest operas,
unruined by a Gounod or a Meyerbeer.
They cannot be cured with meaning
but must sing the very tones of happening.
So tell our father we are blood and soul for him,
we are plainly set in place
as blades of grass, and should we die for love
it will be love of syntax. Who are these
punk phantoms of Pontormo? Who sits fat
in Heaven, looking lovable?

Judgment is all Creation sings.
Here we go back to finding crimes
to match the punishment. Our needs
are music, water, persiflage,
a set of values on a colour card.
No, wonder then our rulers subsidize
an art you are expected to dress up for.

To dress for dreams is dressing up forever.
Mother Goose has loosed her stays
and let her hair in delta flood
a veteran champaign. It is too late always
if you're lucky. A–Major sounds within the ranks.
Sweet dreams, my Master. Dreams may lie,
But dream. For when you wake you die.

ON TOUR

I had just finished the first part
of my recital. Throughout I'd noticed
a small quiet man in the front row
wearing decorations. An Austrian official,
shunned by the Milanese,
but sure to speak impeccable Italian.

In the Interval, he'd have liked to speak to me,
but more importunate faces intervened.
'We look to the North, you know,
we are Italian, we are Catholic,
but we are not backward facing.
In the North lies all our promise,
we hope you will conduct Bach's Passions
here for us when next you are on tour.'

In the second half I played
my 'Variations sérieuses'
but felt that Beethoven, Weber even,
might be more the sort of thing they'd like to hear.
Accordingly I broke my programme
and finished with the *Waldstein*.
I don't think I've ever made the rondo go so well.

Amid the bravos and the knowledge
of all the toasts to come, I settled
my Protestant soul by saying to myself,
'You aren't a real Bach or Shakespeare
but a Jewish convert with a flair
for counterpoint.' The little man was there
beside me, humble but intrusive—
'You must forgive me, we do not often meet
such talents here in Italy.
I am Austrian but prefer this country
to my own. I am not without distinction
but I loathe Vienna. Mozart, at your service,
Karl, the elder son. Won't you please
play something by my father.'

THE LOUD BASSOON

Out of the sound swamp, the delta of dreaming,
Shuttles reluctantly what is accountable,
Warp-words, intrusions, rubbishy mutterings,
Harvest of nicknames, hierarchical slop,
Announcing like radios always left on
Through thin walls of flats in scaffolded towers,
Infusions of wonderment, brought to us daily—
X's great symphony, *The Inconsolable*,
His Number Four, or that tragic opera
Gustav's Vasectomy, a cycle of poems,
Sadder than cypress, *Silicon Mandibles*.

Always a surf of creation to hear through,
Tinnitus feasting on blood and on sunlight
Bringing a past which is parody-present,
Ululitremulant, warning that Nature
Mucks out impatiently, scatters what flesh thinks
Echo-eternal. The ear's on an island
Centuries heavy, lost in geography,
Swum to by marvellous patterns and patents,
Though Self will not find it. Orchestral voices
Beam in so seriously abstraction sounds
Like Swinburnian hendecasyllabics,
But duty sidles up to each wedding guest
And its interruption in story or fact
Spells out the message in mendicant Latin—
Mors aurem vellens, vivite, ait, venio
(Death plucks my ear and says Live! for I come).
We need translations who will be translated,
High blessings bestowed by bloodstream and logic,
Trees to sit under and hear the sky stutter
Arcadian instances robed as statistics.
Now morning unsettles the dust in shut rooms,
Airwaves revive with the titles of living,
The Wrong of the Earth, old words in new harmony,
Listened to lovingly, one cat on your lap
And one in a sun-stripe—how can you bear it,
The clatter your heart makes as it challenges
Air and the universality of air.

PONTORMO'S SISTER

The world's face is a woman's
who died early, the smoothnesses of life
waiting on a ruled horizon—
Consider this in profile even
in my *Visitation*, the four ages of Woman
unable, like God, to be anything but themselves,

and in Mary it seems lit within,
myself there, swept by darkness.
All my people are the same person,
as every artist shows: there grows a face
as hedgerows grow, as water shapes
in droplets when it falls, as we emerge
from the doors of dreams to be ourselves.
Piero's faces never vary, did he perhaps
have a sister who died too young to marry?
That's how I found technique,
a way of bending Nature to the line
of my depression. We say at twenty
and at forty and at sixty, there are
measures and distinctions you call art—
but no, we're in the shambles
with our little sisters and our parents,
we're tied to flesh and death forever
while we live, and out of it our masters ask
'Make me Veronica, the dogs and boys
grape-picking, Jesus faltering beneath
the cross's weight.' I can paint a word
if the word is death, but what I cannot do
is show it to you
unless I wrap it in a nimbus.

O little sister dressed in death,
I have painted you in everyone
and now I beg you draw the veil
across my eyes. It is time for me
to sketch God's face, a smudge of grease
on old familiarity. This is the message
of the mannered style: God looks like
anyone who ever lived, but more so.

CROSSING THE TIBER ISLAND

This is God's Circus Maximus—
a fledgling sparrow slides from pavement to gutter
and miraculously avoiding Rome's traffic
lives to skid by panic wing-power
into the opposite gutter
and crouches there dynastically.
This is no true contest,
Rome has turned its thumbs down
on yet another creature, the Tiber Island
shakes with heat and gravity.
Are not two sparrows sold for a farthing?
They would not fetch so much today
in this expensive city. Gods come here to die
and now a grist of shit and faith
covers Romulus's mound to seventy feet.
We cup our blood for dreams to drink,
thinking we have so many good and evil acts
to chorus us, stones of faith outstaring nerves
beside trompe l'œil ceilings where
bath night fronts a deathless Pantheon.
Each human mind is Rome ruled by a mad
and metaphorical Emperor, or Pope
praised for piddling fountains
and passing barley-sugar baldachinos.
Stepping from the hotel's air-conditioning
you become a city sight-seeing in a city,
your history is just as marvellous as Rome's,
your catacombs the haunt of pilgrims
from Hyperborean archipelagos,
new worlds pillaged of their optimism
to gild a lavishly despairing faith,
the Tiber Island is the food you eat,
the cows ten times your weight, the little
prawns inside their carapace, and lettuce
dressed to ease Christ's vegetarian pain.
The sparrow in the dust

knows neither Pontifex nor Aesculapius
but twitches on its bed of wings
terrorizing Heaven and whichever
deity could meet its dying eye.

PISA OSCURA

You know how images keep coming back,
The lifted arm before the heart attack,
Yet out of all the basket-work of shapes
And plots, those vandalized electroscapes
Of daytime dreaming, how remarkable
The least significant of them is able
To light the mind and flood the memory!
Don't introspect if you want honesty,
And that's what Freudians presumably
Intend when fixing eyes upon a past
That's like a slow vertiginous open-cast
Whose work load is regrettably colossal,
Its every truth impacted like a fossil.
So holidays from thinking look like cards
Of saints in shrouds and girls in leotards
Proclaiming less a haunting charm of face
Than unexpected valency of place,
Or so I felt, midway from sink to freezer,
When there before me hovered dusty Pisa.
The town's historical, a saucer round a cup
Of regional accidie, a dried-up
Vacuumed-out Ligurian emptiness—
I've been there often and enjoyed it less
Each time until this year when suddenly
Of all the history-pitted bits of Italy
I found it most like home, a proper cage
(Not Pound's) to hold the ageing spirit's rage.
Streets almost empty, traffic ice-cream slow,
The silent squares out of de Chirico,

All tourists heading for the Leaning Tower
(The bars have yet to learn of Happy Hour)
And history's ghosts so sullen they won't come
Into the present at the Guide Book's drum.
Of the famed Piazza dei Miracoli
This poem has nothing much to say—degree
Of leaning from the vertical perhaps,
The bombs that made Benozzo's frescoes maps,
Incorrigible youth which carves its name
On G. Pisano's pulpit without shame,
Perhaps to discount in one heresy
The intolerable weight of history
And catch the tired tourist as he gapes
In wonder at the time-defying shapes
And with a CARLO or an ELVIRA
Restore the present in a vandal's scar.
The private miracle the site enshrines
Is in the meeting-up of marble lines,
Geometry inscribed on empty sky,
Invisible gods held fast by symmetry,
And all the dead, great figures in their day,
Not knowing that their names have worn away,
Insisting still in pompous silence that
A Campo Santo is no Ganges ghat
But, filled with dust brought from the Holy Land
And peregrine of faith in sacred sand,
Retains a monumental gesture for
The rotting body and redundant law.
The rest of Pisa sleeps beyond this square,
Few tourists break their scheduled journey there
To wander back towards the river and,
Cascading maps and ice-cream cones in hand,
Quiz Ugolino's tower and Shelley's garden
Or Byron's palace—value judgments harden
When dull façades and husks of buildings lour
On a weedy yellow river and each door
Is fortified by bars and rusting bolts
And echoes only to the Fiats and Colts

And Renaults charioteering the Lungarno,
Italia Martire ma *cum grano.*
Yet here, before a bridge, tucked in between a
Lorry and the sky, the della Spina
Church appears, God's jewel-box, a toy
Created for that icon'd marvellous boy
Italians in their hearts have made of Christ
(His rape of Heaven, His Redeemer's heist!)
To shrine the thorn which tore His silver skin
Before the clause of Godhead thundered in.
This Lilliputian church, not Dante's spite
Brings Pisa from an untransfigured night
Straight to my dreams—this is the grace of love
That Dante's terza rima cannot prove,
The reconciling shape which frees mankind
From murderous faction of a poet's mind.
If medieval wholeness ever was,
This is its only symbol, its True Cross,
This, while the turning wheel of faith revolved,
Showed saint and sinner all would be resolved,
That, with his fondness for 'I told you so',
Dante was just some foiled Castruccio.
A similar anathema still sends a
Shudder through me in the Sapienza—
No university could survive that name
And modern seats of learning trim the flame
To safe and low accountability,
Their Galileos home in time for tea;
Though one emboldened tutor broke the spell—
'Let me be Virgil, I will show you hell!'
For hell, as Shelley said, might be a city
Much like London, dressed in cold self-pity
Fanning-out in grids from dread of death,
Its towers of hate above, its sewers beneath
Where flows the dreck of self—the squares, the prisons,
All at the service of destructive visions.
This in my chill mid-morning I recalled
As Autumn vapour pecked and spilled and stalled

Around my window; a city of the mind
Whose used-up living lives on in its mind,
A Pisa worse than the exhausted South
Despairing ever at the river's mouth,
A shadow city, formed of self and soul,
Its past pristine, its present on the dole.

POSSIBLE WORLDS

The trumpet cries
This is the successor of the invisible.

This is its substitute in stratagems
Of the spirit. This, in sight and memory,
Must take its place, as what is possible
Replaces what is not.

Wallace Stevens, 'Credences of Summer'

NEXT TO NOTHING

The casque of a dragon-fly
eaten out by ants
is living etherialized,
bone round the library
of the brain—
                    One day
when digging in the sand
for pippis I looked about
and saw beyond the beach
a mountain of their shells
a century old
where aborigines
used to come to feast.
One shell is next to nothing
in the dark of being born,
so I dropped it in the bucket
knowing I must offer Heaven
the softer part of me,
my contentious mind,
and leave behind another shell
on the unthinking shore
of the authorial continent.

A PHYSICAL WORLD

To have sat in the awkwardest tree
playing cubby-houses and to be the one
who had to beg his friends to find him
a girl to take to the holiday dance.

To sight the bright bees of ambition buzzing
in a book while the unimprovable sun
blazed down on sumptuous emptiness
and asphalt melted into mediocrity.

So many dead, there was this wealth only
in the family, that you invented the blaze
of extinction: to be such a virtuoso
of yourself that truth remained untellable.

The great world still sitting in trees or looming
over your head in crawling buses—
strange to have no way of touching animals
or comforting a crying face at nightfall.

How ridiculous to be Columbus
offering Isabella the earliest gold of America
when you could be Da Ponte giving Mozart
his first sight of the libretto of *Figaro*.

DECUS ET TUTAMEN

Come with me to vistas of a low dissolving bay
Where mud, fine shingle and the mangrove's toppling roots
Run up to golfing grass, the humpy haciendas of
Unromantic people stretched along a wire of happiness
From self-made history to a climatized inane.
In the tourist season so much shit from the hotels
Enters these discipled waters that the birds fly off,
Though fish increase. Ecology is shit, says the white-shoed
Magnate in his barbican of glass; the universe is stable,
The sewers of LA can take a furlough, what is
A littoral of winding tides upon a fret of mud
If not a model sewage farm? The trouble with the world
Is that it can't be turned to money. We live on a bank note:
The coins are in our bones, their galaxies extend
Through dreams 'to the round earth's imagined corners',
And we still sleep Columbus's sleep, happy to know
The keel will drag upon another slave-worked shore,
An economy of viral flu and feathers.
Praise our intrepid fathers who left swards of stinking geese,

The clog-tympanum streets beneath progressive lighting
(A Rippered dawning of good dividends) to fetch
The future to a sleeping coast. Unpack the corded bales,
You practical romantics, you have a century
Of mercantile weekends before the Tyrian traders come,
The ethnic restaurants and dressing for the theatre.
Meanwhile, exhaustion of newcomers takes its toll:
The flogging martinet no sooner dead than makes a ghost
To ride the river bank beneath the stars' eye-holes,
The heavens a gaol for Lancashire lapsarians
And God on watch. But comes the long-believed relief
As sure as Scottish pipes or camel convoys through the night—
We all can dream ourselves inside Free Trade,
We dip our fingers in the stoup of cash, we bless
The house with pictures of great pioneers on banknotes—
So beautiful is money, it is the nation in low carving,
The miracles by St Democracy among
The bargain car-lots, the blue rinse hyper-rise,
Selling short the wimps and setting up sons of the Manse
As Neo-Emperors. Turn the small disc in your hand,
The coin, the CD of desire; it proves its plastic cousins
Men of substance, it makes the whale-sounds appropriate
To conservationists of the TV twilight,
It sings across all latitudes. Now, on sunny afternoons,
Our yachts at anchor, their cordless phones asleep,
We see ourselves the ancient tribesmen of the land
Telling snake legends to the rainbow trees,
Reverted like the glasshouse hills and mortared gullies
To pure landscape till our very death becomes
A record in a rock, perfection of the will to live.

WOOP WOOP

The backtrack Trebizond of everyone,
it is in a disc of starfish where the lakes
are Balatons and the muslin-valenced ladies
bring library books to town as if it were
no more than six weeks since their husbands died.

Here start the open-shirted young sophisticates
whose fathers took the franchise for a new
variety of Cola, the ones whose poems and whose
gossip-columns are made the more intelligently
decadent by their need to tame the capital.

Out of its famished acres come anecdotes
of men with recipes for 'cockatoo-au-vin',
of fossickers in muddy dams taming Irish tunes
on one-string fiddles—rumours started here
sell beer ten thousand miles from 'Truth To Tell'.

Juggernauts are planned to pass this very place
when six-lane highways from the Bi-Centenary
stride beside the hoardings, but the point
of all this opening-up must be our doubt
that such a site will stay to welcome us.

Although an ancient and austere referent
it is younger than the harboured megalopolis
it backs, since every journey to simplicity
is inland and the parrots dress in ever-brighter
greens and scarlets the emptier the lakes they lap.

The movie industry could not exist without it:
wasp-waisted girls are seen riding after Schumann
to the soup-tin letter-box to hear that London
wants their novels, and following riots in Europe,
amuse their company just naming its odd name.

Perhaps it has no future; we know already,
despite remoteness and the different sorts of fly,
it has suburban aspects: nobody here must wait
a day to hire his favourite video, and one of its sons
read 'The Death of Virgil' through his Sunday School.

It is full of details we agree to love—
the cat called Fortunata, the minestrone
made in milk-churns, an aunt who mounted 'Tosca'
in a shearing shed: outside town, it offers you
the peace inside your mother's mind, the need to get away.

RIVER RUN

There is no source, though something like a bird
distances the very distance in its hoverings
and, tugging at a twig, will mark the start.

Out of nowhere to a little gully, the bits of life
like startings-up of always crying ground
gather and roll forward to a pool.

A pool, a pearl, another pearl, a pool—
the river is arriving where the dew
dries on the early paperbarks as dust.

Every childhood has its playground kills,
the innocentest cruelty and the wet
despair which no maturer pain can quell.

A time of waterfalls, of leaps round rocks
that flash their dignity, a use for history—
our fathers went down this peculiar road.

Where the gorges start, our planners stipulate
well-fenced lookouts and well-hung flowers,
blood smears of bottlebrush and banksia.

Hard-working days of green ambition,
the river and the self are broadening
among short-lived crimes, a gaudy flap of parrots.

As suddenly as afternoon the surge becomes
a modified achievement—where love has stalled,
the four-wheel-drives churn up a path of frogs.

Crops on the shore, a dog asleep upon a cushion
and the arbour heavy with the scent of lily—
out there the water-skiers skim the farther bank.

Wide as a yawn, the slow-coach river now
bastes in itself and boils the leaves
upon its surface: it is going home.

Alluvial plains of age and aspiration
needing great engineering works and
pumping stations—the doctor checks its heart.

Is this the run-up to the Third Millennium
or a ghostly dock of dreams? Each night
we take a boat upon a different thread of delta.

There in the dark, a little distance off,
the breakage sound of ocean—we will dream here
and hope never to reach the pounding Heads.

Instead, make home and common cause
with fish heads and the floating debris
of the wharfs. The river has no start,

How could it bring us to a proper end?

THE BLAZING BIRDS

With their wicker worry wok of claque and claim
the birds play Scrabble on the air. Sky is stretched
and naked nightmare's strung on fencing wire.

On a mat of pier, Australia's noisy birds
are sucking anthems. So much suck comes out
with lumps of sun it spells Magnificat.

Certainly it's a privilege to get up drunk
and leave a note—I'm not inside my ears, I'm
parleying with certain parrots of importance.

All at once and always changing gear
the Sistine servers shrike. Perennial
the praise and every liturgy a laugh.

Telephones are ringing on the wire
but men are starved of epithets. Boiled words,
the birds say, are as close as you will get.

The tirra-lirra parliament sits on.
'Ugly old man with crocheted wobbly hair,
you're wong, you're wong, your curry's doubly wong.'

Give them an inch and they'll take a worm.
A team of locusts trains beside the Firsts,
black cockatoos above a stand of fire.

I almost lose my way among similitudes.
Bird cries may seam into our symphonies
but in this garden only spiders spin.

The 'twenty-eight', the spangled drongo, kooka
with its caco-credo, magpie mutts,
what messages they drag across the sky!

Kings to fish for, larks to scent the air,
a parlement of fowles refuelling,
and Bib and Bub expelled from Paradise.

THE ECSTASY OF ESTUARIES

It is the right time to come here visiting,
Where villagers saved suicidal whales
And sand is constituted white
Beneath blue hulls—a time of times
Precluding death and constantly ahead
Of madness. Rest here, that have no absolute.

What might rock sleep is breaking out at sea
On reefs which bear the Southern Ocean;
Up-river pelicans on posts applaud
Such widening to island esplanades,
A shallow onus of the tide, the whiting
Sketching on the bottom their own shapes.

Nothing is curable but may still be endured.
Voices wait near water for career,
The karri are as various as signatures
And people out of cars confess they find
A fantasy in being what they are,
Slaves to the ancient brightness of the sea.

A magistracy of memory condemns:
Give us your childhood reminiscences,
Fan us awake with scholarship—was that
The famous Ardath pack, the Sydney Silkie's bark,
Were we the partners of those afternoons
Which lounged about in bamboo concert-rooms?

Staunchness of land slipping into light,
Of sandbanks drying from the ebbing tide,
Opens a thinking principality—
It's always a thousand miles from where to where
And will be Sunday by the railway clock,
Apprenticeship to dying in the dark.

To scatter toast crumbs to the gulping gulls
And let the dinghy flutter on the tide,
To be reliving what was hardly lived
When years ago the boat came back at dusk,
A father and a son, strange strangers, home,
This is the storytelling of the blood.

A countryside of changes still unchanged
Where no '*vielleicht*' will travel as 'perhaps',
Remorseless movement that a wayward tune
Has challenged into permanency,
This ecstasy of estuaries prepares
A tableland for time to wander in.

THE WIND AT BUNDANON

In the code of invisible painting
trees are pushing colour to its limit,
a green which parses understanding.

This wind has broken free from minds.
It is assured by sites and measurements,
by the coral trees' red rip-tide
and washing blazing on the line.
The bunya pines' high installation
is a clash of gears and by the lake
the servant oranges are silvering
a black estate.

The wind can't see what we can see.
It is invisible opacity
and slams the shutters on a rising cake.
Cockatoos on a tea-towel
hear it at the window and fear for
their active squadrons in the field.
Its cousin fire
flicks a Draculine antenna from the grate—
the Master's come in glowing granulars.

This merciless blowing has to be
a metaphor of something. The teeth
of this land are worn to stumps but look
at what a gummy grannying can do.
From the river's haunting-point
wind sweeps away stale helicopters,
laggard cloud, complacent quietness.
Taller clouds stand back from barricades:
let Pentecost amaze the visitors,
sky and the four-inch grass are history.

The wind has learned communication's lesson,
these days it rides about on four-wheel drive.
Knowing the public for anthologies,
it asks us to invent comparisons,
but don't ascribe its billowing likenesses
to marketing gone crazy; there was a wrench
when complaining and perfectible mankind
came to Australia. Nature to respond
looked up its entry in the votive texts.
It did this to be kind to Rousseauists
who had no time to preen themselves
before ethnology took over. So the wind
joined terror and the regular volunteers.

Chasing a headache down the dam,
closer to Nature than to Real Estate
and picking up the proofs of rational love,
one sprints in darkness through the rushing air
while another clocks the protests
of the telephone. The wind has helped us
draw the face of death. Suppose we had to find
a passage of the Styx—a goat, a pile of coins,
a strangled chook beside—better this wind
than gods about their business. With fingers
in its eyes, it paints itself a holocaust,
back to our dreams, The Wonder Book of Sunsets,
The Raft of the Medusa, a world on fire.

A HEADLAND NEAR ADELAIDE

In this transparency
hung two aviators,
a hang-glider virtuoso
and a little bird,
facing each other
stationary
in the slipping air.

Talk of thermals is no use,
keep your Physics for the blackboard.
The bird was outdaring the man.
The man slithered
and had to right himself
on a jogging current.
The bird edged a little up or down
back to motionless
unblinking confrontation.

This went on quite a time,
evolution slung in space,
the loss so evident
the gain measured only
by the watch upon my wrist.

DIE-BACK

An early choice among the thousand possible
disposables, let me give you an example—
The chuckle of air which flows from a cloud's
occlusion of our only sunny morning of the month;
the loose knob on the door which rattles as
the cat pushes fifty times its weight
across a well-hinged arc; the papers needing tidying
to stop them seeming nests of spite and vanity.
The subject doesn't matter: words are like colours,
they will fit whatever picture's in the making
and it, in turn, this choice of digits on the screen,
is only made to stop a something else
of more intense concern from getting close
to the describable—that's how we move our readers,
we circumvent the masterpiece, we take the weight
off feet by running a funicular to Helicon
with parking space and trolleys and a crèche
for the sublime. How many of you have ever paused
to think of what you owe the suffering artists
of the world? Little by little, as acid eats a plate,
they use up chances and map at least the edges
of the possible, the unendurable. If I know someone
has tamed a bath sponge with a sonnet,
I will wash my face today; if my fright at moonlight
has darkened a sestina I might escape insomnia.
Some places are quite exorcized—the foxes in the dripping ground,
the thistles on the tongues of Nature Poets.
What's still to do is vast. Each hour a self
is born which may become a juggernaut
no matter how the typhoon lashes at the coasts
of poverty, or new diseases write incipit
on the Immune System.
                          How to spike this bold potential,
this opportunity to make an Enterprise Economy,
is all our skill. The darkness looms: men with ties

adorned with ocelots stand about in suits
at the doors of luxury apartments—this is a Viewing
and the sounds of splashing from the indoor pool
arrive with steam for florid cheeks and collars
till the cheapskate marble weeps—business and desire
outface decay. This unkillable species kills
and goes on being nice to parents, strong on law and order,
its system of despair decked out in hope.
How could our end be uniformly terrible
when our imaginative powers are so confused
we sulk below the level of our fate?
Geniuses may have paid too high a price
for all their optional extras; we do not have the evidence
of their deaths. And information crowds the screen,
a claw-back of the proper passions which should die
but now may live forever. This is the blandishment
of value that our choices are designed to clear,
this electronic smog will activate the systems of despair
until a company secretary screams 'shit'
at a royal visitor, a Chat Show Host hangs himself
ten storeys up, his circuit as he chokes
a half-hour on the clock-face of the dark.

So begins the die-back. The great crowned trees
appear as Light Horse plumes, the branches bare
above the brushed blue tops, a thinning-out
like barbers' rearrangements of the hair
on Managing Directors' scalps. A beetle, a fungus,
a vagrant virus, evolution's other part of the forest,
has changed the whole map of the bush. The cities soak
up soft artesian poisons, the quokkas change their diet
to gleanings from McDonald's, and the desert
seen at night on speculators' charts
scintillates with little spots of death. There will never be
a human spirit equal to the blaze of dying,
no rhetoric to match the chaos in the brain;
but time will save us, ease us to decline
the unsought gift of feeling. As trees gutter to the ground

and alterations to our faces bring on elegy,
we can again dispose of worldliness
by fixing it in a bricolage of words,
our manuscripts left lying on the desk
when wills are read, our mourners struck by visions
we have entertained of nescience,
of lightness once exchanged for consciousness.

A CHAGALL POSTCARD

Is this the nature of all truth,
The blazing cock, the bride aloof,
The E-string cutting like a tooth,
      The night that crows?

The cock has seen the standing grain,
The bride is shrouded by her train,
The violin is strung with pain.
      A cold wind blows.

From earth to sky the cry ascends,
What breaks will threaten where it mends,
Proud lovers end as pallid friends,
      These feed on those.

WHITEBAIT

A multitude of fervours comes to this,
a shoal of silver crispness on a dish:
one man equals ten-thousand fish.

See all the frogs writhing in a pool,
feelings coming in from the cool,
and who'll do it this time, who'll . . . ?

The genocide of creatures which
is the support of life is also life's rich
riot and keeps our howling up to pitch.

CAPITAL AND INTEREST

From the discovery of penicillin
and development of the pill
to the clinical diagnosis of AIDS,
the world had two decades of safe sex.
Such a wicked interregnum
could not go unregarded.
How appropriate, say those
whose highs are power and money,
that we should now be punished
through our sensuality.

But consider it this way.
The human urge to love
can take no stricter path
than through the sexual membranes.
Who then could blame the virus
for crossing to its future
on such a perfect bridge?
A text the New Right might discuss:
market forces pledge success
to the best-equipped contender.

COPYCAT

At least his funeral might be followed
by some of the books he didn't review.

And his notices thrown into the grave,
something to read for a wet eternity.

The stoppage of bells tells that another island
is gone down, the horizon snapping back.

Copycat had grown to love the arbitrary,
maddened by the injustice of good sense.

He'd lived through enskied angelic days
of young Puritans with gourmet needs.

And dons who left their desks on Sundays,
a promise with no need of enemies.

He'd done his best by jokes and syntax
but was a tabby tabbed with unimportance.

His last call to the office asked, could he have
another week, there was still so much to read?

HE WOULD, WOULDN'T HE

He'd say, if pressed, the bomb has kept us free,
We sing the future in an awkward key
But, look, the orthodox revives in me.

As well in acid rain command the tree
To stop its leafing: the moving hands decree
Time has not changed by even one degree.

In whichever place the Emperor chanced to be
The capital was set: the royal we,
Like this man's ukase, came subconsciously.

From Chat Show Host to Superbard we see
The world made new by new ambition, 'The'
(So to say) 'Comedian as the Letter C'.

Apocalypse is followed by High Tea,
Prevailing winds blow fallout out to sea,
The war will make a series for TV.

There still are those who want the CBE.
Bad-tempered diarists praise the Family
And say the Poor live irresponsibly.

Adam, when told by angels that his plea
Had been refused by God, just shrugged like Mandy
And answered, 'Well, He would, wouldn't He.'

SERIOUS DRINKING

It comes from wanting to be perfect.
All human pain from spite to rape
Is just a reading on the grape
And all these living counterfeits
Are for philosophers' defeats;
A discontent so undivine
Moves water one notch up to wine.
Put it away, here comes the prefect.

The sinner is paid in his own coin.
Blood is love's apotheosis
And brings the liver to cirrhosis,
The flowers of sleep which towered stand

Are the famed brandy of the damned
And Wunderkinder who begin
With champagne lights may end in gin.
A drink, lest I forget thee, Zion.

Which human host can match the Devil?
God's watery water is no use—
The anthropologists' excuse
States every known society
Makes alcohol and poetry
Which in their likenesses explore
Creation's toxic metaphor.
Sober I shake and drunk I drivel.

NIGHT WATCH

You sleep less as you grow older
As if it were wiser to stay awake
To be ready for the angel's shake,
The chill of the exposed shoulder.

But it isn't easy to make good use
Of the time you've gained at 3 a.m.
Warm-footed us becomes icy them,
The witty saint the cracked recluse.

To die might be to be fully mad
And sanity to stay open-eyed.
How many of the sane have died
Trying to remember dreams they've had?

TABS ON DICKINSON

Body and Soul drift homeward now
In less than perfect sync,
The Soul which made the longer vow
Impatient of the link.

But none may speed the end of this
Grey firstling of accord—
The Soul is greedy for its bliss,
The Body's seen a sword.

THE FAREWELL STATE

Waking, being glad, not blessing
another day yet taken by surprise
by accustomed miracles, the duvet's
hill of cats, the radio through hiss
coughing fantasies and trivia,
you sense the comfort of your being
momentarily beyond the power
of dreams, their tricks and calms,
extruded on to a world
which feels the cold and sees the point
of cruelty. Remind yourself,
for once, this bourne you live in
owes you nothing—even words and music
float to you from a distant star
whose diligence is unconcerned
with pain or cunning. What then
of wrath and politics at 9,
the shouting and the banging-down
of spoons? The discontent, the poor
gas pressure in the bathroom,
the sky of angled slate beyond
the window—these are commas

of the working day, not needed in
the seamless punctuation
of your dreams, those parables
of Emperor and worm. Make the most
of anger and discomfort then,
and people's grating voices:
tomorrow or some other likely day
the cats will wake and feel they're cold
and seek a warmer contiguity.

SACRED AND PROFANE

They hurry from their storeyed layers
Down to the wet and littered street,
They have not met their far betrayers
But only self and self's defeat.

Nowhere at all is where their home is,
Their greed is small as any mouse
And like a mouse their unfed moan is
Trapped in a dark and shuttered house.

We call apocalypse to flatter
Their pain and say the world's the same,
And yet we know it's no such matter—
Though all must die, not all may blame.

The government of words is vicious
And fills the writer's mouth with gall;
His indignation adventitious,
He is the torturer of all.

THE UNFED APHORISMS

parse this, as boiling water said to steam
trial by train became the fashion-plate

kept up by incompatibility
the weary Devil's nominative muscle

sell a Porsche, be lyrical at last
the consequence of several heavy harvests

wide verandahs magnify the dark
the moon encrusted in the atrium

work had spread to shadeless corridors
vocalize of birds on midday watch

Psyche gives her vote to Cinderella
laburnum transepts cross the tabby's path

to be inscribed on pin-heads: charity
holidays with all the ferries running

corrections in green ink may yet convince
below the salt but still above the mice

after the trepanning homely ghosts
a code is broken in the billiard room

no parking space was left outside Valhalla
their female orphans learned good housekeeping

a friend's polite review is soon outfaced
envy was found more natural than hope

sexual trooping—something from the Raj
gone from the menu, everybody's choice

an ear in your word, the gritty Janus joke
untiring fountains falsify the grounds

ON MALLARMÉ'S ANSWERING MACHINE

Leave the sink to serve the sonnet, Maeve!
After eves of old dove's feathers when
Twilight hangs pegged-out towels and hen
Cries follow, as the bathers leave the wave,

Trudging past your door, you bend
Low, cooking a generation to the grave,
All your elbow's vanity a slave
To these inheritors, your house of men.

This is the call: the saving gesture must
Come from those who clean the moon
With sighs and chamois. Under the dust

A sermon lingers. Put down your cloth
And follow love—who services will soon
Be soft and dressed for dying like a moth.

SUN KING SULKING

In the park the peacocks
have made their own Versailles
but the sparrows prefer a universal slum.

We are classic because we live
so briefly: the ant tells the dung beetle,
'Labour on, Hercules.'

Saint-Simon's entrails exploded
in their funerary bottle—more fun
than the levée of a constipated king.

I said to Molière,
Virtue is above Morality
and my subjects are beneath it.

(I am not usually so easy to follow,
my oracles are toll-gates
and arbitrary confiscations.)

We have always welcomed strangers—
André Breton introducing Henry Miller:
'Gentlemen, the Big Sur Realist.'

Anachronism. I lift my cane
in time with Lully. Elliot Carter
beats down Boulez.

When asked for my reign's greatest
achievement, I've sometimes answered,
M. Perrault's Puss-in-Boots.

Port Royal never interested me
but the cannon-fire at Oudenaarde
made sense of Protestantism.

Dutchmen, Dutchmen, no less,
have resisted my diplomacy,
but I am old, so paint me a victory.

A Mass is worth Paris
as my grandfather didn't say.
He wasn't really an artist.

I recall my chamberlain: 'Sire,
a thousand musicians were born this year
but only one of them is Rameau.'

A fire in the West,
the sun in my window,
I too am a spectacle.

ESSAY ON PATRIOTISM

Compared to my true patriotism
the imperialism of my legs and bowels,
the suzerainty of my eyes,
grave hemispheric rulings
of the wide Porterian peace,
my love of country is a pallid passion.

So when they say
we've dwindled to a Third Class Power,
a Banana Republic without
a decent satellite to spy from,
I recall those old inheritors
of fear, dirt, snot and rickets
who crawled out of their burrows
to hail Ladysmith's relief
and bray the victories of their rulers
on air they couldn't warm.

Let us therefore handle the word 'great'
with circumspection. It fits Blake
and Milton, is much too big for Cromwell
and generally should watch itself in mirrors,
bearing down like Yeats's Nobel head.

When commentators write about
'the patriotic proletariat',
imagine week-end articles—
'From flat-cap to cat-flap
in one generation', 'Dinkies
are not toys today', 'Designer
Murder comes to Sicily'—
and hang wild garlic round your ears.

Let what people really love
invent an island tongue:
'a gemstone cantilever . . .
hearing it in Noel's SOTA
Dynevector/Spectral/Threshold/
Acoustat/Entec . . .' no wonder
Rambo gobbled up the gooks
if he had such voices in his head.

Patriotism is not enough
of a scoundrel's last refuge
even if you love
your neighbour as yourself.
When I fell from the long tree of light
I didn't know it was going to be me
or I'd have checked all these quotations.
Where I landed I named *ours*
though it was never *mine*.

True patriots all,
the still-swimming lobsters in the tank,
the lambs that face the ocean through steel bars,
the opals in the open-cut—
I left my mother's and my father's house
and stepped on to a road beneath the stars.

AN INGRATE'S ENGLAND

It is too late for denunciation:
That the snow lingers on the sill
And that there are too many newspapers
Is the same as telling yourself
You've given this country forty years
Of your days, you're implicated
In the injustices of pronouns
And the smarter speech of sycamores.

This is the England in your flesh,
A code enduring Summer while
Tasteless birds flap at the edge of
Civilizing concrete. Some have found it
Necessary to reimagine Nature
And stop importing Wordsworth
To shame the bugles from the evening air—
You were born in not the colonies but God.

Yet the brain cannot be Gloucestershire
And vents of human hate are viewed
As old cathedrals across osiers.
The selling of the past to merchants
Of the future is a duty pleasing to
The snarling watercolourist. Prinny
Used to ride by here, and still the smoke
Of loyalist cottages drips acid rain on voices.

The trains in their arched pavilions leave
For restless destinations, their PA Systems
Fastidious with crackle; nobody
Will ask you to identify yourself
But this will lead to hell, the route
The pilgrims take—down the valleys
Of concealed renewal to the pier-theatre,
The crinkle-crankle wall, the graveyard up for sale.

THE CAMERA LOVES US

This is a lucky century, we have more
To leave behind than just our bones.
The minutes of our relaxation
Cry for record, and where a spasm
(Call it hope or pain) might once
Have languished just in some sightseer's

Slight recall, we have the lumps of light
To keep it fresh, to turn reflexes
To investments—finally to harrow Hell
With specimens of timeless platitude.

And that is just the start. The camera
Will paint us backwards. More than our
Disappointing mothers it will love us
And groom us into shape. It doesn't merely show
Us to the world but sprays us with its own
Invention till deep-seated ordinariness
Is lacquered by its gleam; the self,
Used to cracking knuckles in dark corners,
Is beamed out as a worldly figurine
Festy with the lens's afterbirth.

It's real, it has been photographed.
The tears aren't sticky but the smile's stuck down.
The soul gets up and leaves this site
And is not missed. Archives are oracles,
No other hell presides beside the grave.
We wonder what the pictures would look like
Were we to see a print of Hadrian
Breakfasting at Tivoli—perhaps
As disappointing as pornography
Where cocksmen camber with their socks on.

The artist came before the camera:
Such fanciful misreading! Walk down
La Rambla past the lines of cages
Filled with doves—do the people eat them, love them?
Or are they what Picasso had to bank
Before he drew his bird of peace? The blood
Runs down the wall, the soldier hurls his rifle
From him as the bullet strikes. People
Are walking to their deaths and will not know
What hits them till the camera christens it.

CIVILIZATION AND ITS DISNEY CONTENTS

Dear Readers, I offer you this impassioned book,
or, should I say, this disquisition on culture
as impassioned as I know how to make it.

It has been so often observed that what we want
is usually to do with food or sex or comfort,
but there are no systems in printing such conclusions.

And systems are what separate us from the animals;
they are the sublimity of our reasoning, the jolt
to eye and brain of the façade of San Miniato.

Our duty is to find them where others see only
a jumble of contrivances, a slogging resonance,
or the dirt-caked misery of the way the world survives.

It will never be forgiven let alone laureated to say
that the trouble with systems is that no one system
can cover everything—to work, a system must be unified.

And so you have before you my Hellenic-Hebraic law,
the tables of which I brought down from the attic,
the universality of family trunks and secrets.

But yet, like a hidden second diary or codicil
to an unfair will, I offer you a few contrary
commonplaces further to my systematic thinking.

We are not put on earth to be happy but to ensure
The effective production of Daihatsu Hatchbacks—
not even the Japanese could want to live in Japan.

Though our lives are short, time is a terrible burden.
Masters think that slavery is necessary to their riches
and slaves know that rich men constitute God's grammar.

You must have met reverent aesthetes patting rarest icons
and have known, while biting on their exquisite food,
their incomes derive from Mail Order jugs of Charles and Di.

Nothing is too far from the grave's edge, or the curtain
slung before the fire. And all the Micky, Dopey, Bambi bits
are to keep your eyes from wandering to the dancing dials.

And yet, why not? To be serious you need a grant
or to have secured tenure. The rest is journalism.
And here's a serious documentary on the survival of the beaver.

At night cicadas mourn the beasts prepared for market.
Tuscan hills vibrate to generators and to rock-and-roll.
The majesty of the Trinity wafts past an old cess-pit.

Bind up the sticks for strength. We are not Fascists.
What will they dig up afterwards of us? Donald Duck is quacking
his charges off to school. He will not tell them he has cancer.

THE POEM TO END POEMS

This poem will get up and off its bed
And let you have the mostly left-out facts,
Such as, it's getting written round about
A theme it's following whose doubtful tracks
Are somewhere in the poet's dusty head:
It fades to life, its past ahead of it.

The theme it's following has special pegs,
Such as, '11 o'clock one day in June,
The trees enleafed, election vans proclaiming
Words as meaningless as opportune,
The mind blocked like a sink and all its dregs
Demanding form but unconcerned with meaning'.

The writer senses that his work must be
Like archaeology on some distant dig
And should he paint the throne-room and declare
It must have looked like that, an endless gig
Of beards and timbrels, bulls and minstrelsy,
He'll turn the serious to the picturesque.

Demanding form but drowning meaning is
The sort of sub-Platonic joking which
An art which flees the sacral is left with:
High Tech should go without a single hitch
And arrogance should never lose its fizz—
You pay the Freudian pension off in myth.

What's new? What's old? What even smells of life?
Today the theorists are the avant-garde,
The artists make it in the Supplements.
The cultural Michelin is stacked and starred
With every genius and his nagging wife—
We keep the templates safe in our bank vaults.

But as I write this down I may uncover
That ring of majesty I know is stored
In words, and by retrieving it I may
Dredge cool reflections from the image-hoard:
Thus while each word remains I will discover
The source from which the magic rays are sent
And publish it this once, the world at play,
Our single sphere which purrs with measurement.

A BUNCH OF FIVES

for Kit Wright

Caveat emptor? or buyer, be choosy.
Buyer, be choosy and hope to be saved.
Hope, to be saved, must last to the end.
Last to the end is the cringe of the slave.
Cringe, be enslaved, but get your Jacuzzi.

*

Time was the *Greens* were a team
of vicious charioteers. Now the colour
stands for everything the Liberal soul
most desires to save. That whales may roll
through Haydn, the Emperor must dream.

*

Shakespeare on original instruments:
bear-baiters' breath, the Walsingham snivel,
Jack Cade's diphthongs, Douai's Jesuit screams,
boy choristers' simpers, the King's dribble:
an end to RADA decadence.

*

With cognate syntax, you're too far in
already, so Lichtenberg thought.
Every aphorism should abort.
Those are words you're playing around with,
you won't piss wine or grow a fin.

*

The poet Alec Hope has a building
named after him. Birds come to the living
poet's window every day. They grow
accustomed to him. He says, 'I don't know
what they eat, but they'll drink anything.'

*

Rhyme's coming back. Hooray! Hooray!
And stanza and metre and narrative.
Our old hack, metaphor, is blooming,
but under the dressage and the grooming
trot the spavined nags of yesterday.

*

Mallarmé was wrong. Poetry is made
of intervals, the spaces between words.
My Collected Works are all the white
of all the pages I shall ever write,
my First and most victorious Crusade.

*

Here's my crack at Zen. Existence
is the notation of an untranscribable
melody. Art is the incandescence
when you pass the current of the present
through the past's resistance. And then?

*

My mind is like a bookshop chock-a-block
with weighty, plate-filled tomes, all listed as
Porteriana. Customers reconnoitre
for pornography; they loiter,
fingering, not purchasing the stock.

*

Then, as they say, it all became a blur.
I woke in Paradise and it was dark,
I had become my double; there we were,
the carnivore listening to Bach,
the gentle, vegetarian murderer.

*

Why do libraries fill me with unease?
They make me think of God the Great Curator
whose mind stores all atrocities that were
and every death which has yet to occur.
Churches are better, the dead there are at peace.

*

Music begins where words end
(Goethe). But he didn't like the sound
composers added to his words.
His place was on the ground,
the point from which the larks ascend.

*

Planet Earth now boarding through Gate One,
everyone aboard! So these are who
you're flying with, an unimpressive bunch
to find yourself among. Cabin Crew,
doors to manual. The Sun. The Sun.

*

I woke from my dream crying.
It had been so beautiful,
love personified.
Earlier, I'd woken terrified.
Both dreams had the taste of dying.

*

I stand outside the prodigal's door,
on my own now, my one good angel gone
back to the canton where sun never shone.
O shattering of jugs, O tears unfurled,
I leave the world and am young once more.

LITTLE BUDDHA

'Ich bin der Liebe treuer Stern'

To see its porcelain smile
    Is a surprise in that room
With the electronic junk,
    The albums, the morning gloom,
The empty Pils neatly piled
By the futon, the light sunk
    To a hangover of dreams
    And yet, whatever it seems,
Whether indifferent to
    Fate or expectation or
Luck, its surveillance tells you
    Love can't walk out through the door.

Unbelievers, still stung by
    The need to construct a trust,
Like to set some piece of kitsch
    In place, a Madonna, bust
Of Shakespeare, Sports Day trophy,
Anything numinous which
    Shines in the Humanist dark,
    For they are set to embark
On an unknowable sea
    And the call-sign from afar
In darkness and light is 'I
    Am love's ever-faithful star.'

You sing this and try to prove
   It by rational choosing,
By doing without the bounty
   Of high romantic losing,
Keeping instead to a love
Durable as accounting,
   Traditional as the rhyme's
   Approximated sublime,
And you let the Buddha fix
   On you its unchanging look
Outfacing digital clicks
   And the brandishing of books.

But the warp remains in the soul,
   The obscenity of faith,
The creed that runs in the blood,
   The seventy years of safe
Excess succeeding control,
A dream of desert and flood,
   Of God at the index points
   Whose gift of loving anoints
The numinous animal
   With lyrical avatars,
The lure of impersonal
   Truth, a silence of the stars.

MARKERS

Your death came between Auden's and Britten's
and a few weeks after Connolly's (C.).

The first two you met but hardly knew—
Auden at Heathrow and Britten in Aldeburgh's Post Office.

Connolly you'd seen only on TV
yet you cut his obituary from the paper.

Just as you once cut Randall Swingler's,
a child reaching to the past for an adult's hand.

The long march of the trivial needs markers:
we have to guess if there is terror at the end.

But something tells us to watch the shining
of certain lives as if they were our beacons.

A single plot involves each one of us.
We nestle in the dark against generics.

Then, instead of home and old humiliation,
the starless night of human love appears

And with the great exemplars of our race
we walk out in the cold and pathless air.

OPEN-AIR THEATRE, REGENT'S PARK

In all truth-telling there is waste of art,
Too much of what the soul knows
Can't be said in any working shape
And if an excavation of the heart
Were made for all to see, what grows
Would just disgust and bring no tears.
So I can start sententiously to ape
My feelings, feelings brought about
By words upon a stage. Thirteen years
Since what I hear now was acted there,
The Two Noble Kinsmen, with its plot of rivalry
And the gaoler's randy daughter, out

In the open at Regent's Park, the Morris dancers
And the Bavian round and round each bush and tree,
The audience darkening as the lights come on
And you beside me with your groping stare
Trying to fix the limits of despair—
Did Shakespeare write the speech before the goddess?
Auden finds the power of love so strong
It is humiliating, and says Shakespeare loathed
All masculine vanity: I confess
I hear only the multiple inclusive sadness
Of what Human Beings want
Vibrating in the words of Palamon;
I see a dying woman packed with pills
For whom no words would ever be salvation
Yet loyal to the social gestures till
Her heart's punctilio
Faded in mid-sentence. Time comes on
And we won't meet again on this kempt grass.
'Thou that from eleven to ninety reignest
In mortal bosoms, whose chase is this world
And we in herds thy game . . .' of you I ask
The power to disbelieve in you, to protest
At the vicious heraldry which boys and girls
Renew before my eyes, even my own children,
Cavorting along the margins of the grave.
Remake the world so the disappointed live
In a decorum of their usefulness,
Intervene in theatres of despair to save
The humorous and timid—it was your altar
Which we visited one bad summer in the park
Because we thought Shakespeare's hand was there
And liked collecting rarely-given plays,
And sucked from you the poison of your art
And heard your words die in the timid greys
Of what was green with love before the start.

THEY COME BACK MORE

And I thought they all had gone. Through doors
They hardly knew were there, the sick bays
With their yellow curtains or into legends
Of hard starts in life, of families losing fortunes
And long years of night school, the maimed and poisoned
Ancestors who take the place of history
And Marxist arbitration. And take the place of love
So that my life has been a pilgrimage
To safe refinement, the arch and etching of the cry
And not the cry itself. Where I should have packed
My sandshoes, taken a striped towel and zinc cream
To the sun, I sulked instead on Genoa velvet
For Old Vienna and old manses. Now I see the outcome;
These ghosts are as rich in real estate in heaven
As they were in Surfers Paradise; they have endowed
The trees; the city takes its pallor from their smiles,
My father the only spirit exiled from
A world he couldn't hate. The fire of his death
Became the Queensland sun; he's trapped in me
And I would wish him sky's forgetfulness.

And he's first back, in braces over flannelette,
Boiling cigar butts in a saucepan, planning
A lethal spray for aphis. Details for my mother
Are a harder bet, and betting was her florid best,
Having dreamed a winner in the darkest welter
Of her flesh—always willing to concede
That Eden had a tradesmen's entrance, she
Passed to death from exile, fearing both.
Yet she's the spirit of all cake-baking,
Laughter, kitchen-prowess, which inheritance
Proved to be a love of art: she may have thought
Mozart the favourite for the Seven Furlongs
But she knew instinctively our brains
Must be as intricate and wonderful a score
As anything he wrote if his great pattern

Should delight us. However she appears, in tan
Shoes and white-brimmed hat, or flaming
Pubicly from an afternoon hot-bath,
She and I will recognize each other,
The playful faces in the scowling crowd.

And such strange friends return, so say hello
To the iceland poppies and the zinnias,
The male and female pawpaws and the passion-fruit,
Straggling a drop of sixteen feet from our
Back landing to the wash-house and its copper—
Between this underworld of stumps and palings
And the long back hedge of bougainvillea
Was where I filtered Europe through Australia:
Ranunculus and asters loved to learn
The Magic Flute and William Walton
And cared for Ansons more than Wirraways—
It helped them to endure the Brisbane heat
While my father scanned the wasps and buzzed about
The garden scolding Natives, emptying
Love on his more brittle blooms. If 'under-the-house'
Was sex and guilt, the garden was salt Paradise,
The field of art. I knew to an instant's blick
I came from nowhere but had somewhere dire
To go, that we are granted lease of sun
And sounds of water to console us here,
An interregnum in the war of flesh
When Caliban and God sunbathe together.

And a tousled sunburst opens up to haunt
The daylight's overdream, an impromptu ballet
Of things which live because their owner died.
That bag with green and orange leather patches,
Gawky handles and a hardihood of hessian,
Bought beside the Vatican walls before
A morning gin blurred judgement—it went, I think,
to LA to outlive another's death;
The mirror ormolu'd to seem as if

Someone had been robbing Shaftesbury Avenue,
Preserving guilty looks no matter how
Clear the conscience of the glass—and will it show
Her face in Heaven? The plain watch on my wrist,
Repeating its warning of the end of things
Though it only winds and isn't digital—
It was her gift and keeps near-perfect time,
A calibrator of the perished hours
When hurt and humour raced us to the dark.
She's not come back but sends her artefacts
To represent her; nothing wipes the pain
From dusty surfaces, and as I list
The souls of these inanimates I know
They'll turn to flesh in death and guide me to
A warehouse of unclaimed identity.

And they come back more, the more to kill.
Till now my own dead body would have been
The first corpse I had seen but here these close
Ur-Revenants and friends are sent to shroud
Me with their occult shadows, to lounge about
As half-official yuppie psychopomps.
The traps are laid by language, the Judge's jokes
Hang everyone; our ducts of sense are zones
Of Eros, himself a god who forged his past.
They come back more, hoping to appear
On diary pages not to be indexed;
They know the world to be intrinsically
Evil, that whatever sense we make of time
To write *Finis Coronat Opus* will be
Some sort of privilege, and nobody is waiting
To meet us when we land. They will not live
As shades but angle forward to enjoy
The pluck of life, the pressure of their ichor.
And to resume? To live again, to stare
At eyes which happily occluded light
And pain of light? This must be banishment

And must be what the dream is dressing in,
The joining of our hands, the ampersand.

And the axiom asks always to be proved.

FROGS OUTSIDE BARBISCHIO

How reassuring to listen to frogs once more
From stagnant water in an old brick cistern
Beside olive trees run wild and the unprogrammed
Flight of a butterfly over hot fields and terraces.
One grandfather frog stays on his stick to watch
A self-tormentor return to his book to trace
His anatomy of melancholy. He's in Italy
To surprise an old hopelessness known long before.

The cosmos of frogs inside its wet-walled fort
Warbles and cavorts in the all that there is.
Wise frog rejoinders have challenged that book:
Come down to our waters so pulsingly black
And lose all your stubble of fortune and truth.
Here's art inside art, incision and sign
Of the purposeless minute outlasting its span,
Of the gloat and the plop and the stick still afloat.

PORTER'S RETREAT

Once the difficulty had been
to cross the Divide, to follow spurs
which seemed to end in air,
to swivel about the cobwebs where the creeks
dripped below their spiders to
a contrary encircling of your steps—
to keep on through the undergrowth

with only stripes of sun above,
to get beyond these endless-seeming vistas
and look out on the plain which might contain
a sea, a minareted island, a mirage,
whose common epithet was Felix,
appointed place of all felicity.

There are, of course, bland natures
back at home, whose only earnest
is a theory that your expedition
means to straighten out the land with names,
to fit a grid of the accounting gods
on plastic otherness. You'll have to give
a hostage to them—do it now.
Here by Disappointment Bluff, gaze
across the Vale of Sixty to Uncanniness;
beyond the rock-strewn creek
is an escarpment called Incalculable
and the fields are more elided than Elysian—
mark this tree the point of going back
and set it on the map—Porter's Retreat—
the place at which all further progress
ceases to have consequence.

But expeditions never go as planned.
You're given a foretaste of the future:
a set of barbecue emplacements,
Olympic Pool, koala sanctuary,
suggestions for a heliport—
journeys inland have moved Nature
from the coast: this is the people's fort
where families collaborate with the sun
to make home-movies of divinity.

You're far beyond here now,
digging for nurture under balding trees,
only too willing to fold up the map
and start the evening's diary entry—

tomorrow will be another scorcher,
meanwhile this heap of gutted granite
shall be named Mt Misery
and the muddy tank-full where the river
dips into the underworld will make
a just impression as Lake Longevity.

MUSICAL MURDERS

Tromboncino and Gesualdo,
two composers killed their wives.

Their temperaments were 'molto caldo',
Tromboncino and Gesualdo.

From Sabbionetta to Certaldo
sung notes were not as sharp as knives.

Tromboncino and Gesualdo,
composers who killed faithless wives.

*

Two others were stabbed in the street,
Stradella and J. M. Leclair.

Their lives and loves were indiscreet,
these others murdered in the street.

For journeys end when lovers meet
a jealous step upon the stair.

Composers murdered in the street,
Stradella and J. M. Leclair.

THE ORCHARD IN E-FLAT

The waves are weeping vaguely. Confessional dust
Plagues the opacity of ocean and a book
Lies down at angles—scene-setting by our sons.
A god is rising from the ambient air
As though there were no griefs and nothing died
But there appeared a wholesome vanity
For us to live in: evangelizing light
Is spread before a holy picnic, goats
And men move down the isthmus to dark bells.

The numberlessness of stones is speaking for
The helplessness of people—debts, deaths and
Spoliations are a tuning of the world,
A chord of limitless additions, but
Anywhere a road leads over hills
And temperate dawns to some encumbered cabin
Where the bruise of exile turns to timeless rose.

Sequences are set by leaves, the ripplers' coven,
Even as Aeolian sounds are congregated
To pick up yells of history or the bubble-breath
Of dying, separate conveyances of truth,
Some convected into keyboard plausibilities
And some to concert strokes of sanity.
Evil at its console feels for carpet-slippers
Choosing the classiness of the baroque.
Surely such categories include the double.

Behind us is the deep note of the universe,
The E-Flat pedal on which time is built,
Spreading and changing, both a subtle
Growth of difference and a minimalist
Phrase, with bridges crossing it and staves
Of traffic on its tide, a broad bloodstream
To carry to the delta full mythologies.

A mother and a boy come to the orchard
To turn a cow back to its field; they see
The ducks in line-ahead among the crimson
Pointillism of the windfalls and,
Overheard by them, the everlasting anthem
Changes as injustice starts to sing—
There's wood enough within: it fires the earth,
The creatures coming home, the buried bones
And pairs of ears poised, the weeping waves.

STRATAGEMS OF THE SPIRIT

You've reckoned without the world. The soil
Itself is pure sententiousness, the ocean
Argues with it when the wind springs up
And corpses won't stay buried. So many saints
Are unemployed, they can't turn down a part
Even if it's no better than a minor role
In some low-budget Tempting—feasting
Out of bounds or tripping up a donkey
In a culver, raising billhooks from lake bottoms.
The artist praises God according to
His pattern book; it's wholly orthodox
And worth his modest fee—but look aside,
He's really interested in something else:
A young girl pouring milk, a skiff the wind's struck
Going about. That's his Te Deum, rushes
In the evening swaying to the shore. We're so far
Into history, we relish the cordon bleu
Of abstinence, our stomachs and our bowels
Are training for the confidence of stones—
All this continues years beyond the Age
Of Faith: we just have uglier pictures now,
Paler credulities: the earth will not
Co-operate but sulks inside its tent
Of miracles. And we must watch our crude

Interpreters muddy up the halcyon—
If the slit in the Madonna's dress
Is sexual and she fingers it, the tent
Above her like a conquering glans, it's God
Day-dreaming a new gender for the war
In Heaven: a marvellous smile which runs
Through flesh *del parto*, headlong on to love.
Think too of angels which no man but Blake
Has ever seen—yet how everyday and picknicky
They look just holding back the curtaining,
How like the cousins you'd have liked to have.
They could be Stevens's invisibles,
They wouldn't need to borrow trumpets in
A land of intervention—might they be
The plot, the shining embryo, the blot
Of Jesus on his mother? It's too late
To be religious in the census sense,
The sons of Benedict have so baptised
The landscape, it's all hungry soul—No,
The spirit's excellent stratagems are set
To bring on other platitudes: we
Must think ourselves alive and newly-landed,
Star-faced Linneans hearing musical
Communiqués no erudition robs
Of freshness—we must pace our footfall on
The temple steps and listen for the sun.

HAND IN HAND

They are always together, the two who travel
But never know when they must separate,
A gravely frowning pair in gloaming who
Cast such savage shadows that the beasts
Stir in their tiers (sweet macaronic pun)
At this invisible portage, that the rivers
Etch their banks to fine-drawn lines

And music forms a gum upon the air.
They are hand in hand; no looking-back
Is necessary, but their fear is palpable—
Their Hermes is a harvest of remembering
As if they had been born to gather in
A future lived already: it must be this
Since tiredness was their starting-point
And faith like sunlight faded in betrayal.
The onwardness is strange; they grow old
But won't believe in time; they are fed on words
And every disappearing trick; an abbey
Is a schoolyard and a paysage
With carrion birds reveals its toothy fright
In pictures of a mother. By interchangeability
The world subsides to sex, its surfaces
All lust, its membranes history's odd halves.
That hand's in this hand, so no one sees
Their partnership is change, that love is like
A signal passing which may startle air
Only by its afterglow: is this a death,
Not of the one or other but of all?
Huge horns stake the mountains in their places,
A damning rung of darkness widening
Until the sea itself withdraws to show
The puny two still wearing eyes like hats.
One hand undid the swaddling wraps of pain,
The next one vanished in a coffin's echoings,
And yet one further bent down further to
Raise love to love, hydraulic vanity;
The last hand and the best enskies the heart
Along this path grown Mannerist where gods
Quote from their memories. Dark and darkening
Are the Furies' tails, whip-lashing light
On snow-tiled Erebus. Avert the eyes
And do not glance aside to question who
Is there. The species is the soul on trial,
Its pilgrimage a handclasp from despair,
Walking with Hermes to the upper air.

TALKING TO THE LIZARDS

It's true. Nobody should live all his time here, away from the dust
    Of delivery vehicles, away from
The knowledge that news is arriving which turns men's complexions to
    Maps, tells them that labour's relentless as life,
With queues of fine spirits sold up for breaking. The city is there
    At the end of all roads; may it forget me
If I forget it. I won't even tickle a letter, watching
    The lake, or savage the swans' punctuation—
Instead I'll endure the bad prose of the insects, their redundant
    Lyrics. Dance early death, life is escaping.
You wouldn't expect this: Cicero, master of morals, his grim
    Jar of precedents shut, sitting in sunshine:
The songs of first days are as sweet as smoked honey, the hazes of
    Noon in a month without rain—the upside-down
Landscape says walk on the air, this dust is from planets as lucky
    As Caesar. Thus we deceive ourselves, country-
wise, country-slow, stooping to scratch the hog marked for
                        slaughter, his snout
    In petunias. My books are my truffles,
I dig them in dreams. Last night when mosquitoes like bores in
                        the Senate
    Sang me to sleep, I saw a face open which
Had been a Roman's, a hard politician's whose love was on sale,
    Whose words were like nightmares where lampposts become
Portable gibbets—this gruesome effigy was too everyday
    To terrify me: a waking disturbance
Rocked me instead—a drunk screaming death at policemen and
                        tourists—
    They dragged him away but from his foul frothing
Caesar's great conquests appeared like prisons, the world he is
                        making
    To lock us all in. Hate is a flag which flies
Above rulers: they know our weakness, our envies and spitefulness;

The sum of our decency to them is mere
Anarchy, the state falling apart in kindness and service. I
      Fear that the gods are awake after sleeping
And mean to be noticed: the Innocent Age has slunk to its cave,
      The Epoch of Turbulence waits at the rim.
On nights when the moon is a sliver I shudder to see beyond
      Darkness the countryside's monster uprooting
The farms, the roads and the vineyards—the spirit of timeliness
      Washing in blood. I wait then for morning to
Show me the lizards convecting the flagstones, a sensitive
      Ballet of substance and shadow, the spring
Of their probing convulsed beyond truculence. A politician
      Should study lizards; their ludic rehearsal
Will clear his head and then when he sits at his desk again writing
      He'll think of their dart and release, their having
No path to prepare. He'll say to himself, We make music when we
      Act, almost as beautiful as real music,
A patterned disinterest like the movement of limbs across marble.

COPYRIGHT UNIVERSAL PICTURES

An immensely gifted palaeontologist
Shard-sifter has brought his virtuoso
Teenage viola-playing daughter
To the island to join him on the dig
And so encourage her to forget the quite
Unsuitable roller-skating son of a rabbi
Now proprietor of a pineapple cannery
On a remote bayou in Cajun country.

She has already noticed the only brother
Of the schizoid Alexandrian owner
Of the Crusader Castle where they excavate
Mosaics of Pyramus and Thisbe and airborne

Ganymede, the oldest of their kind in Paphos.
He has published one book of sonnets privately
From Keele University entitled *Atlantis, Atys,
Attica*, and brought his Burt Reynolds videos.

Professor Fuori Sanguinetti, who has had to leave
Catania University hurriedly and who hopes to
Acquire some Hellenistic artefacts for a firm
Of antiquarians in the Veneto to whom his wife
Is seriously in debt, suspects that our
Loving father is not everything he seems and that
The Manager of the Phylloxenia Hotel
Is either an agent of the KGB or CIA or both.

The poet is on a deserted beach breaking open
Shells for the viola-player, telling her how the fish
When boiled made a purple dye called Murex—
'Gee, you're a bore,' she says. 'I came here to get laid.'
The little waves like Aphrodite's feet lie down
In the spume and gulls snatch wrappers from the sand—
This is the scene she said she wouldn't do nude
Which will be on the posters when the film's released.

The Professor has followed them and watches from
The dunes; above the bay a helicopter circles
While a fishing boat is anchored out of sight
Below the Rock of All the Romans. Along the road
The Manager approaches in a Pre-War Chev.
We are not shown what will become of this
And pan back to the diggings where we see
The child-god simper in the eagle's claws.

The poet has begun a sonnet and from a room
Just over his the sound of Paganini studies
Drives an alto nimbus through the evening light;
Reynolds has beaten up a man in an all-night

Diner in St Louis, and the screen goes blank—
The girl and her father come into the lobby and greet
A man in a panama hat whose sweat-circles
Below his arms spread almost to his waist.

Articles of clothing catch the moon beside
The hotel swimming pool. Arpeggios of bubbles
Accompany naked limbs. A blue fish from Murano
Swims in air above Reception and trunks are loaded
On a BMW. The story will move on to Rhodes
And leave this cheap-to-film-in corner
Of the great inane. Leave, too, the unimportant
Like ourselves. Next shift, it may be Athens.

THE NEW MANDEVILLE

I

The people of this place are activists
Of the spirit's incompleteness, living
In expatriation from death, a state
Always anticipated, never known,
And so they place their clocks on traffic-lights
To tell the time of immanence. Missing death
Their value models are phenomena
And pictures borrowed from their neighbour state,
The Adversarial Isles. Decorum and good taste
Are taught by Masters of Imagination,
Proposing such Last Things as rage in orchards
After hailstorms, or Trecento altarpieces
Abandoned in some distant gravel-yard.
If we could die we could have history,
That rosy cause of all exhaustion,
Plus multi-layered books to write it in,
They like to think. Their exports are their mirrors
Which reflect the soul and not the expected face,
Very attractive to the vainer peoples,

But their afternoons are stunned and effortful
With everything from sex to conveyancing
Confined to morning hours. Missionaries
Have laughed to say the only beads attractive
To them are the rosary and that
A pear-shaped mole of orange hue found on
Their faces has been named 'The Lacrymosa'.
These then are people who define themselves
By one great missingness undoing all
Which love and speculation should insure.
The change they never fail to pray will come
May yet be drawing closer: not a wind
Like whiteness from the East waking disease,
Nor some Messiah raised on ruby yoghurt
Setting out to cross the tall Sierras
To an entrepôt, but economic shifts
Which foil both Planners and Free Marketeers—
So many have gone missing in between
Two latitudes of one peninsula
They coin the phrase 'Consumer Triangle'
And warn the esoteric seekers-out
Of ploys to counter boredom that a false
Connection with mortality is worse
Than floating down eternal afternoon,
So they should keep their patience for their sleep
And dream an intimation of an end.

2

Our captain entertained us with tales
Of haunted floatings, of the *Marie
Celeste* and drifting Zeppelins with meals
            Still hot on tables.

Good preparation for our landfall,
The twilight archipelago named
Archivia. The mist here is dense
            With unstopped music.

A land without population but
Rich in society: pictures
Freed from Museums posing beside
      Their unpainted selves,

Books, as punctual as newspapers,
Sitting at tables over Happy
Hour, swapping parricides and dram-
      atis personae.

Tantrums here are tantric—watch a note
Cut from its tonic contemplate some
Passage into joy to change the course
      Of modulation.

This world, so beautifully inscribed,
So underpinned by scrupulous pain,
So ruled by registers of others,
      Will last forever.

And has, the records show, outfaced its threats:
The Deconstructors' Insurrection,
The Death of Summary, then Silence,
      Exile and Cunning.

It's always Conference Time. Hotels
Advertise such comforts as 'Bring your
Own Death' and 'Permutate confession
      In our dream language.'

Tonight they're playing 'Exit, Pursued
By a Bard' and 'The Passion According
To St Bach', but jokes are seriatim's
      Ectoplasmic end.

Visit the Museum of the Future,
Goggle at the Dance of the Unborn
Masterpieces, try to imagine
　　　Living in a world

Where Sviatoslav Bimbo never
Existed, where the triptych 'The Mass
At the Trocadéro' wasn't hung
　　　And Brut was only

An aftershave. Prayer-wheels turning fly
The flag of ecstasy, The Serious
Squad arrests a frivolous graffitist
　　　Caught in the act of

Spraying 'Penis Angelicus' on
The windows of a music store. Time
Is the supreme swear-word, the last
　　　Emancipation.

The Mega-Store of Harmony stays
Open every night to harness
Exclamations of the million words
　　　That triumph trod on.

Each watering-place and Crossroads Cap-
ital affords a Festival: 'The
Parleying of Photographs', 'Redan
　　　of Recusancy',

'Salon des Diffusés'—the racks of
MIMs* are raised to light from underground,
A Demo-Pantheon assuring
　　　Immortality

* 'Mute Inglorious Miltons'

162

Its quarter of an hour. Ice-cream
Emperors, seconded to the parks
And crematoria, lend leaves their
      Best metonymy.

We tourists feel forlorn as if we'd
Lacked a chapter heading at our birth
Or got through childhood glued to the box
      With no memories

Of Sunday School or nominating
'Black Beauty' as a prize. Yet there are
Copious compensations: Book Wars
      On the Bioscope,

The trenches winding through Arcadia,
The Glossary Grand Tour, and for the up-
to-date a kinesthetic keyboard with
      Finger-tip control

Of metaphor, a sort of 'Chips with
 Everyman'. The afternoons are hung
With sentences which Sterne bequeathed to
      Universities.

The elaborations last. The lion
Lies down with the lamb, desire spins its
Cool cocoon and love is free to love
      Itself as syntax.

3
After the Tableland of Dreams our next
Intention was to kick the switchback to
High End, that showland, ever-changing Expo
Of the newest redeployments of the Spirit
Where greedy fables are precisely nimble
Whichever laser-digits phrase the murk
Of history—instead a fever took

Our bodies to a very different place,
A veiled occluded territory
Haunted by a tribe of disparates,
A sort of deep defile like Syracuse's
Quarry prison. To some its title is
'The Swamp of Suicides', to others 'New
Samaria'—patterned like a hand
Which clenches and unclenches constantly.
Its calm is voices ceasing, and its hope
A closure of all doors, its air-free sounds
Proclaim there are no questions here, the end
Of ending is so beautiful. This lie,
Consistent with each other lie, permits
The pain of stopping to persist as pain,
The images of human unredemption
To come back as 'The Generation Show',
With teenage fury always at rewind
And envy cataloguing its CDs.
The true books came as liberators, they
Reproduced the best historic hells,
The Lagers, Genocides, Apostolates,
But nothing here would print such images,
Their documentaries faded when the self
Looked from its attic to the childhood lawn
And saw its shape, the grass beneath the blade.
A nation whose last words are not to be
Esteemed makes this its only poetry:
'I die' (iambic), 'death comes' (trochee), 'dead
As dust' (dactylic), 'Thou shalt die' (an
Anapaest), 'Proud Death' (the spondee)—hearts
As much as God are spiked on prosody,
The silent voices chant and are not heard.
And then we set out from this backward Cave
Of Cadences to rejoin the world and felt
The breeze of commerce moving on our faces,
The sun re-focus on our skin, and birds,
Which had been idling in our wake, construct
A future round our ears with fervent cries.

THE CHAIR OF BABEL

For my granddaughters,
Amelia and Martha

A YES AND A NO

A Yes includes a No the body says,
absorbed in its unhappiness,
and music will not let the ears forget
that 'saved again' sounds very like 'as yet',
the old placebo of a guess

No wonder rapists hear a No as Yes.
Repentance tastes like *Punt e Mes*.
The fleet is still at sea; the ports regret
their one-time empire, all its rudders wet,
            now Yes includes a No.

Every cruel commandment more or less
will find its sacrificial Tess
and poetry from ode to triolet
can alter nothing, merely put its 'stet'
on each unfairness, pleased enough to stress
            that Yes includes a No.

THE CHILD AT SIXTY

The harpsichord plays out of black or silver grooves
And undulant air receives the message of
A past where with the rhythm of hard hooves
Each inexorable part of you vibrates
At memories of gardens, faces, loves,
The hiding behind doors, the padlocked gates
And backs of friends, the well-invested hates.

Such fear and palsy in the grey will then compel
The greedy child to claw back sixty years
And find himself along the path from hell
He missed first time, and being old but now
Replete with charm and cunning trim his fears
With bright armorial lies and mutter how
What time condemns the music will allow.

ENCOURAGEMENT TO SLEEP

The things beside the bed will wake with you.
    To wake with you your mind must live through sleep.
Alive through sleep your dream keeps you in view. ·
    What dreams can view will not be yours to keep.
What's yours to keep is all the world ahead.
The world ahead is things beside the bed.

And there you enter when you close your eyes.
    Unclose your eyes and see what time has made.
Time has made a tomb from its supplies
    Since it supplies such brilliance as will fade.
Such as will fade is brilliant at the centre.
Things at the centre touch and there you enter.

GO SOME OF YOU, AND FETCH
A LOOKING-GLASS

When Hardy looked into his glass he saw
A younger self of real not ghostly pain
And knew the travelling law
That youthful loss is framed as adult gain.

The reader reads and thinks he understands:
He's still inside the huge machine which time
Put in his parents' hands
And staved on paper with confirming rhyme.

They are themselves and so they can't be him,
And somewhere as his ancestors retreat
Intrusive Cherubim
Make singular the general defeat.

Always the present lingers in the glass.
The lawn is mown and soon the daisies rise
Above the new-mown grass
And looking in the mirror blanks the eyes.

NOTHING NEITHER WAY

I saw the world cease at my cradle's foot.
Beginning life with knowledge of its end
I wasn't told what acts would come between.

I meant to be a writer who put down
the truth dressed in its absolute brown clothes
but found myself in motley in my dreams.

I learned to live with my contending powers
and feel the warmth of being what I was
the while my species swarmed beneath the sun.

Natural History Programmes pictured mice
alive beneath the desert sand, clusters
of ants like music's notes on wide patrol.

And all the while a silent ticking told
my individual fate, my siege of self,
I was the screen where history would show.

'War declared today, went for a swim',
'got my *Zauberflöte* 78s',
'came home to Father choking on the floor'.

What do the waggons roll for, who will weigh
a Butlins in the pan with Buchenwald?
Death is a word in English. Gott is God.

And when I crawl from this cold absolute
of pointlessness I only step into
the meaner worries of the middle way.

Why are the ones I've loved so treacherous?
Where's the escape from unoriginality?
What courage could command a quiet end?

'I am myself indifferent honest but
yet I could accuse me of such things . . .'
Ophelias feel the heat of our self-hate.

And so fate faces both ways. My close loves
are matches for myself: can they forgive
my seeing my mediocrity in them?

DESKTOP CONFESSION

It is the brain which publishes our lives.
The fingers fight on any keyboard to
Invent the self, the total which survives,
The secret fundamentalist who
          Loves me but hasn't heard of you.

The screen lights up, the processor reveals
Its hoard of words, its everything that is;
The little brain is shocked, so it appeals
To death and summary, and 'Hers' and 'His'
      Are timed and ticked, with *sic* and *viz*.

Consider the girl whose head's between her legs,
Think of the minutes stalled in days and hours,
Making novels fly, grading rhymes like eggs—
The evanescent words, the paper flowers,
      The shifting Freudian lakes and towers,

These are confession's public instruments,
The only way a private voice can win.
Great houses send their several compliments,
This time you really get beneath the skin,
      You lift the lid and peer within.

Alas, there's nothing there to see; we come
From an unprinted blackness, one by one
Into the light; our books applaud and some
Live in our minds longer than things we've done,
      Old desktops warping in the sun.

BEDRIDDEN

There in a space like Lear's fired upland
We see them, the beds we've dreamed our lives in—
High, iron-framed, they wrap you like a mummy
In the cloths of dying, the toenailed sheets,
The blankets of the memory's understain—
Stored beneath them suitcases of letters,
Wine in cartons, tissues loved by moths,
Books fallen out of hands on to the dust.

These are the mirrored portages of life,
The tracks we took and once more didn't follow:
On their calm and terraced tracings
The sleeping mind has played the Emperor
To Everyman—a sort of slavery
Is all an ordinary terror can expect
Remote from the magniloquence of dreams,
A breakfast mind still sniping at its mail.

Such were the great ships of planning which
The Pharaohs built to sail in after death,
Made from what limits even gods on earth
To a belated laugh, and this is what
Your parents did for you, conceiving you
Upon a frame of casual fortune where
You'd lie in turn and make the world look down
To turn the pages of a picture book.

Now, like abandoned churches, beds adorn
The acreage of memory, lecturing
On treachery, quoting apocalypse,
Pure archaeology of randomness—
Here we hand on to others treasurable
Satisfactions of the race, a son's
Invisibility to God, a daughter's
Sacrament of beauty solemnized.

Danger is seen too late, the cry unmasked
As waking from a half-familiar storm
Devised by faces always swearing love
You feel the sides of where you lie, a real
If coffin-shaped, twice-reassuring place,
And start the channel where your parents passed
And feel the flow of paraphrase and reach
A wordless haven words might shelter in.

COAL SMOKE

He filters to the back of throat, a young man
        rigid with uncertainty,
breathing coal smoke from the evening air.

The writer in his sixties welcomes this
        returnee from eventfulness
and shows him to the body which is theirs.

The little cake dissolves, a sulphur taste
        deliquesces on the tongue—
evidence that the world exists for love.

1952 in London: fog closes in.
        The young man, older than his ghost,
looks to be delivered from himself.

1990, Lothian: the old man
        prepares to kill the forty years
he's fattened for his pungent prodigal.

THE VILLAGE EXPLAINER

The art of life is to be provincial;
to have sat in a plywood studio
for one's audition at the Quiz Kids'
Saturday Morning Jury,
to leave the shopping at the tram stop
but get home safely with the Cyclopaedia
of Submarines; to miss the waves of finches
in the wattle's volary because you wouldn't
lift your eyes from Audubon.

This way the fiction of assertion starts
and all the trumpets of controversy.
See the baby in his cot lift two fingers
in rebuke or benediction—dare his mother tell him
he's not the Pope? The blessing started
with the Fall, a myth to leer at
in the canvas seats of matinées, shared with
stencils of delight and death. Your ministry?
Café pulpits, those long hours at dawn
when the confessional cup is passed
and Mahler on the gramophone
abrades the torn wistaria—to travel,
to win disciples and to be depressed.

And so to the Enlightenment.
There will hardly be a Panel or a Column
you can't grace, or Round Table where Reality
is more than the rotating Chairman.
The March Past of the Words is now
a daily trooping, Understanding
plays its miniature overture, and
Self-Effacement looks into the glass.

Time makes even the autocue a blur
and this not uncourageous certainty
slides on to after-dinner mumbling,
the room emptying to your anecdotes—
back to the comforting provincialism
of dying, and if brave enough your joy
at finding out what can't be known.
Lastly, a reasonably long obituary
in the paper where you got your start,
The Village Explainer, in which old friends
remember how you milked the words the tribe
entrusted to you and the way you held
them spellbound, putting to them what they were.

BAD DREAMS IN VENICE

Again I found you in my sleep
And you were sturdily intact,
The counsel you would always keep
Became my dream's accusing tract.

Still I dared not think your force
Might even slightly slack my guilt—
This wasn't judgement but a course
Which self not knowing itself built.

It scarcely mattered where I dreamed,
The dead can choose a rendezvous:
You knew that nothing is redeemed
By blame, yet let me conjure you.

And this was Venice where we'd walked
Full tourist fig, first man and wife
On earth, and where we'd looked and talked
Your presence could outlive your life.

But now Venetian vapours clung
To every cold and wounding word—
The spectres which we moved among
Came from the phrases I had stirred.

They could not harm you but they bit
Into whatever had not died;
However we might reason it,
Your face and mine marched side by side.

And those old harshnesses which you
Muttered to me unrestrained,
Like Venice, loved but hated too,
Were all the closeness which remained.

BAD DREAMS IN NAPLES

My mind, that privatized Maecenas,
Has struck a bargain with my penis:
I dream a violent cityscape,
My feet stuck on with sellotape.

The boys of Spacca–Napoli
Are on their bikes pursuing me,
With girlfriends perched on hot machines,
Their labia outlined by their jeans.

I'm drinking Ischian white wine,
It's someone's piss, not even mine,
And now instead of riding pillion
My head is under Hugo Williams.

Around me genitals and faces
Appear in unexpected places—
A tap I chance to stand beside
Unzips my fly and feels inside.

I know what hurts me terribly,
The jokes and lack of dignity—
That fear should show contempt as well
Indubitably smacks of hell.

Yet this is better than the tilt
Which moves the action on to guilt.
A terrified and dying man
Is seeking his estranged wife's hand.

The Manager croons, con amore,
'No credit cards, please, Professore.'
I say my poetry will pay,
He shrugs and looks the other way.

They're packing me into my shroud.
I recognize it as the cloud
Always above Vesuvius.
My soul hangs round for God to suss.

So much for transcendentalism!
All the colours of the prism
When blended make one living light.
He breaks them up to keep them bright.

WISH WE WERE THERE

It would be our garden of scents and Spitfires,
it would be our yard for exercise,
it would go on for ever (and ever)
it would, of course, be Paradise.

And be fitted like a German kitchen,
every pleasantness at eye-level,
the cats on their curly yellow cat-mat
unequivocally of the Devil.

Mother and Father in frayed straw hats
and swatches of angelic flannelette,
the nimbus of childhood spreading wider,
the milkman trying to place a bet.

Getting old would be growing younger
as the CDs turn at 78
and Haydn's No. 97
provides a coda for Beethoven's Eighth.

The pet dogs buried by the roses
should rise from the limed and clayey soil
and the Council steamroller-driver
bring belated tears to the boil.

The post come twice a day from Youville
with letters of triumphant love—
you and Joseph on the river,
you with Fyodor by the stove.

And there too Indestructible Man
would keep death lurking by each bush,
clipping and pruning tirelessly,
the old lawnmower hard to push.

The voice of friendship calling up,
can you come down today to play
so time shall not move round the dial
and after-breakfast last all day.

The macaronic air refresh us,
taking pity on a poor linguist
till it's Pentecost and Schubert's Miller
takes his withered flowers for grist.

The end is nigh but will not happen
as tea appears on the lawn—
the synchronicity of Heaven
is owed to us for being born.

VERB SAP

Nothing they say of this
Infinite mystery
    Love could disparage
More than its usual
Course through extremity
    Safe into marriage

High expectation of
Personal happiness,
　　　Magic achievement—
One takes on dozens of
Lovers, another stays
　　　High on bereavement—

Each plays the cold self game,
Seeing in love's face a
　　　Secret opponent
Where the advantage is,
Mirrored attraction or
　　　Pious atonement.

Poetry knows its role,
Lending its rhythms to
　　　All that's enduring,
Servitude, blandishment,
Irrationality,
　　　Even procuring.

STILL LIFE WITH CATS

Once more I thank you beasts: you have delivered me
from the scrutiny of time's inspectorate
nor have you insisted on alternative philosophies,
endurance, love of limits or the world in little—
you know expectedness and a sort of
charity keep meals arriving and a few good rubs
attract a stroking if the biped god is kind:
the rest's captivity, the freely starving birds
mocking you at third-floor window sills,
the tray behind the door a sponsored graveyard
where dreams of freedom waft the death-smell out,
but you are moving firmly through our rooms
defining objects, a whole cosmology of glass

and cushions, stipulating with a yawn and outstretched paw
the anti-matter of the visible. Supremacists
of what is there, cats are the Chardins and Latours
of inner-city living.
                        This room has lost its focus,
no cat is in it. I am left with vanity
of pens and speakers, panel-lights, chrysanthemums
drooping now to dusk. Our human scale is sadness
giving readings of selective understanding
and when some happiness obtrudes it weighs like ornate bowls
bearing the fruits and flowers of imagining.
                        Then the cats will say, trotting through
a suddenly opened door, 'you had forgotten us
and our sharp needs, painting your pretty picture,
unnatural living is still life, you know . . .'
                        and I will lead them back
into the kitchen where the sacred loaves
and fishes wait in tins and boxes, and the light
switched on makes sermons of necessity.

AWAKENING OF PLEASANT FEELINGS
UPON ARRIVING IN THE COUNTRY

I was talking to a tree near Kettering,
admitted straight away
I didn't know its sort—a kind of
beech or hornbeam, rather spindly,
not well placed beside a fallen gate,
too close to the railway and scuffed
by cows and sheep—
                        Nearby and all around
more nearly noble oaks and sycamores
and even the odd cedar rubbed the sky,
with semi-undismantled hedgerows,
willows scraping the canal
and gardens dragging through
the lees of autumn—

I could barely envision
a less romantic landscape,
one made more derelict by men's
necessary sad encouragements—
        Imagine my surprise
when with a dark percussion of its leaves
it answered me—
            'Vain as your fears
of dying, the contusion of the planet
in a frame of fire, is your love
of Nature, the tall Wordsworthian glare
which turns green fields to templates,
douses in a swill of Technicolor
the rooted struggle of articulation.
        We have no Pantheon,
just a clinging to the soul of water,
a light-filled ruthlessness which hoists
a canopy on every hurt.
            Argue with the earth
and lose your way: the only life which counts
is any system which won't shift its ground.
Set in the soil, it lives and dies
where it was made. Life was a jousting
of two modules once: it's now a raggedness
of old survivors looking at the sky,
ungraded, blank, beyond nomenclature.'

PIGEONS, GULLS AND STARLINGS

Imagine a heaven where every one of these
is known by bar codes on its wings or tail.

Where someone cares beyond importing them
into an apophthegm about survival.

Better for them to stick to their concourse
of things abutting, edges without flighting.

We like to think they clean the wounds of feeling,
the scabs which form around dependency.

It's not that they like scorpions will survive
the fire storm, just that they aren't concerned.

A philosopher might teach one how to talk
and find it walked right past philosophy.

Yet a bird could share with a philosopher
the poverty of dreaming one dream always.

The syncopation of our kindness: we
shoo them from the lawn when wood-doves land.

They can't be rare and lovable, or mime
their gratitude like hungry ducks ashore.

Come *The Last Supper* in the Park, they know
France's premier chef is named L'oiseau.

They've been with Jesus and at Venice, viz.
renowned St Gull's, St Pigeon's and St Stare's.

Pray for the sadness of intelligence,
the many lives envisaged in the one.

IN ROSEWELL

These small, well-built and greystone Lothian houses
Seem full of sadness, ringed about by sky.
Unlike the flock of birds my presence rouses
Their dignity will wait till I go by.
Perhaps they feel that one who lives in books
Is hardly worth a turbulence of rooks.

The birds have high trees and a castled river
To underwrite their screaming senate's noise
As down the wet roads juggernauts deliver
Animals to death, and cycling boys
Pass kennels where impounded dogs and cats
Howl to the lonely lawns and council flats.

How should a writer better test self-pity
Than standing soaked outside the Miners' Club
With letters of importance for some city
And far too shy to go into the pub?
I bring my quiet burden to the post,
A lifetime's correspondence with a ghost.

OVERHEARD AND UNDERPHRASED

It was Happy Hour
at the Café Helicon.
Ever since boredom
made the ratings
a good crowd had
beetled in to hear
the big ones talking
or just to look
at the ever-changing
faces at top table.
What was the conversation like?

people wanted to know.
It's not a pick-up,
it's an eavesdrop place,
Olympian mirror-alley,
they knew that. One
asked a waiter. Well, he said,
they'd been rabbiting on
about the new faces
in the Sundays, not the slags
and gossip-writers, but
the communicators, bards
and moralists.
They didn't like it. It cut
across their territory.
But they could wear it.
After all, said Zeus,
just take Sappho
and Cassandra, what
does it come to, their stuff,
surely it's just that people like
hearing girls talk dirt?

THE IRRADIATED POEM

It has been exposed to safe bombardment
Of formalistic and idealist rays,
Hölderlin's mad Hellenism and Dante's
Tuscan spite; Grand Masters of the Usual
Have lent their dailiness to what it says;
It will not stale through evenings of
Impossibilist ethics; nor will Modernism's
Janus gaze unsettle its decorum,
Reading backwards to a heritage
Or forward into unsupported shapes
Of art. The world is learning on its way
To entropy: we can keep our poems fresh

With digital robotics, dots for deeds.
The secret is in essences—consider
A strobe of Wordsworth on his lake patrol:
To separate the wonder and the fervour
From his paper stamps and stale rememberings,
The cottage diction and the drying nappies,
This will show now on the modern screen,
A self-insuring shadow, lettered love.
Untouched by human mind, this packaged work
Is yet encoded with those proving slights
Which sound technique has raised above the mire—
Haven't poems always snuggled down
In stout anthologies the better to forget
The wrecks of hate they were constructed from?
These things are now themselves but troped
In sunshine and in cleanliness,
All made in factories of insightfulness
And marketed responsibly. The rare,
The suicidal, calamitously dreamt,
Become pure style, an ogling of the dark,
An epic for our breakfast rooms compatible
With toast and radio. The Odyssey
Is on a jug and someone is collecting
Rebel Angels, the whole series, out of packets
Lanced by winter light. A Golden Age
Which cares for poems dawns once more and they,
Delighted to be useful, give interviews
To busy journalists. Who says the world
Can not unlock its brutal doors or that
The Muses will not wear white coats? The Inward
Shines through outwardness and we no longer need
A sickness in our words to make us write.

This poem is certified safe to read.

APOTHEOSIS OF THE SHORT POEM

It has to run to thirteen lines to kit
the Devil out and yet avoid the sonnet;
death should be reflected in its hub-caps
but never named; rhyming, scanning and devices
of ludic and linguistic stitching-up
can be to taste, and so a field
of lightly-planted language poetry
might suffice; Blake and The Palatine
Anthology, Altenberg and Landor,
Mabel Lucie Attwell, Emily upstairs—
the enormous Self attains apotheosis
in a bonsai belvedere, its elder eye
misting over as Susanna bathes.

THE CHAIR OF BABEL

We are in the fashionable Republic of Evil
for an especially relevant conference.

My neighbour has been first on his feet
after each paper with a question.

I see from his conference entry
he has the Chair of Babel
in a taxidermist's country.

Unfortunately it's so hot
we keep the windows open and the noise
of traffic fillets every sentence.

Half of us speaks one language and half
another, though their half knows ours well
and our half's monoglot.

The official translator is a genius—
'The lady says her case is near-Hegelian'
he likes to start —

This morning my neighbour asked
'Why do Schubert's lieder hymn the sea
and fisher-folk when he had seen no stretch
of water wider than a lake?'

The translation went: 'The landlocked mind
will ever seek an amniotic . . .'

I turned my headphones on and heard
'The camera runs, the wildcat eats the hare . . .'

The noise at coffee-break is settling down
at about G below middle C, I guess.

At lunch yesterday two conferenciers
had their bags stolen by youths who rode
mopeds through the restaurant.

Case histories tend to leap from
shit and bonding to repair
ignoring counter-transference.

We are united in distrusting one old man
whose sense of humour is exaggerated.

Viz., he said, 'This reminds me of
Judge Schreber's childhood harness which only
Houdini could have masturbated in.'

I've seen one car which halted at the lights
but that was when they'd turned to green.

A Venezuelan hung around with gold
suggested we imagine suicide
as a function of God's Repo-Firm.

The conference is in a palace
with *trompe l'oeil* walls
seemingly adjacent to Arcadia.

I dream of people making love inside my body
quite unconcerned that I am watching them.

But now I know what we are here for—
it's in the Bible, that club of confidences—

A buzz of international cooperation
doubtless held hubristic somewhere else.

Stuffed melanzane and fizzy wine
are served beside old fish ponds
by the light of floating tapers.

I say to my neighbour,
daring to speak to him at last,
'Is yours a big department?'

'We have Gossip, Pentecost,
Green Vocabulary,
Eye Utterance
and Cultspeak,' he replies.

The plane to take us home
is blessed by several Cardinals
and provided by
The Cooperative Society of Ghosts.

WITTGENSTEIN'S DREAM

I had taken my boat out on the fiord,
I get so dreadfully morose at five,
I went in and put Nature on my hatstand
And considered the Sinking of the Eveninglands
And laughed at what translation may contrive
And worked at mathematics and was bored.

There was fire above, the sun in its descent,
There were letters there whose words seemed scarcely cooked,
There was speech and decency and utter terror,
In twice four hundred pages just one error
In everything I ever wrote—I looked
In meaning for whatever wasn't meant.

Some amateur was killing Schubert dead,
Some of the pains the English force on me,
Somewhere with cow-bells Austria exists,
But then I saw the gods pin up their lists
But was not on them—we live stupidly
But are redeemed by what cannot be said.

Perhaps a language has been made which works,
Perhaps it's tension in the cinema,
Perhaps 'perhaps' is an inventive word,
A sort of self-intending thing, a bird,
A problem for an architect, a star,
A plan to save Vienna from the Turks.

After dinner I read myself to sleep,
After which I dreamt the Eastern Front
After an exchange of howitzers,
The Angel of Death was taking what was hers,
The finger missed me but the guns still grunt
The syntax of the real, the rules they keep.

And then I woke in my own corner bed
And turned away and cried into the wall
And cursed the world which Mozart had to leave.
I heard a voice which told me not to grieve,
I heard myself. 'Tell them', I said to all,
'I've had a wonderful life. I'm dead.'

HIS BODY TO BLAISE PASCAL

Dear Monitor, I have lived too long
with discipline, I have become a boil
of parable; I can hardly stop myself
making pus from meditation.
                    I am vain of green,
of salad gardens; roses my carbuncles,
water for carnations my recourse
to free blocked tears; nature seen in windows
not on pen-stands. You have promulgated
*No other religion has proposed that we
should hate ourselves. No other religion then
can please whoever hates himself.* Steam
unfolds in wrappings of the sick-bed, pain
tastes like lightning, and in storms I see
your torn connectives building Heaven until
the world is one ridiculous proposal.
                    Truth's a freelance god
and mathematics is his muse. I have
been converted like a Janissary and
compelled to serve the lord of immolation;
you have made me one of dying's mercenaries
ranging through the morning's hapless streets.
                    *To exclude reason,
to admit no other thing but reason*: your arrows
miss the butt—to have the flush of sickness
by equation, politicos of splendour
built on dreams, and think it all from Moses

not the body's storehouse!—O stars
far off, spread light on me; you only glow
inside a mad humility.
                We are being trained
to live our very living without life—
instead of narrowing through glass the sun
on pigeons' wings, a shaman-spirit toils
by candlelight at revelation, yeasts
of fear to make deception physical.
             Cromwell was about
to ravage Christendom but a little
grain of sand got into his bladder. You know,
my host, we cannot bank on grains of sand
incising us on God's memorials.
             You gained me as a mule,
today you walk me like a hospital;
I am your body and would be your friend
but can't act as confessional: my grille
shows nothing of a face and ears beyond,
no listener with untainted breath. Job sat
in chiaroscuro while the world recoiled
to salt, his cities axioms of comfort—
are Hebrew letters your false comforters?
            Incomprehensible
that the world should be created
and incomprehensible that it should not.
The starlit stairs, the movement of a viol string,
an adding-machine's projection of the soul—
whichever mystery you choose will prove
you wrong. To doubt the animal in me
will not goad God. That's death, an ordinary
fellow difficult to dislike—he knows
that you and I pay taxes here. He's coming
with abrupt continuo to liberate
the one and many from innumeracy.

TRICKY LITTLE MAGDALENE

The membrane separating this world
from its other is wafer-thin
and only sex sustains it.

The Last Post and the Lost Past sound together,
childhood through the rain-swept queues
shows dogs fucking at your trouser-cuffs
and Uncle Mick leaving Circular Quay
with Resch's Dinner Ale and a bottle of oysters
wrapped in the evening paper.

After the light shows and the Edwardian whiskers
a gift for drawing—grandeur and decline
are chiaroscuro,
the knights ride on the ice
and here a drunken woman falls to the ground
masturbating through her skirt
outside our chic Belphoori.

This androgyne Belshazzar
giggles as a hefty Rapunzel
curtains his genitals with her hair.
What's going on behind? Certainly
he's got his toes in her ravine:
it helps the ecstasy to find sex funny,
then you can put these things where they need to go,
in the hole created for our trickiness.

No, we are not doing the dirt on sex
or finding it repulsive
but considering Freud's pet vulture
as she parts our lips with her tail feathers
and brings us to the world's workface.

Is this the Obscurity Principle,
the laziness of imagination,
a doing-without-significance,
or is it instead the Obscenity Principle
where all the happy tales of hobbits
and witches inside mirrors
are pornography for men afraid of women?

The sex-chain is a food-chain.
Eat your mother till you are her,
steal from Daddy's well-stocked plate
and go down greedily on Goldilocks.
The chants of cannibalism
float down from a cantoria
so quattrocentro, such a frieze
of angels proudly edible,
The Last Supper everlastingly laid out.

Of course, the best course is Repentance
for which you need a feast of sin.
God's little joke is in two worlds
and coming from the other
we have no memory of it
and going thither again
we will not know what we have been
once back in that occluded air. The scene's
a football crowd, an orgy, a party
at the zoo—the caption reads
'They shall not die', and Magdalene
stands up for Jesus, your parents open
the picture books of history,
the cruiser Aurora fires her salvoes,
jacaranda smoulders on the garden path
as Granny Main, stiff in her lacy black,
lifts her veil and shows you down the steps
to the dark places of inheritance.

A TOUR OF THE CITY

In the tenth week of the siege
I discovered I could triplicate my limbs
and looked bemusedly at my six arms
lying parallel in the bath.

The enemy had built a tower
which out-topped our walls and thus they must soon
move against us. Sieges, of course,
had long since ceased to happen
but fear of dying musked the air,
a seriousness glossed by caricature.

Suddenly I could not bear to look,
the gods were walking by our gates,
star-poultices against their eyes
to stem the glare of our carnality.

The body can't hold ecstasy:
I clasped them to me
knowing they were exactly what they seemed,
the huge and radiant intercessors
whom books and nerves have sanctified
in every generation—and the joy
of talking with them raised the siege,
I could tell my friends we were beloved,
these ancient specialists would contrive
an exile for us, not a final death.

The timed naturalness of their skin,
enjambment of intensity and fate,
could co-exist with tractable delight—
their conversation was of Irish priests
who baptised long cigars, their choruses
a clawback from Euripides
and chocolate nightingales.
I cried for sheer simplicity

as though I took an everlasting heart
from my long-buried mother. The siege was time
and would be brought again but they would know
a passage through the vines, a blood funicular.

They had the dryness of encyclopaedias,
a wide disclaimer like a page which opens
on a saffron lake with fish-nets drying
and a castle lapped by water; their halcyon
was the opposite of miracles,
the first hours of a holiday, your mouth
finding its own way to hot bagels,
ahead a terrace lunch, a via dolorosa
lined with moulting figs. The blurred gods
were the first tourists and true pathfinders—
it is hilarious to meet them, Lady Hesters
under veils of lightning, translating
the epodes of a Montenegrin shepherd.

The whole world was their city and they took
my hand and led me to the parapet
and showed me which great doors were closed,
what cupboards Bluebeard kept the keys of
and which departing buses knew the road.
In my bath two arms now seemed enough,
the skylight garlanded the sun—outside
the city simmered and the gods were gone,
back to the paper of their ecstasy.

THE CARTRAC QUATRAINS

The deaf man at the ranting rail
Thought Uysses by the mast a liar
To dare the supernatural lewd
Yet give it flesh in which to dwell.

They'd travelled troubled miles through maps
On nothing more than hope and spam.
From figurehead to galley rats
The whole crew sought a landward star.

The Chief would tell their chancy saga
To any girl, call it a gas—
King's daughter, sorceress or diva,
His salty words made each one avid.

They'd passed beyond the sucking pool,
The chute of soot, the strangling loop,
They'd trembled at the giant's step
And put baits out for Circe's pets.

Up at the helm, an unmoved slob
Swilled his mouth with heavy Bols
And from the sleep of tainted pork
Devils came, a spectral crop.

Philosophers had taught them time
Is infinite, that skies emit
Ill luck alone and in the trap
Of hope endurance plays its part.

And now they sulked in Venus' cart
Along some star-directed track,
The sea their home, a final coma
Where death and memory run amok.

FLAGS OF CONVENIENCE

His trouble was he was too easily awed
Yet when absurdity and fear were wed
His speech of warm congratulation made
Implicit reference to a world gone mad.

Then twice he was the hero with the wound,
The Magic Bowman, The Keeper of Christ's Tear,
Discovering as bandages unwound
That where the soul would speak the flesh must tear.

And looked within a vile and feasting pie
For childhood faces; set sail from the pier
When dawn winds fought the harbour undertow;
Hid as the decoy trundled through the town.

Asked of the tongues of aunties on his couch
Above ancestral streets if this might lead
By creeping groundsel and suburban couch
To confined scarlet or laconic lead.

The language knew its duty, what to know
And how to make him say it, so that now
He found his words insisting what he said
Be packed in stanzas ready like First Aid.

NEIGHBOURS

I am Ceccho de Cecchi
who died in 1493
and I apologize now
for troubling you.
This is my chance to speak,
all because a book
is open at my entry—

that's my name, a key
record for the month, but nobody's
heard of me I've been dead
so long. I was important, I led
a useful life and was a devout
Christian, true husband and
a businessman of good repute.
You who read my name,
quite a few of you will be nobodies
compared to me—please
understand how I long
in this dark to be back among
my fellows and my reputation,
how lonely it is here
where we are forgotten. Days, I know,
must lengthen into shadow,
but let me talk to you.
I remember we'd sing Mass
and beyond our voices we would hear
the cries of pigs being slaughtered
for the coming feast. We listened
to our own ends but we felt
only the excellent wind
of fortune which fans the young.
Now time has torn out my tongue.
On the opposite page, level with me,
is another faded entry—
for October 1492—
in the Libro dei Morti
of Borgo San Sepolcro—
'died on the twelfth, Piero
di Benedetto di Francesco,
painter'. Pray for me
and for all immortality.

A PSALM BEFORE THE SAUSAGES

Enter now the irresponsibility of ants
whose workload is sheer slavery but whose
hearts are hardened by inconsequence.

The little plums are rotting on the tree
uncultivated: a beautiful holiday sky
hangs over a land which smells of shit.

Every part from hoof to anus goes
into these calm torpedoes on the grill.
Their benediction spatters on your glasses.

And the lost alluvial finch sings on the roof
above the prowling cat. You could believe
some mighty hand made these arpeggios.

The constructed and the natural conspire together:
trucks head into Vence and at Coursegoules
clouds arrange a meeting-point at sea.

Transfiguration seems just rearrangement,
the foot in sandals near the naked breast,
equivalences without synonyms.

High above the baou a spotter plane
circles for fires, the country's soul on show—
they drag Madonna through the air at Nice.

The labouring woodlouse needs a miracle
to live another day, and we have plans
which reach into the next millennium.

'Slink-tink', 'slink-tink', cicadas start: the sun
undoes the knotted brain and the great harp
of sausages plays to its only Lord.

THE RIVAL POET

His work shines through the spaces of your thought
So crystalline for being words in stars
And phrased as if our blood itself could speak.

The world he sees is cuneiform for God
But he is free of moral adjuncts, dining
With names and beauties in allusive dachas.

He has the dangerous beard of a Tuscan
Innovator early dead: you see
Him strut like Tolstoy on his own estate,

Each peasant pregnant by him; he has flowers
At his fingertips which praise the land
While you are keyboard-bound and colourless.

Call him a louche Longinus and he'll smile
And dangle a child upon his knee and scan
The family snapshots for sublimity.

The first to make a picture picture its
True self in diagram, he lets his mind
Recapture infantile omnipotence.

His pre-shrunk paradise is metaphor,
A crossword puzzle running out of clues
Till even death-beds start to stink of skill.

It is your vanity to be his Other,
Erecting trellises of words to keep
The world suspended in the winds of time.

Two politicians of the printed page,
You both are talking to a vacant moon.
The tongueless stones have said it all before.

LISTENING TO SHAKESPEARE

I was at school with him
that Will Shakespeare,
carved his name on his desk,
pissed on it to make it shine,
edited a magazine called *Nova*
the name of our river spelled backwards—
he said we should always remember
that words were the way you told lies
and got out of a walloping—
he got us to compare our penises
and said one boy's was Small Latin
and another one's Less Greek,
he kept us entertained with faces
and wrote endless essays
when he wasn't courting.

When he went to London
I was really sorry. Or was it Lancashire?
Anyway we heard of him in London,
then his Dad got into trouble about church
and his Old Woman sulked at home
and we had several discontented winters.
One day I met him in the High Street,
he seemed a bit furtive,
said the chap loitering on the corner
was a government spy,
'haven't I got trouble enough with Coriolanus?'
I loved his stories from the classics
but it only made him gloomy,
'You know what Marston told me,
all Penelope did in Ulysses' absence
was fill Ithaca full of moths—
why come back when the moths at home
are never going to change to butterflies?'
I showed him a review in the local paper,
'Stratford author's sour-note sonnets'.

He wasn't interested and talked
about the price of real estate.

But he was big in London,
you heard about it even here.
And all the time he bought up property
and made himself a gentleman
like his father had tried but failed to do.
Then he came home, old and tired,
saying if life's race were run from eleven to ninety
he was at the ninety end
though all of forty-eight.
Once at an Open Day he said mysteriously
'Congratulations, you have just invented
a new art form—let's call it Local History
and hurry it along to Heritage.'

We listened when he talked to us.
I used to love his high haranguing
but it died away. He died too,
quite suddenly. Managed a good tomb
before the altar and no digging-up
and stowing in the ossuary. I've kept a note
he passed me under the desk once
during a long grammar lesson.
'No man may know a neighbour closer
than his own defeat. The unfolding star
calls up the shepherd. Soon there'll be
nothing of the world to listen to.'

IN ECCLESIA

1 *For the Honour of Italy*

Oh how they feared my caterpillar rages,
I sang in flesh as robins roar in cages.
Siena the well-pleached would slumber on,
The truant Pope skulk still in Avignon.

I brought him home, I wrote a thousand letters,
I prayed with axemen and harangued my betters.
To starve the faith the Commune practised caution,
No loaves, no fishes, just the sinner's portion.

God's secretary once, now Italy's,
How can I pray, I cannot bend my knees?
In Santa Maria Sopra Minerva, boned,
In San Domenico, a skull enthroned.

2 *A Field-Day for the Baroque*

Chill water everywhere brought by the Popes
And high tech ruins clinging to the slopes—
Whichever Rome you like is on the clock,
The hands, alas, keep pointing at Baroque.

From Sant' Andrea al Quirinale
To twisted baldacchinos of God's barley-
sugar, Baroque has loosed its loyal genie—
A Berni Inn compared with Borromini.

Now try St Ivo alla Sapienza,
The dome's a calibrated light condenser.
Geometry has lanced the site for pus
To spurt on God, but shower gold on us.

SACRA CONVERSAZIONE

We're here to help old Dosso out,
there's gentle Joseph, John the Bap,
a saint the donor heard about
and Mary, me—and Him, of course;
the Babe I'm holding in my lap,
no room for angel, sword or horse.

We were alive once—that's to say
I think we're more than legendary
but what the picture has to say
despite how very real we look
is Keep your eye on Emily,
Make sure the keys are on the hook.

You'll have to ask this little Bugger,
the focus of our family pic,
doctor, lawyer, rugger-bugger
when He grows up, the point of it,
this lovely world which makes us sick—
we don't know how the hell we fit.

You doubt that folks like us could get
our picture painted by a top
professional (so hard to get)—
we hear you sniff behind our back,
art lovers scoffing escalope,
'This lot's the sort for a Big Mac.'

It's symbolism, can't you tell,
the low raised up, the high cast down,
as paints and words and notes foretell:
Heaven's a sort of Hollywood
and Dosso's hot on evening gowns—
who gives a shit who's great and good?

RULES TO THE EXCEPTION

The great good of the one is not a cause.
Effective power settles into laws.
The liturgy was made from broken rules.
The words of love become the names of schools.

To imitate the Saviour stay obscure.
The brightest object in a trap's the lure.
Theology, we're taught, makes better art.
How many angels surface in a fart?

Until the rules are written, no one wins.
The bits which fall on that side are called sins.
Most gods have tempers like their worshippers.
The cat that's tickled is the cat which purrs.

This church was built to house a piece of bone.
The stair to Heaven rises tone by tone.
Ecstatic truth includes the ludicrous.
What people die for must be serious.

Id, Ego, Super Ego, Trinity!
The Devil's bell calls hermits in to tea.
It happened long ago in picture books.
The brochure for Mt Athos is at Cooks.

Pascal took issue even with perfection.
You see the danger of divine election.
Great minds exhibit great credulity.
This fervent space of doubt is filled with Me.

The possible begins with a Big Bang.
The dawn of pain was what the angels sang.
The seventh day was set apart for rest.
The Blessed are hard to tell from the Depressed.

A CLUMSY CATECHISM

What is the purpose of our life?
Question the butter why the knife
Goes through it, clear the pond of weed
And watch rapscallion beetles breed.

What power put us on the earth?
The lack of rhyme, the pious dearth
Of consequence, the one-way flow
Of dripping curds through calico.

What is the challenge of the New?
A freshness of the morning dew
Turned automatic hosing–down
Of thoroughfares throughout the town.

What do we mean by tragedy?
A rather bigger you and me
Than any that our neighbours know—
Fire in Heaven but lights below.

What, after all this time, is truth?
Research reveals that Pilate's tooth
Was troubling him, he couldn't stay
Debating with the Bench all day.

Where may an honest man be found?
The singer hears a different sound
Inside his head than discs record,
Herbert alone can say, *My Lord.*

What is the reason for our death?
To find the only rhyme for breath,
To bottom–out both Blake and Dante,
The genius proved, the Profit scanty.

BRIDES COME TO THE POET'S WINDOW

Birds, it should have been, but pleasure quickens
As the white and peregrine performers land.

Such chattering of all the hopeful starts
Like trees renewing their hay-fever wraps;

Cool shadows, straight and ordinary,
To startle the recluse's whisky dreams.

Each bride is decked in her uncertainty,
Her jokes are uncles, sex a limousine

And in the ride to the abyss she hears
With doubtful face the radiant hymn swell up.

These are the frescoes of a fallen world,
The flocks of sulphur-crested cockatoos,

The parrots which don't read the City Pages,
Corporate worms indifferent to Darwin.

Where else, how otherwise devise a world
Where God is in his place and Heaven's a sight,

Where boredom does the artwork, misery
The economic planning and petulance

Sends the invitations? Our daughter's wedding
Was the day we decided to separate.

The poet in his cell is sneezing with
The pollen of the breeding world; he blows

His nose on sheets of multi-stanza'd white—
Is he obliged to fizz his own champagne?

O Brides of Solomon, did no one tell you
You're merely symbols of a loving God,

That high erotic temperatures are just
Visions of Paradise on fading silk?

In the painted garlands of the Farnesina
The melons, halved, glisten in future light.

YOU MIGHT HAVE RHYMED

But I was busy putting things in order,
like language so Shakespeare could write his plays,
and stamens and pistils for the bees
and waves to carry surfboards to the beach
ending up among the winking needles—
The details can be peculiar, viz.
something I saw on television, a tray
of skulls seeming like arteries in mutton
or gargoyle mouths from Gaudi's own stockpile—
These details have the numbers:
think of me as the biggest chip of all
and always in the present. In the poet's play
you get a video of important men
fighting over a backyard and its souls—
The immortal liveliness is mine,
I underwrite it with a fear of death,
a monstrous burden on my conscience, yes,
but you won't expect me to face everyone
who has a clause to plead to, nor amend
some workable few rules which can't be made
to square with justice. Originally this was
to be an experimental place, a sort
of trout farm I could leave apprentices
to run, but it got out of hand. The trouble
must be language—I know you think it's tears

and blood and all the mess that's left behind
at death, the swellings of incontinence—
But words are worst, the devil's advocates
(I can pinch a good phrase when I need to)—
they're ratchets on the running-on of time,
my most precise invention. Worse still
they're plausible simplicities that woo
the brain from complication. I stir the avant-garde
(my best fifth column) to put a shine
on this opacity but meaning still
pokes through—It's Vallombrosan leaves
and epigrams at sundown as the world
gets out the chairs for its crepuscular chit-chat
and puts it nerves on watch. And as I said
I made the stuff originally, the words I mean,
not just the sexual nucleii and space
so limitless it must engross itself.
I've watched the human creature come
into his inheritance and known he'd scatter
his poor bones among the charcoal glow
of Nature. I'm tired of perfection
almost made, of legends born in gardens
and words of faith exchanged at dusk
but just this once I'll listen to your prayer
and so amend my well-loved son's quatrain:

> *For thou dost know, O Damon dear*
> *This realm dismantled was*
> *Of Jove himself: and now reigns here*
> *A very God because . . .*

EXHALATIONS OF THE ABSTRACT

It's right to take the key of family terror
And so unlock the old bureau to find
Some estimables to offer to the market,
And the key will be inside a drawer stuffed

With dreams and hankies—the old key furred with fear
Fits every strong-box when the one tune plays
In manner as a friend epitomized
Beside the hospital TV, his cool
Enjambment of security and fright
Approving all the engineering words
Which publish Babel and defy concern—
Then with the proper slinking gait of one
Elected to portray Pandora watch them fly
To do their patent harm, the photos, packets,
Feathers from the Punjab, filed under
Stranded love and streaming out to kill.

Thus even the phlegmatic principles
Of true responsibility relax
To watch those starry whirrings up above
And trace through some black text book what this means
As inner fire: worlds of ice and dust
Appear on monitors and say they're real
Though mouthing electronics as they go
To amplify credulity, and this
Cohabits with the dugong's smile, the lights
On tuners and the panelled envelopes.
All language is of objects and the rose
Surprising you above the window sill
Is one strayed word returning to the fold,
A dividend exacted from abstraction.
Among the dead the aunts have not relaxed
Their stark vocabulary and prune for hope.

So, craving all the sharps and flats, the ear
Explores its puffy mathematics and
The ups and downs of rules which make the earth
A sheet of paper from a tired computer—
Give me a child at five and I will make
Him numerate with God, say fantasists of line
Whose blood can analyse to triangles—
Watch me sail like Bach across the moon,

My feet on pedals of the Saxon greed,
States one maturely, all his variations
Claimed in canon. Otherwise in gloom
A tiered inheritance must bring the gout
And grief of genealogies to
The present door and only hackers of
The screened sublime will taste the honey made
For us and stored in combs of inequality.

THE CAMP

Nobody believes it will be permanent
yet none is just a visitor—
those are the visitors, the horrified with low-calorie drinks
and flowers in candy-strata'd paper,
trying to identify their cards
among the book-and-fruit-strewn chests-of-drawers.

These inmates hate the outside world
but not their kapos
who if they are good will one day
put the all-forgiving pills in magic quantity
into their night-time milk.

Nurses excuse a sentinel complicity
with self-abstracted smiles.
If they were to break the high taboo of truth
their prisoners would know beyond a doubt
they had been wicked
and would recognize their punishment.
'Look-who-I've-brought-to-see-you'
is camp language for the cull to come
which may even be tonight.

Say six are in a room,
each his or her Sargasso moored around,
none will want to know who these five are
nor tell an outside spy one fact or name.
To pity noises in the night would be unthinkable—
the breakfast angel wheels a new day through
the straggling outer cantonments.

Now comes inspection by the Commandant
who may prefer preferment
in the open air to these exiguous duties—
he has a nod for each inveterate
and an eye for change
as finely calibrated as a rain gauge.

Yet there are annunciations.
Perhaps one plaintive afternoon
touching on the sibylline
hope's cruel consistency
condescending out of memory
will conjure eyes past cloudy windows
to a place where luck can happen
and show between the bed and shadow
something leaning over whispering love.

There has been a brief rebellion.
A veteran spoke of terror, screamed resentfully
at the pastel walls—now all is quiet
and experiment is started once again
along the corridors: one day we may know
what brings about this ruthless alteration.

Soup and messages, sitting-up however hard,
more tough assignments gargling at the spoons,
'O-you-haven't-even-touched-your-lovely-flan!'

Of course not. What they eat is end
as grammar is uncoupled from their lives.

THE SECOND HUSBAND

He was a selfless man, beautiful
In all his actions if not handsome in
Himself—look through all his Orders, The Finn,
The Swede, The Turk; powers from Istanbul
To Christiania honoured him, a pin
To wear before the Emperor, a four-
starred crucifix, a jewelled watch the twin
Of Baron Swieten's—I keep them in a drawer.

Marrying him, I swam away from need.
The servants stopped their answering back, the bills
Arrived with presents; I discovered skills
I didn't know I had; the Court agreed
My figures for back pay; the last quadrilles
Sold first, those manuscripts I had to hand
He saw I wasn't cheated on; the quills
We never washed, the ink dried in its stand.

He was the most magnanimous of men,
One sign of it, I ceased my pregnancies.
Those days have long since gone; I have to please
New waves of pilgrims asking how and when.
My sister-in-law and I like two old trees
Live side by side; each plays the oracle.
Her mind is on those childhood prophecies,
Mine on the man who rescued me from hell.

And my misunderstood much-loved second
Husband wrote my first's biography:
I wondered at such generosity.
Now Europe listens, for the world is fecund
And everyone forgets reality
And praises the most marvellous of boys
Who drew the face of God for all to see
But was to me puerility and noise.

AT SCHUBERT'S GRAVE

They took their calipers and measured
      Dead Schubert's skull,
So Science was by Music pleasured,
      The void made null.

What could that space of fleshly tatters
      Say of its time,
Of keyboard lords and kindred matters
      Of the sublime?

The integers took up the story
      In fields of snow
And dreams through every category
      Were leased to go.

His was the head which notes had chosen
      To move within—
What gods and scientists had frozen
      Melted in him.

HISTORY

Friedrich Kutsky, known as 'Mac',
a lawyer's son who worked
with Russian military intelligence
and sent them warning England
wouldn't fight over Czechoslovakia,
was pushed off a grain freighter
in Lake Superior by an NKVD man
disguised as an elevator mechanic;
Manfred Löwenherz, 'Tom' to their circle
of University Marxists, helped organize
the destruction of the POUM
in Barcelona (Orwell had heard of

but never met him) and was himself
arrested in Moscow three weeks
after Catalonia surrendered: he is
presumed to have died in prison;
Frank Marshall, called 'The Englander'
because of his unlikely name, went
straight to Comintern Headquarters
and survived the show trials of '36
and '37, only to disappear from his flat
on the evening of the Molotov/Ribbentrop
Pact: his name is mentioned often
in the few authentic papers which
survive from Yezhov's office:
The Szymanowski brothers, Andrew
and Jerzy, led a Soviet expedition
to Zemyla and authenticated
the reports of nickel deposits—
both were murdered when their boat
was strafed by an unknown plane
on an expedition in Bering Strait:
the MVD uses more than ice-picks
was said in Moscow in 1940;
lastly Willy Marx, alias Oskar Odin,
'Old Grandad' to the group, jumped
in front of a Viennese tram the day
before the Anschluss, with plans for
Hitler's assassination in his shoes—
no one knows which Party organization
ordered his death. Six middle-class
boys from a racially-mixed Galician
town, three of them Jews, and only
one with a widow at a New England
College. Their story will not be told.

LE JARDIN SUSPENDU

Among the garçons edging the High Table
Of the Success Society were several pimply youths
Who never making prefect had a lot of yeast
In them; a funny thing, one older member said,
No matter what the Götterdämmerung,
How black and stiff each green initiative,
Some bunch of brazen never-readers
Turns up, shouting 'This is Now, This shift
Is What There Is and I am its Vizier.'
So much for tiredness and the vellum robing it,
So much for digits dripping down their columns,
For Third Worlds, Total Exclusion Zones
And bucklings of the plates of history—
A small moustache is working at the world
And won't be interrupted—you will hear it
When it croaks its beating need. Do you think
They knew they lived in an Age of Eloquence
Who were arguing with stars through fiery glass,
Who took perfection of the artist's form
For granted, working instead on how steam fell
And rose in tubes and how the ugly module
Of just seventy years might blaze a golden rose
For Demos? And in The Age of Epigram
When an out-of-kilter cummerbund
Or a wrong caesura in hexameters
Was most of what was worrying in art
Some brutal primitive was marketing
A colossal apparatus raising myth
To high symphonic shouting. No one
Can escape the garish present; it brings
You face to face with the Napoleon
In your mirror; your very nervous system
Is fundamentalist and knowing death
Instinctively it outlaws it,
Imagining committees to sit on
And hunting lodges still at planning stage,

A full obituary of accomplishments.
They raised their glasses then to fame and let
Those parvenus take up the light: the night
Was young, just like the world, and there was
Room in The Success Society for all.
In another part of town a curious band
Had come together, seemingly not talking,
Just looking at large folios of battered blue
And calling continuously for further drinks.
Someone named them to us, The Failure Society,
Pretty important people once whose books
Of hopelessness brought royalties flooding in,
Whose visits to mosquito coasts caused wars
Or burning of the staple crops. For years
They'd tinkered with the liturgy of hope,
Adapting social engineering to
The real face of evil, so they sat
At dinner parties on the host's right hand
And sauced the duller hates of millionaires
With rich lapsarian links: they didn't like it
When opponents asked them why the wickedness
Of worlds went hand in hand with personal
Success or what those prophets really meant
Who, choked on locusts and sand apparitions,
Called down the fire of heaven on Babylon
Or Rome or Rickmansworth. How wicked was it
To seek promotion in a PR firm
Or grow the largest marrow on the lot?
But now society had phased them out
And found it missed them—that tone, that dying fall,
That lyrical sussurus of despair
In novels or in sonnets lent relief
To people keen to learn a sense of style—
What could it be, that artful knowingness,
But the ancient acid of defeat, the sun
Which shone on tombs and Paradise alike?
So now behold the veterans convened
Again, as in the old days, swapping stories

Of why the Nobel Panel loved the dark
And where the flood of evil had its source.
They nominated one, a velvet bard
Too long in exile from extravagance,
To make the keynote speech. Tonight, he said,
I shall recall a golden age; I shan't
Speak of our exile in the provinces
Or how we washed the lavatories for Stocks
And Shares and ate the dead sea fruit of doubt.
My treatise is a poem, visionary
And full of an hermetic indolence;
To give it extra unction I shall make
Its title French, 'Le Jardin Suspendu'
Or 'Hanging Gardens' to the journalists—
As rich as *Salammbo*, as high above
The ordinary as *Sardanapalus*.
It covers death with that anticipation
We know as music when we lie awake
Chalked by the moon on bed and pillowslip—
Nothing of the vernacular will underpin
The picture, just a hocket of the desperate
Adding another note to consequence.

And he began. 'The king was sad and so
He ordered gods, not just his courtiers,
To raise a garden in the sky where plants
Might be the grander close to sun and rain
And standing tiptoe when the king approached
Would point him into heaven with a touch
Of leaf or stamen. A flying garden would
Have pleased him more, but this interpolation
Picked up the interstellar gossip so
The king could eavesdrop on the voices of
The dead, who told him men would not live long
But work much evil while they were on earth.
Saddened at this the king addressed himself
To welfare and the public good and works

Of art, to gates and roads and aqueducts:
He was not heard in heaven and the stars
Shone on regardless. If God could stoop, the king
Was told, He'd preen the smallest fly for fun.'

MILLENNIAL FABLES

For William Trevor

'*The best in this kind are but shadows,*
and the worst are no worse, if imagination
amend them.'

A Midsummer Night's Dream

I

THE APPROACH ROAD

They didn't tell you how you were to go,
Only that you must start and having started
Should keep in mind the big road up ahead,
That what you swore to do as you departed
Would be forgotten in the contraflow
Of signs you followed, skirmishes you led
While wilful herds went slow and insects darted.

The twilight thickens and the darkening road
Appears to narrow through its banks of green;
The clouds and trees have fossilized together
As if they wouldn't let the car between—
Here are the megaliths the route-map showed,
The dried-up lake, the starveling moor of heather,
Yourself the image on the startled screen.

FORTY YEARS ON

It was notation of the English air
which brought me here
that blood not words in books might share
with me this working hemisphere.

Which brought me here,
hope or despair? I knew I took
with me this working hemisphere.
What was inside the final book,

hope or despair? I knew I took
a step which could not be retraced.
What was inside the final book
if it were shown must be outfaced.

A step which could not be retraced,
(it was notation of the English air),
if it were shown must be outfaced
that blood not words in books might share.

LITTORAL TRUTH

You are discovering one of the mimetic truths
About Australia—it is a long and silver littoral
Within the sound of surf, a country rhymed by waves
And scanned by the shifting outlines of the bay.
We are all still strangers on its shore—the palms,
The Norfolk pines, the painted face of concrete to the sea—
No matter how far from the coast you go you only
Leave yourself and drift in double legend to
An old impossibility—no wonder those explorers sought
An Inland Sea; it was the pool of madness in them
Fed by rivers running into nothing. Relax instead
Along the endless shore, the mountain seas of sand,
The various heads and raging bars where change of tide
Rips channels to a narrow bottleneck—you can be
Odysseus or Captain Cook, forget the package tours
Flying into Cairns, the washed-up stubbies on the beach,
And step into a balanced darkness, mangroves, mud
And soft withdrawal at late evening. Your inheritance
Is welcoming you, and as you flap along the sandbanks
Look out to sea and watch the tourist preen himself:
'Thus sung they in th' Australian boat' but not to praise
The land, themselves or God, but with a level voice
To mark their presence in a sky of perfect stars.

THE PICTURE OF LITTLE P.P. IN A
PROSPECT OF PHOTOGRAPHERS' PROPS

See on this oval stained by time
A burial's beginning smiles
As last makes first its paradigm.
Here childhood's milky background teems
With brightness rushing out of dreams
And guileless charm itself beguiles:
              The photograph
Shows 'Eden 1930', minus staff.

A middle-class concern looks out
From coloured cheeks and tousled hair
And carefully modulated pout.
This Darling of the Gods is sure
Of nothing but there must be more
To love than his allotted share;
              Between his knees
The world, a coloured ball, is held with ease.

His two fists like two running shafts
Stretch out to greet the tug of life;
His feet are well-tried rubber rafts
On which he'll float till out of sight
He rides the waves of lurid night—
Inside his head desire is rife:
              The tinter's hand
Has lightly coloured all the seeming sand.

This studio's the world at large
Where decades of the worst which man
Can do are immanent: the barge
He sits in burns on mystic waters,
A scion of transplanted Porters
He stays as distant as Japan:
              The marvel is,
Of democratic riches, all are his.

Time which lingered in the shutter
Has wound a universe since then
On yearly reels, yet puerile stutter,
The prelude to full-grown despair,
Seems still to haunt the pictured air
And apprehension broods again:
                    The only child
Is cramming all disguises in one smile.

CONNECT ONLY

I'm drinking illicitly
from a bathroom mug
in a Writers' Retreat
some Montepulciano d'Abruzzo,
not my favourite wine
but usually the one
inside those carrier-bags
sold on Italian stations
to hungry travellers,
and I am back again
with a pretty companion
I don't get on with sharing
lunch en route to Ferrara
where we won't sleep together
and I'm happy to allow
this memory of the train
to remind me of the time
my wife and I encountered
a man who entered our carriage
at Padua and masturbated
against her thigh all the way
to Venice, and I wouldn't
say anything to stop him
out of embarrassment
and he justified me

by pointing beyond the causeway
and welcoming us—'Eccola
Venezia'. A simpleton,
he more or less resembled
a beautiful Renaissance male
in a portrait on a postcard,
and my wife is dead and she
didn't resent what he did,
only my cowardice, and I
need forgiveness of them both
which is why that postcard
is ample occasion and reason
for my mind to wander to
other postcards and other
parts of Italy and on to days
before we went from England
for our holidays and the kids
were tucked up for the night
and we'd sneak out to find
a pub and look to see if each
could somehow find the key
to the other's doubtful heart
and failed, I'm sure, but still
felt closer for the try,
yet somehow this won't fix
and back comes drink, the days
of scouting bottles locked
in drawers of knickers or
stuffed behind old shoes,
the death watch born of life—
all this was years ago
but who believes in time
whose body bears him on
to where all memories meet
or has the style to face
the picture of himself
when wine must have a stop?
Now gadarene the words

run headlong down the page,
old symbols no one trusts—
alas, we're trained to tell
back to ourselves at night
the endless consequence
of being alive and hands
revelling in such trust
reach out as well they might
for wine in bottles rich
with the red threads of death.

NIL BY MOUTH

Life enters by the mouth and so that's closed
to all but air. High drips are spider-lines
to bring relief. How beautiful when young
these bodies were which now lie wrecked on sun-
framed catafalques. Life never ages and
the mind is breakfasting on horrors: it
saw death with death's permission, a tall screen
of glass on which was scripted a cascade
of algebraic formulae moving up
and down and from its inhumanity
evil shone in lights. This final change
revealed how life began on earth, a conflict
of prime numbers tending always to equate
to nothingness. But on these beds there lie
the casualties of that incarnation,
strange numériques engrossed by flatulence,
forensic tropes made man with catheters.
If we were spirit only we would have
to burn all records, shun the eight o'clock
white-coated caravanserai and give
despair its due. Instead, we lucky ones
will soon go home—until one day ahead
a choking food will fill our open mouths

and scrutineers will take down warning signs,
the screens be drawn and loyal sun shut out.
Ask the chaplain what he always says:
'Language is the only thing which we
possess at death we didn't have when born.'
These buildings rose to audit any gain.

COVENT GARDEN IN THE SIXTIES

Here where bridges to the past
may be trodden by a team of cheating gods
or carry the companionable dead
back to life from their long overcast
empyrean, we sat, not quite at odds
with one another, staring ahead
at the usual muddle on the stage.
Maestro Solti's dome, tympanum
of a Straussian downbeat, bobbed
above the pit. Two ladies of uncertain age,
tiara'd, satin'd, shifted bum to bum
through three long acts, happily hob-nobbed
with their kind in intervals
and made our evening comic at the end—
one asked, 'What did you make of it?'
'Too long, too loud.' That memory annuls
for me the real pain the music sends
straight to my slow conscience: I admit
that marriage and the seed of life need Strauss
to fill them with appropriate harmony.
Human creatures worsen in the light
and cannot make a temple of a house;
the birds which clamour in the family tree
are vultures and not falcons; every night
the court of dreams must pass its sentence
while scores and books and pictures rush
to judgment on their makers—why else

come where the trials of gods commence,
where Neo-Babylonian tiers of plush
pretend they wait on pleasure and our hells
and heavens are strictest shuntings of the air.
I know we courted love and couldn't believe
that it had come and then that it had gone—
years later in a park I saw a pair
of birds like us—she streamed, he had to weave,
hopalong goose who thought himself a swan.

TOGETHER AGAIN

I was strangely back—here, there or somewhere—
And these were my old friends talking at lunch
And he who was dead was brilliant, his hair
Never grey its full chestnut again. The crunch
They were saying, when it comes to it, is who
Outside his body can be sure of his work
Or companionship? Not so, I thought, this too
Is involuntary, each dream is a perk
Of the moment's perfection: this unity
Is waiting in time and compels us forever.
Then they were gone but one voice said 'See,
Our reunion's as unsure as the weather,
As slippery as dreams always are—for instance,
You thought that our dead friend was happy,
But he came on parole that terrible distance
Out of their custody, Time's KGB—
"Nightmare Shepherds" he called them, the ever-grim
Shadows he'd borne in his blood, and rather
Than fail us had let them arraign him—
Poor ghost of a son, despising his father.'

SERENADE

In manner of a mystery we hear
in one man's choice of notes played then by trained
musicians complex valencies of ear.

So in unfairness fairness is explained;
that beauty should be felt the felt is hailed
and all are gainers by desire detained.

If changing of desire to action failed
just once, a million times or sometimes never,
potentiality was yet regaled.

Each night the dreaming self has sought to sever
all lines to consequence, but dawn proposes
a serenade both opulent and clever.

We all own shares in what one mind composes;
it is our nerves which temper the full scale
and ours the compromise its passion glozes.

That human chances, like the working snail,
live in a house of slowness is a fix
on fruitfulness, a halo of detail.

And music, that most serious of tricks,
puts on its wig to pose as justice here—
the gods give up their Zimmer-frames and sticks

And walk upon the waves in perfect fear.

LATE IN THE DAY

Following Yeats's *Cold Heaven* is nominal
Suicide, says the soul, always in its place
As careful accuser, sound as the Binomial
Theorem, waiting its call to the Palace.

Risktakers Anonymous meets on this page.
If you speak up you may find your words
Opposed to your desire, taking it down a peg,
Still wielding archaic symbols like the sword.

So sort out eternity on the retina,
Try to see what Yeats saw through marine
Astigmatism in Ravenna, retsina
Made old Chian, Lowell lapped in Maine.

The hemstitching to God, an eyes-down draw
Where any word may fill the card: our pens
Drip with effrontery as we edge toward
The Grail—inside its lip, EPNS.

Late in the day of language, life below
Is blocked by souls thick as cloud on Carmel,
Resented by the living who must bellow
At a Heaven cooked to caramel.

HAPPINESS

The world's a window on to death
With killers closing in to kill,
But love of life's a shameless zest
      Persisting still.

The sun eclipsed by passing cloud,
The icicle upon the sill,
With feeling in their gift were proud
　　　Of standing still.

To have survived another night
Is all the pelting bloodstream's skill
And purpose through the octave's height
　　　Sounds surely still.

Our language lacks George Herbert's nerve,
His more can only make ours less,
And yet we cross his lines and swerve
　　　To happiness.

SIXES AND SEVENS

　　　Of equilibrium
the Spirit must speak as of the blood's once garden
　　before leaves fell on the blackened sundial
　　and loquacious floribunda stood trial
　　　　by tempest: then pardon
　　was for the ugly bug at the very brim
　　　of existence,
　　　born judge of distance.

　　　Ur-chaos, disorder
and the innumerate span of the warm bird-table
　　was a nescience needing to be tamed
　　in a republic of nerves: so they blamed
　　　　the set gods of Babel
　　who must be acknowledged at the border—
　　　of course these were
　　　the ten digits of fear.

Ever-smooth decimals
though not asked to be widely or crudely divisible
unlike their harrowing neighbours followed
a strictly formulaic code
and being biddable
took then to the policing of cells,
their cold heavens
at sixes and sevens.

Achieving due balance
consequently required a lunatic proportion
which right thinkers consider tragic,
not science nor philosophy, but magic,
as on the gold valance
of Alcalà de Henares height's tortion
keeps protesting
at two storks nesting.

INTO THE GARDEN
WITH THE WRONG SECATEURS

The soul requires a second for repentance.
An afternoon can seem eternity.

The Open Verdict or The Open Way,
each leading to the unrevolving door . . .

The Press reports Police recruiting's up,
the crime statistics are encouraging.

Bring back internment for our terrorists,
imprison them in decent people's thoughts.

Lifting the vagrants in the park to gaze
across the reins of Elijah's chariot . . .

Spring tides bring duckboards to the Square,
new ways to rout the sickly pigeons.

The gorilla agrees to masturbate more often
to encourage visitors and save the Zoo.

Courtesy of a top team of researchers
this virus enjoys a photo opportunity.

The Government rebukes those cynics who
doubt the range of choice in its Rapist's Charter.

Psyche was consumed by revelation
but caught a glimpse of dirty pants.

Because you can't make your poems modern
don't say Shakespeare found it just as hard.

Since privatization of the means to fame
Post-Modernist thugs control the Book Reviews.

We who hate metrication still agree
the working syllables be fixed at ten.

The Party's manifesto promises support
for elfin epics as well as villanelles.

The angel who appeared to Constantine
was doing PR for a new anthology.

Trapped in their fortress by unlettered troops
the Imperial Army lived on epigrams.

Sin is content to work for very little
but Virtue insists on a minimum wage.

Theory One: we need language to invent *King Lear*.
Theory Two: we need *King Lear* to invent language.

Hier ist kein warum.
Ne pas chercher à comprendre.

NOT THE THING ITSELF
BUT IDEAS ABOUT IT

It wasn't the blackbird at the window
but the colourless bird inside his sleep
which he could hear. It was saying nothing
about the world the blackbird praised
and nothing about a God among the pillows.
And so it had an end-stopped beauty,
being sheer idea, however redundant
to imagination. Something in him said
there is no new knowledge of reality,
just the idea of self still hovering
above each thing, a halo borrowed from
masters who believe in what they see.

ADDRESS TO THE STARS

These points of light which metaphors debate
Disclose a separation so extreme
Infinity awakens from its dream,
A tongue-tied horizontal figure eight.

Since they are unimaginable, we
Invert them till they shine through inner space:
Up close they act as gods whose laws replace
Extrapolation with sublimity.

O stars encompassed by our measurements,
Your integers show where belief may build
And adding noughts until the chart is filled
Exchange eternity for immanence.

A GEORGE HERBERT WORD GAME

So this contestant, ever keen to win,
    Seeks the big prize, his name in newspapers;
He's come to the bright studio, opinion.
    And looks through light at ranks of seated gapers
    And names his first word speedily—CONTRIVANCE.

The odds are gathered and the Quiz Master,
    Whose glowing jowls no cynicism shades
And whose dress suit is holy alabaster,
    Double-pumps his jet of accolades
    And cheers another win—SINCERITY.

To go for broke the highest word is sought.
    In Durables brief fame is soon consumed
Though to the cheque they add another nought—
    Blame each of us in whom the world is doomed,
    We all contest a golden NATURALNESS.

CONTRIVANCE is CORRUPTION in advance,
SINCERITY is SIGNING what you see,
NATURALNESS is NOTHING more or less.

WE 'SEE' HIS POEMS WITH A THRILLING FRESHNESS

What do we see
when we read 'his' poems?
We are encouraged to leave the page.

A boy in an ironbound boarding-house
reads a book about Dragut the Corsair—
he is lounging on a candlewick bedspread.

237

He is not coursing through the famished roads
beyond St Elmo. He is seeing, so to say,
inside quotation marks.

'We too make noises when we laugh or weep.'
Now the quotation marks
are a gesture towards copyright.

'The physical world' too is a phrase
most of us knew before we discovered
it belonged to Wallace Stevens.

It was part of our first great poverty,
after which we met one greater,
the rational poverty of poetry.

Instead, this exercise in sound: C,
The Good Shepherd, is translated to the See
of York, from which you cannot see the sea.

WORLD POETRY CONFERENCE WELCOME POEM

Brothers and sisters, whether joined or singlish,
    We bring you greetings from our lovely land—
Everything will be exposed in English
    so delegates and lovers understand.

We are in no doubt publishers of Man
    and Man has thieved the spark which fires the clay,
so welcome everyone and sparkle soon
    and we will have for certain a nice day.

Our country has great dams and several sorts
    of mentionable fruit—what has yours?
Our friendly poems like to go in shorts
    and your hotel will have the cricket scores.

What do we need with Scuds and Dreadnothings
    when smart's the word for pantoums and haiku?
Our Minister has made war so disgusting
    that we love peace and poetry like you.

We say our neighbours are the sun and moon
    and we make love to ocean with our feet.
We hope that you will couple with us soon
    to join our satisfactory élite.

A GADARENE PROJECTION

Between two pillars of the mind
    ten feet apart is where they shelter,
loudspeakers, humanly designed
    to make their air a sonic delta.

But these are markers of mere space
    to them—cats can unreel the distance
rolling past each loving face
    without the help of Brahms's pistons.

What has it done for them, this surge
    of music surfing in their hearing?
Theirs and the moral world might merge
    if seeming were more like appearing.

And then perhaps the notes would pump
    a blend of God and mathematics
through their veins and make them jump
    from flowered balconies and attics

with parts of us inside their heads,
    a truly Gadarene projection,
out of their calm and sultry beds
    with no consenting recollection

of feline meals and murders to
    abate their abstract apprehension,
a strange self-immolation due
    to J. S. Bach's Two-Part Inventions.

THE GOLDEN AGE OF CRITICISM

After so many crowded centuries
consumers have their say, with extra helpings
of old Gainsboroughs, recorded round-ups
of an epoch's tabulature. There in a pale
among the factories of Arcadia some are working
at packing time into its crates of knowledge
(rather like binding children's feet or getting
Paradise Lost by heart). They have staunched
the flow of the Castalian tap and now
put down their heavy wrenches: they are happy
saying of Sylvia she paid a higher price
to the Ferryman, or of Sam he made the sun
stop above a cemetery. We play
at their feet, our timeless childish shouts
reminding them of filing systems and
the supernatural codings. Suddenly
they see, on the Grammarian's height,
just what serenity there is, a sort
of 'characteristic landskip' drawn
with the pencil of a Claude or Corot
and they know this is The Golden Age
of Criticism, and as darkness dawns
on the inverted sky they sing vesperal
hymns to old humanity, the gods
that rise in rivers, shepherds calling to
their flocks across a sculpted quadrangle.

ESTATES AND SUNSHINE

And the poet stressed the flies. Metaphorical flies,
But we have real ones settling and rising
From curled-up sheets of veal, their noses pressed
Against the windows of the restaurants
With punning names, and sheets of sunshine
Unexpectedly on dried-up river courses
Where the birds, unlike the cattle, cannot vote,
The SAS at practice by the largest broiler-farm
Before the Marches, then an industry of piano-legs—
It's keeping-on, it's Heritage, survival,
Heartbeat of the flags, and what could satire do
Against the need to live? It would say the world
Is glorious to its summer friends and spends
The substance of its titlement to make a show
For privilege to sprawl in, coaxing
Glottal shifts from Underclass to Underpass.

The writer throws his hands up in despair
And gives his vote once more to saintly Herbert.
Here's beautiful thought immaculately engraved
And God Himself in all His jerseys playing.
Perhaps we should conclude that writing verse
Is gas and water, little bits of good concluding
In depressed assessments while unfairness
Hits the fan. After Adam, only an evolution
Nobody believes in could alter things, and death
Attending patiently is the single democrat in sight.
Go for the round journey, travelling against the sun—
There may be somewhere favoured by true progress—
Finding it will put you in the corner-seats of boats
Or ordering coffee in uncleaned Transit Lounges
Remembering the pilgrim's modern text:
I to A, 'We're off again.' A to I, 'Oh, goody!'

STILL IT GOES ON

The numbers are such we cannot
      hope to evoke them,
all mankind rising to God,
      filling his cloakroom

And passing the door beyond death
      into full Judgement,
every wrong straightened out there,
      love all ungrudging.

But how can the creatures we are
      cease to be fallible?
Great crimes may be excused, yet
      self is indelible.

When mine and my rival's bones are
      unearthed together
our words will be mutually as
      hostile as ever.

ABOVE THE VILLA LINE

Importance grows sparsely at these heights
marked off from the valleys of trout farms
and geranium-flanked gardens
by several lines of concrete pylons
and their curving cables. Here, so far above,
the seekers after calibration come
to look down on the ranked achievements
noting nothing stays the same—a hairpin bend
is being widened, a new 'Caves' is opening
beside a family florist, and out of sight
beyond the row of trees now reaching heights
intended twenty years ago a truly monumental

half-palazzo wins the echo-prize of envy.
Yes, all is and must be well where time's
a neighbour and decay and growth are pairs
of equal opportunity, the modern gravamen.
Above the villa line live those who heard
the death-cry of success. They bring their hopes,
scenes poorly dressed and lacking all
equivalence: life is jumbled and its order
sheer occurrence. Charcoal-burners' huts
alternate with ragged radar-posts,
the grass imagines record frosts through
statutory summer and sheep slip down
to pasture by the drawling brook
if once the old dog turns his back. But we
are drawn to this imagined place—
here we may find the attributes
which furnish our desire to praise
(failure must sing as sweet an anthem
as success but cannot settle for
the lushness of a valley life)—
you find us now attempting monodies
to rival the *a capella* of the towns,
our ego-stained and envy-nurtured tunes
becoming lambent objectivity
while those who choose to leave on looking back
are graced to see a chute of fire descend
and stern observers turning into salt.

THE PAINTER OF THE PRESENT

Living in the present is well yes perhaps.
The present has a nasty attitude,
it reminds you that everyone's gone out
and left you all alone, that someone
on a bike's in danger on a crowded road,
that there are more snails drying in the sun
than could be saved by a rescue squad of Buddhas.

Which is why the past is more hospitable.
Say of this old castle scarcely visible
through the oleanders of the autostrada,
Castruccio erected it in 1423
and you cleanse it in an instant
of blood and history and even disinfect
the car of all the sulks of family outings.

But to be serious about both past and present
is another case. It strikes you suddenly
that reality has no style; to picture
it or represent it you will need a handle—
that's why you told that tense young man
that cadences from Bach won't work today
though every note he wrote is humming still.

So, contrive a style and let the subjects come.
Good Heavens, what a soiled and circumstantial
set of applicants! And how unworldly.
Last night I dreamed of being snubbed by one
I'd done great harm to. So I woke afraid.
But now my pen insists on frisking through
the drains of medieval Sinalunga.

No, not unworldly, just unserious.
The oilcloth on this table is itself,
my stomach is itself, but these my words
belong to no one, are on the coat of arms
of nowhere. Stevens had a window on to
Truth? Reality? . . . something anyway
his poems spoke for. Someone pushed it shut.

Putting his black cap on the Judge is sure
his words make proper sense. But the true tyrant
needs only a gesture or a change of smile,
his syllables unfolding in our screams.
And for a bonus let us now propose
two frightened enemies whose webs of hate
fill with the self-same flies of petulance. ˌ

The painter of the present lifts the shutters
from the window, opens his pattern book
(Leon Battista Alberti, courtesy of Phaidon)
and aided by despair takes up his brush
to claim the scene, and it can be the past,
the future, any platitude he likes,
but what he sees will change its blood in him.

UNSICHTBAR ABER SEHNSUCHTSVOLL

The record of one's wickedness, open before
The Almighty on the Bench, is not a book at all
but half a page torn from a scribbling pad—
worse, the police have hardly felt it necessary
to tamper with the evidence—
                     And a high waltzing
                     of the jargons beckons:
The Left all documents and indignation,
The Right a tribal talk-back from the floggers'
triangle—
                     When the lambs are sprinkled
                     on the hillsides like silkworms
                     on their leaves and leaves themselves
                     have feather-soft pollution
                     on their undersides,
we are at the barricades of Middle-Time.
History has cleared the boulevards to ensure
the enfillade will cover every angle
and the Wizard waves his decimal-stark wand
to mark Millennium. Surprise reveals
that every old instruction is in place,
each dogma is as polished and restored
as some pre-war Bugatti and the phone-ins
fill with sing-song admonitions to espy
'a thousand years of rolling-back of Socialism'.

Our critics are so right—
we need a key to our emotions,
an algebra of art
which sounds the same
on any keyboard outing.
Why bother to be clever if your feelings work,
why not cry on cue (or cry at Kew)
and please the millions waiting to be pleased?
Soon they'll clear the files and publish every
crazy secret the Nomenklatura
kept of everybody.
At that time
(or at the hour of death)
you'll know what rings evasion's left
inside your heart and which of all the words
your feeling brought to mind still testify
beyond their written shape.

THE GRAND OLD TUNES OF LIBERALISM

They're the ones we never sang, we had it so good
but could always hear them through the decreed
miseries of classicism, the well-fee'd
alla marcias and symphonies of greed—
unheard melodies are sweeter, we understood.

All the great composers were heresiarchs
of happiness. They believed in it in notes
if not in lines, but a looking-out for votes
converted their long melodies to simple quotes
and Orpheus & Co's sound-bites in Sunday parks.

Just like the Church, the deeper thinkers held
that misery's modes and scales were Nature's voice
from the abyss, that modulation's choice
precluded choosing and equality was noise:
since Art was Fascist, Nature must be as well.

But yet the notes kept going cancrizans,
insisting on imbuing the human mind
with a glory it knew it left behind
in childhood—a sunburst for the blind
was the deaf composer's bequest to his fans.

It could never stay so even—back on earth
The Field of Folk turned out to be The Mob,
scholarship sat late assessing *Blow Job*,
an Epilion, and genius proved a snob—
everyone hummed the one tune from Perm to Perth.

Today we're trapped in faceless symmetry
as the white noise of Demos disputes air-time
with the monkish runes of Heritage, when chime
is held a wonder and accident a rhyme
and faction shouts beside the well-tempered sea.

Somewhere outlandish, perhaps above the blast
or more probably beneath it, a human sound
continues, pain and joy on common ground,
the Liberalism our fathers thought they'd found,
a bridge-passage to the future from the past.

WHY THE BARBARIANS KEPT US WAITING

They knew they were some kind of a solution
But wouldn't risk their legendary horses,
Battle wagons: they'd read about pollution,
High-rise slums and poisoned watercourses.

To keep their army healthy they ran races
On plains and let our cameramen record them—
Nightly the same professional drained faces
Fronted clips on TV and deplored them.

Their Great Khan broadcast from his tented city
His moderate ambitions while Supremos
Wrote for Sunday Papers and the witty
Juniors at the FO shredded memos.

This westward surge while seeming so dramatic
Required another horde pressing behind them.
Perhaps therefore our fear was automatic,
The need for devils showed us where to find them.

The Stock Exchange, the markets and the churches
Couldn't resist an 'après moi' prediction,
The think-tanks called for cross-the-board researches
And sad colloquiums defined our fiction.

Time might insist each was the other's Other,
The building-up and running-down of power,
But brother's empathy can offer brother
Only the fact of death and not its hour.

TRINACRIAN AETNA'S FLAMES ASCEND NOT HIGHER

What sights the world has raised to soothe itself
        and filed away to serve as history
for its prophetic gift may still recur
        through blackened sands and obelisks of fire,
past cows like cut-outs of a *danse macabre*
        or well-oiled seabirds legless on the shore,
and fetch salutes from any public day,
        though sore despair, the wicked twin of self,
finds second options, settles down in towns
        with civic lakes and glassy streams for fate
to cast its sure and end-stopped lines into.

That's when the terror starts, when what's inside
        the mind exaggerates its syntax to
accommodate apocalypse—remember how
        one Sunday, pestered by the drizzle, you
sat on a beach whose windlass waves raised balls
        of shit along the promenade and where
behind your callow wincing flames climbed up
        the sky to paraphrase necessity—
lost and faceless in that stinging draught
        you narrowed God to make him fit The South
Durham Iron and Steel Company.

Just as the lines which grow now on the page
        espouse a hope that somewhere more complete
the ends of things make sense, that skies won't burn
        unless a saint is rising in his glory
or new volcanoes promise wonderland,
        so too transfiguration must expect
to turn the other cheek and do without
        the perfect food of truth, living for love
of this one planet out of millions where
        unrest is drenched in feeling and you are
a witness to the courtesies of fire.

HUDIBRASTICS IN A HURRY

If only my poetic slot
Like Pope's to Dr Arbuthnot
Might scold in so abrupt a wise
Its later urge to catechise
Should be forgotten in the jar
Of my superb vernacular,
My 'bar the door', 'turn up the Telly'
Smack properly of Machiavelli
And not be just a desperate hope
To fit millennial shades on Pope.

To plunge in Hudibrastics is
The only way to make them fizz
But when the masters set them going
They could expect no reader's slowing
Down since indignation then
Was poised on each poetic pen
And relished at enormous length
By connoisseurs of satire's strength—
It's doubtful if they thought reform
Would be the outcome—but the norm
Was biting, wounding without quarter
(Distortions faced by their distorter!),
A curious consensus that
The thin might prosecute the fat
For moral self-indulgence while
The fat in just as sure a style
Damn as politically correct
All members of the skinny sect—
So politics and satire screen
The simple things we really mean
When wrapped in indignation our
Blame's as righteous as it's sour:
We couldn't hate the fault if we
Hadn't first loathed the he or she
We castigate it in; a tort
Is little more than afterthought—
A shape of mouth, a cast of eye,
An uncleaned shoe, want of a tie,
Too loud a voice, too big a car,
Injustice of things as they are,
The world proved wrong inside a minute
Having such paranoia in it:
Thus huge moralities may be
Constructed on mere enmity,
Theologies of punishment
Brought down to squalls of rates and rent
With Janus-like the hates we had
Polemicised as good or bad.

The satirist is hired alas
To hide this truth and hold a glass
Up to Nature, warts and all,
Outside the plastic surgeon's stall
And with anathema instruct
The scalpel where to make a tuck.
Would it were so, that what we read
Were not diversion but a creed
And wicked-doers skewered by words,
Paleo-Gadarene, in herds,
Gave up their vices to confess
We'd saved them from the precipice,
But all along our pious urge
Is just where interest meets the verge
Of self and self's imperial thrust
(Oh for one friend whom you can trust),
All stoked by sullen entropy
And published as morality.
At last admit that satire's bite
Is germane to The School of Night,
A version of cold pastoral
Where simper is replaced by snarl,
Composed by everyone but Germans
And like Savonarola's sermons
As much to heat its own position
As to lead on to Inquisition
Though ending up, intent or not,
Insisting deviants be shot.
Must then all wringing of the withers
Or grading by didactic sievers,
High stamping on the moral ground,
J'accuse etc. be mere sound,
A recognition that the norm
Departed from gives us a form
To dress our crude ambition in?
To run the gauntlet of man's sin
We build a violent edifice,
A Souk of Wickedness and quiz

When its sad cast is long since dead
The reason why the work's still read,
Its annotated lines debated
And iconography collated—
The hard conclusion must be reached
That art is indignation bleached,
And urgent works of edification
Survive as texts in education,
The only use of their philippics
Tone registers and style specifics,
And when we judge them years after
Hear Swift through unembarrassed laughter
Declare with pride what genius
He had in youth when he wrote this.
The problem will not go away;
We must believe that what we say
Can change the world to some degree—
To halt the felling of a tree—
Or topple some outrageous bully
Or work like Herbert's pious pulley—
But Auden warns us what he wrote
Hardly rocked the Nazi's boat
And things he told us we should do
Failed to save a single Jew.
Of course not! But we might examine
Not how best check Idi Amin
But test that other Auden maxim,
Committed poetry which packs 'em
Into sites of True Correctness
Or self-identified Electness
Will only draw attention to
The poet's own loud ballyhoo.
Unfair perhaps, but now recall
Those readings in our public halls
When bards would fight and scramble for
The chance to damn the Vietnam War—
Their reputations are intact,
Bank balances still in the black.

They've changed their brief to planet-saving
While ills of history like slaving
Are quite enough to damn a nation
In retrospective indignation,
And should good causes grow more scarce
There's internecine strife in verse
To keep their instant anger hotting
At names an epoch finds besotting—
Ho-Chi-min City *was* Saigon:
That cause is won—and they've moved on!
And yet this scorn may not be fair,
A writer cannot change the air,
He does no more than other men
When holding views and lifting pen
Or switching on his processor—
It's just that real events like war
Are hardly touched by authors' rage
In books, on TV or the stage;
Establishments for good or ill
Lick off the coating, spit the pill
But might as sop to probity
Dish out a bromide CBE.
The real danger's vanity—
Consider Yeats, a self-made stoic,
Who sneered at Owen's unheroic
Warning from the stinking trenches
That blood and pus and phosphorous drenches
Are not chivalric—this same Yeats
Posed high and mighty like The Fates:
'Did that play of mine send out
Certain men the English shot?'
And did it? Writers should reflect
That in the war with intellect
Emotion holds the highest cards
But more importantly by yards
The words we wrap emotion in
Like those our intellect finds kin

253

Are forged in every human heart
And don't need priming by high art.
The awful vanity of writers
(The grown-up fruit of nail-biters)
Is forgiveable perhaps
Since, of all men's, their inner maps
Show most that dragon-haunted Terra
Incognita, The Swamp of Error
(And pity those who have to rhyme
In words employed time after time)—
There, from the first autistic shock
Till Domesday, lurks the dreaded block:
What shall I write? Who shall I blame?
Have I the courage to name names?
This Devil I met in the dark
Is he the genius of The Ark?
What of a world where seeming seems
Less present than the idlest dreams?
But simple torments hurt the most,
When at a party your bland host
Asks 'Should I then have heard of you?'
Enough's enough—an end is due,
It's time to recognize this foray's
No TGV but mud-caked lorry,
That names like Butler, Pope and Swift
If claimed will get the shortest shrift—
I mustn't think that my iambics
Are biting satire or svelte tantrics,
But more resemble, when they bat well,
The lines of Mabel Lucie Attwell
Or doggerel on Birthday Cards:
Forgive us all, we headlong bards,
Whose inwardest investments are
To follow a deceitful star
And be brought face to face at last
With everything we thought was past
Only to find that memory
Recycles life perpetually.

II

HOMAGE TO
ROBERT BROWNING

GIVE A DOG A NAME

And soft, two parents come
from luncheon to
a church athwart a stream
and notice as they pass
the ribboned weeds like eels
racing forever to the weir.

Treviso, San Francesco,
once an army commissariat,
restored to God and his free market
by the pious tourist trade.

Inside, two poets' children buried
with memorials appropriate
their fathers' names—
Pietro Alighieri and Francesca Petrarca,
still solemn in unversified content—
so long ago, we say, but fame
is not as brittle as loved bones.

Ourselves lost children
of a famous father,
we pray for peace as long
as Italy, for congruence
that's closer than a name.

AESOP'S DRESSING GOWN

The spillings on lapels and cuffs, according
to his fellow queuers at the bathroom door,
were sloppy eggs and greedy second helpings,
but he knew better—they were what healthy
overreachers of commercial mornings
make of conscience: he would study them
and see the fox and grapes, the farmyard shapes
these others never could construe. He fought
consensus with his smelly feet; if truth
came up as lumps it meant that lice
were called again to be inquisitors—
meanwhile that gravy stain should be
a pond for pompous frogs to trumpet in;
a crumb might make King Log but certainly
he'd blown his nose down one sleeve as King Stork.

What may an underdog perform if not
squeeze fables from occlusions of his brow?
Since Everyman is unreformable
he must be entertained with heavyweight
impactions of his own imagination.
Aesop set out for his appointment at
the portraitist's in his coat of many cringes,
more bad breakfasts than Achilles' shield
had ships and warriors, better shadows there
than death knew how to frame for underlings—
he might be thought when brash posterity
circuited the gallery some old
and grave retainer with a book, rather than
what he knew he was, a hired explainer
of the gods' obtuseness to the gods.

GUANO

'The man I call *The Sulky Sperm*
Still eats his garden dirt and drinks
His urine, yet from him I've learned
Just what Le Bon Dieu really thinks.
I curse this war. I'm in my prime.
Write soon, dear friend. We'll win this time.'

'My colleagues are all bigots; they
Oppose your theories since you're German:
I spent some hours yesterday
Searching *The Forsaken Merman*
For any signs of Transference—
Our country fights in self-defence.'

'The new act is superb, it's worthy
Of your immortal genius.
But send me more—I cannot see
For tears, and even set the Bus
Timetable in my haste tonight.
This stupid war upsets me quite.'

'My Estimable Colleague, I
Suggest with great respect that you
Temper your lofty spirit, high
And noble-souled, with that most true
And sane corollary, Good Taste.
The war? Call it Eugenic Waste.'

Islands where sea-birds nest high-steepled
Above the ocean become rich
In guano. Culture likewise is peopled
Layer by dead layer, the which
Say artists, selfish to the core,
Explains the altruism of war.

HELPING THE POLICE WITH
THEIR ENQUIRIES

Could the verandah have been so wide,
the boards so rotten and for God's sake
whatever happened to the two-stringed hammock?
How back-to-front my childhood was:
a house surrounded by roofed openness,
the cluttered darkness like a keep within—
other people had their flowered atriums
and benison of moons;
they lived in different ports where ships
were bees among the stiffened derricks
not our sand-fly niggardliness of masts
and stories reaching town too late
to magnify the equipoise of books.

Back-to-front but never upside-down!
I didn't think there was an orthodoxy
of time and season; I lived in a climate
of staged paper where without experience
knowledgeable dreams spoke with the force
of ideal parents. They said, as if they'd guessed
I'd settle down in poetry, one never should
look back, speed was the thing, the mind must skate
above its deadly pool—they saw the frowns
of critics and knew that love and comedy
retreated from such phantoms; they used up
light and sinew to sit down at last
in grooves created by their commonplace.
And there before I learned to read
I saw the endless volumes truth has bound,
its glitz gestalt, the rainbow-bridge of self
spanning an abyss of consciousness.

Good God, this is romantic. But what
can any human mind be conscious of
beyond its being there? Fear is the cousin

you remember best, your hard headmaster
with the change of clothes. The river banks
pile up with debris, there have been such floods
the landscape looks like mining on the moon,
yet just as you are handing out medallions
courtesy the Overseas Explorers' League
that horde of ancient haunters bounces in
hallooing passwords and old College Songs—
girl-friends, women you could not unscramble
from the Lovers' Decalogue, tread this ground
with no need of permission: somehow they fit
coordinates, even the darkened parts
of childhood—each loving presence though it lied
desires your good and nestles up to you,
completely sexual but chaste with tears—
they wear the uniform of Hermes and one
will take you off on that official ride
where all the verbs are running, life's analogue.
Knowing the dream will fade you say to your
custodians behind the scene, 'We're all friends here,
we're helping the police with their enquiries.'

THE WORST INN'S WORST ROOM

You face it now with terror, but it seemed
while still far off a simplification
devoutly to be wished, a happy tugging
at the curtain of the airless archive room,
not wondering or caring what the sun might make
of such empowering.
               Immediately, lights
go on in snappy phrases: *descensus Averno*
says the dust which every printed letter makes;
nothing will be wasted in this palimpsest
of penetration; forgiveness even

must be looked up in the Grand Concordance
while Paranoia's name-tapes are unstitched
from mass psychology and none can tell
whether *terra clausa* is the anus or
the painted desert.
                              Perverse remembrance
trying to account for dreams of cruisers
and Zapata-like assassinations
can do no better than assume you know
what Anne, Countess of Winchelsea,
wrought on her napery.
                              'In fading silks compose
faintly the inimitable rose.'
                              When Bougainville
brought Aotourou to Versailles from
his South Seas expedition, he gave a boost
to ballet, and the native, growing rich and fat,
died in Mauritius going home. I could
have made it Bennelong but as they say
what a gain for gourmet cooking if
the French not the British had settled
in Australia. Yet, on the other hand,
what a loss to ballad-writing.
                              Thus far unable
to make progress with what's serious
and must come soon, this calculation
moves to another page as if the world
were in a book and now at last the final
chapters were in sight. Age and health
are not the issue—just intertextuality.
Finest dislocations of the avant-garde
turn out to be the simplest captions of
disease and the pocket-book of dreams
is all that's left when fire destroys the libraries.
                              And we emerge
like bomb-disposal experts in the ruins,
tapping at a drawer of microfiches,
decoding lettering on toasted calf—

'Through Borneo on a Penny-Farthing',
'The 218 Plots of Kotzebue',
'Function and Disfunction in Amnesia'—
and suddenly it seems so beautiful,
printing's aural mysticism,
a low sea-wall of objectivity
against whose groynes time surges every day
until a smothering subjectiveness
overwhelms the sky.
                    Meanwhile a god has landed—
stepping out of Auden's borrowed craft,
he dries his wings and trills his generalities
in proper Viennese:
                    'Du schöner stiller Gott'—
your dust is dancing in the final beams
declining from the uncleaned windows—you
compose the patient on the bed with stars
inside his eyes, the barque of Pharaoh warping
to his side and chroniclers on hand—
time to forget all childhood mysteries
and dotages; each pronoun must renounce
its birthright and the catechism start
with namelessness, alarm and ecstasy.

From THE MARIA BARBARA NOTEBOOK

. . . I cannot understand
how, like the ease and precision with which
he puts his notes on paper and boxes their ears
when choirboys turn them into travesties
of music, we are so very numerous
and yet so solitary—the one,
the self, the single, a paralysis of numbers,
the pain of ending at our fingers' ends!
I am an accumulation of particles
but have to be a system emulating

death's preferred design. To be caught
apprehending like Prometheus
a veiled intention, one hand on the rock,
stealing a little fire scarcely enough
to warm a lying-in—there you have it,
woman's part in creativity—
he couldn't get his sounds if getting lives
were not both pious and responsible,
a tempering of the not-yet-perfect scales
of love. And so I write down in this book
the trivia he sprinkles on the day
as if he's watering an office plant
in bureaucratic sunshine. The little gigues,
musettes and cats' cantatas emulate
the great phantasm of Jesus trapped in words
while out of sight hooves of the Lutheran
Cavalry ring their deliverance on
our Sunday faces. Where does he get such texts?
—the howls of sin, whispers of repentance,
Jordan stealing through the banks of truth,
an oboe's outline like a planet in
the dark, the camels in C Major to
their hocks. I see a stranger in the house,
a person from Pforzheim come to call
with some unmeaning message—several times
today I've met him in the hall. Dark angel,
what will become of us when the music
has to stop? Strange that everything seems used,
familiar from some other life, perhaps
before or even after this: my children
climb the hill to peer in at the Crib
like junior Magi and I hear the horns again,
the rolling 12/8 caravan of God.
Take me Lord when this life is complete.

. . . and yet I cannot go
when this bewildered air is beating with
the wings of children. That's my firstborn son

at the harpsichord learning disappointment
and an aptitude for drinking. I fear for him,
I fear for me. 'Before Thy Throne I stand
at last.' But who may abide the hour of our coming?
There's one who may, for whom the city slates
are pedals of an everlasting glory,
whose trees are rushing in discursive quavers
over printed graves: he faces both
the end and the beginning, cadence of
our purposes on earth—how glorious
the work he does, how impulsively his health
is measuring out my death. He'll remarry
and the published world renew its catalogue
of wonders: choirboys will hang on notes
like bells when my Exequien is rung,
the trumpeters be changed to dovelike
cooings of despair and memory unhinge
the darkened windows of our afternoons.
Ah, such fatal fluency—another
foray into F Minor—Friedemann
has all his father's skill except his love
of God. How long a road we tread and yet
we always wish it longer. Now a fugue
in three parts with a tortuous subject
and overcast by dissonance. The garden
fills with rain but through its veil I see
the shapes which come to tell me I must leave.
They urge me like a child to say my prayers.

. . . our cat has dribbled on
a hassock I'd brought home from church to mend—
I'll stitch it when it dries. I dreamed
God's tongue was licking me as I sat through
a sermon catatonic with theology,
and then he asked me to assist him
in the kitchen: 'Who can digest Melancthon
and Luther, and who likes tripe as old
as martyrdom?' I knew the voice, part love,

part niggling courtier, and I thought
shall I never escape my husband's wars,
his stormclouds in the organ-loft, the knock
which means a visitor who might present
himself as psychopomp or onion-seller?
The sun is up, there's madness at the door,
prepared to haggle—I feel my heart
fly from its anchored place into the sky,
amazed by sunbursts, by curricula
of angels calling out the odds, by domes
of the celestial pavilion, and my family
isn't with me where the palms give shade
to Jesus and in strictest canon voices
sweeten time with just a tincture of
chromaticism. My husband's pupil draws
the stops, Sesquialtera and Principal,
and squirts his diapason down the aisle—
my tears dry and nothing gives alarm
except the tinny echo of my voice,
a cantus left on earth, prehistory to
the lands of Paradise, and no one now
will save my children from the dread of death.

WHAT DO WOMBATS WANT?

On the Great Day of Division
when the swimmers swam and the womblers wombed
The Lord was already laying down his rules
to help psychiatrists.
                          Before the cloud could clear
and language fit for by-laws straighten
itself out, we had the Super-Real
for lunch and all our happy needs could keep
in touch by touch, leaving words to rocket up
like Sickert's circus-folk. Oh how ready
were the prepositions then to join the gang

of show-off verbs, how innocent as dogs
sniffing at genitalia each adverb
not required to be accountable!
Language was all lift, from ballads to
soft burblings in the bassinette, and said
what critics think—it's onomatopoeia
all the way: the coach is leaving for Aeolia,
the team is singing out its heart.
                              Long since however
we've woken with a hangover and found
our words as serious as any modern student,
the pert rococo jokes and mock façades
which hide our sexiness changed by decree
to insignia on security vans—and who
could doubt that categories mean just what
they say? Our caring doctors are as young
as our policemen, the patient sits in rooms
of chosen shades and hears the laughter from
a Game Show while his noose of terms draws tight.
Even those great savers dressed in light
on TV screens, smiling calmly as
another rare and half-blind creature
passes the safe thousand mark, have dark
inquisitorial urges, shouting in
exasperation, 'What Do Wombats Want?'
                              Therefore we hug
the pure exceptions, denizens of grieving
glades whose natures are not ruled by
trained interrogation, the ones whose names
have launched a blessing on them. Who, if called
Donatus Katkus, could be anything
but a viola player? These become
our heroes and compel our hearts to beat
apace when high despair appears dressed
in its official verbals, when we read
'Workers rally to a Queen of glass
treated with the proper pheromones . . .'

                              Back in the jungle
Surrealist feasts continue, sponsored by
the best environmentalists—these things
may yet be doomed but all around them Nature
flaunts its platitudes and quail and gerbil
never ask their Shrinks for an interpretation
closer to the classic. What are we left with?
The doorstop snake widowed from its house,
the china finch, the pencil-sharpener snail,
the banzai good-luck cat—it's no surprise
that what a crowded planet likes to love
is its intransigence, the wastefulness
which lies beyond morality, whose life
is never Puritanical though high
on disapproval. Somewhere in all of us
the riskiness resides, the link to sounds
of love and hate, so like whatever made the grade
before the Lord set out his options—thus
as we prepare to stroke a furry friend
who's brushing by our feet, we dare to hope
even so very late that we'll be lucky
underneath the tree of life, not good.

THE ARTIST'S DONKEY

The Lord giveth and the Lord taketh away!
At the moment he's offered this barrel of a barn
dedicated to a dimbo saint and I'm
to paint it. Today I'd rather settle down
and write a monologue of crunchy poetry
(or lump of prose if you prefer) than fret
in fresco. Good-boy acrylic knows to wait.

When they painted like the movies—Apocalypse
with half a hundred Supermans above
a sea of bums—they always put their friends in
and sought a shine might please or petrify
some dicey Pope. I leave the cave of dreams
to pace a polystyrene altar-front
like Luca at the wall. The word's made flesh.

It's best to see yourself a chef, dressed
for the fire, belly hanging out above
the restraining belt, with not a fresh-washed ladle
on the bench. You have to go by metaphor
till paintings cook the world—a green sauce
for unctuous Eden, a peppered steak when Herod
lets his taste buds flay the banqueting.

Holman Hunt had half a dozen goats killed under him—
the great age of seriousness! My borrowed donkey's
grazing in the yard. He looks as if he knows
I'm putting off the task. My *Flight into Egypt*
may hail a punning plane and he can go
on hold, but when the buzzing in my eyes
subsides I need the creature-calm he brings.

Imagine those in Heaven painting us—
their backward fancy, good Orpheans all,
is limning what they left behind: grace, lust,
uncertainty, as words and sounds and shades
hobble on as many legs as work
back to the Vale of Tears: we come, my Brother Ass
and I and all the Is who fit into a face.

LISTENING TO LEOPARDI

Who is this speaking to you?
Just some dusty spirit,
a bibliophile's 'Gespenst'
(those Northern armies brought
their barbarous language with them),
a warning from the tower
there are too many books
already in the world.

I was a healthy boy
until I crept into my father's library—
I became the ghost of sickness;
from my bowed back imagination
shot an arrow at the world:
for what? My countrymen
still stew in their ridiculous
mellifluous tongue—when was there ever
either sense or poetry in Italy?

Yes, I know of Borges,
all art being simultaneous,
another library Caesar—
but look here on my balance:
one pan, a moon, a village after storms,
wild broom, a dozen perfect poems—
the other pan, provincial boyhood
(even if a palace), death in Naples
(once a royal city) and cobwebs in between,
oh, and some prescriptive pensées
with thick Italy looking up at me.
If it isn't in your head it isn't art,
there are no libraries in Heaven.

What would a scholar want with love?
To write about it? Do without it?

We're a multicultural lot in Italy now,
so *fango* has to rhyme with *mango*.
And all the rhymes are riddling in my head
and all the everything there is
which I pronounced was vanity
goes on being vain in poetry.

THE BLOND ARM OF COINCIDENCE

The scene is Venice, the streets as crowded as
A Browning poem, with confirming details such
As spider crabs in plastic tubs awaiting
Their apotheosis in a *vongole*,
Blue-suited businessmen downing a quick
Prosecco in bars sans stools or chairs,
Tourists galore you know look just like you
And the Piazza's pigeons pecking underfoot.
I meet my old friend William Dunlop
Unexpectedly, crowding through a calle
Near San Marco: unexpectedly,
Since two days previously we'd spent some happy
Hours conversing in a restaurant
And didn't plan to meet again until
I left for Florence. 'You're a dangerous man
To talk to' are his words immediately
To me. 'Why?' I ask. 'Do you recall
Discussing William Empson and Ralph Kirkpatrick
Over lunch? Not together, but both came up
In conversation, and you talked a lot
About each of them. Well, both died overnight,
The radio reported—Empson in England,
Kirkpatrick in America.' I am horrified,
I'm not superstitious usually,
It's just that suddenly creation seems
A throttling mesh of interactions
With gloating gods encroaching on its ends

And fleshless angels leering in through space.
'Willie, I'm sure we need a drink,' I say.
He tells me I should think of it as rational
Coincidence. There's no *mal'occhio*,
God isn't listening. We walk back to
His rented flat in the Castello where
We talk of divas and his PhD,
His sabbatical on 'Shakespeare as Opera',
Not 'Shakespeare in Opera' or 'Operas
Based on Shakespeare'. We don't meet again
For several years. I still read Empson happily
And listen to Kirkpatrick's records of
Scarlatti, consult his book and try to use
The Ks and not the Longo numbers. What is
The meaning of my title? Just that the girl
Who served us in the bar that time had long
Gold tresses and blond hairs along her arms
Glistening as she passed our drinks to us.

WINCKELMANN AT THE HARBOURSIDE

I tell the man
standing by his sloop
we come down from the North
to get away from hope

Water oils around its keel—
to spit into the wake
won't change anything,
what's classic
is repetitively new

History, from Herodotus
to the boy at the *Pensione Mercurio*
is infinite desire
mocked by timeless need

BERENSON SPOTS A LOTTO

It takes me back to my beleaguered youth,
Chiming across an Italy where carts
Rocked down dirt roads and crones without a tooth
Unlocked the doors of chapels, and bleeding hearts
On banners, flung aside, revealed an altarpiece
Whose dim and long-dead donor thought to win
A sort of immortality, his Fleece
Of Gold in Heaven, sitting painted in
A flock Annunciation or some ghetto
Holy Family. Year after year I roamed
The provinces from Como to Loreto,
But this was just the fieldwork: I had homed
In on the big boys from the start and knew
That not just railway magnates but the scholars
Wanted certainties, the only true
Account of Europe, and beyond the dollars
A secret map of Christianity
Waited projection by a doubting Jew.
So these my lonely forays were for me
And for my conscience: I felt the world askew
But told it straight: as Burckhardt was the first
To show, the art of Europe's a crusade
And universal culture is a thirst
In conquerors whose vanities have made
Our palaces and charnel houses grow—
The story must be written, heroes found,
Masaccio, Piero, Michelangelo,
A triumph set to pass its native ground
And bear the Western spirit into space,
With me its true evangelist, the one
Who'll say authoritatively a face
Is duly a Farnese, but not shun
The central mystery, the major-key
Colossi, men whose grandeur connoisseurs
Can only blink at—thus it falls to me
To play commander, wear the holy spurs.

And, yes, you've heard my word's corrupt, my voice
In grading minor masters built my villa,
And somebody has rhymed me à la Joyce,
A prophet, *Teste David cum Sibylla.*
I'm the greatest art expert the world's ever seen,
I make attributions for Joseph Duveen,
From tycoons and bankers I draw a fat fee,
So here's to Vecelli and Buonarroti.
The grandeur falls away and Duveen's dead,
And Europe sinks once more into Avernus.
It's good in one's old age to leave one's bed
And young again to stalk such joys as burn us,
The glorious anarchy of what we love,
All stupid scales of value tossed aside
So that a Dosso Dossi seems above
A Titian and we'd die to prove our pride
In Credi or Melozzo: exhausted now
With rugs about my knees, in a wheelchair,
On this my final pilgrimage, I vow
To praise the greatness of that inner air
Which blows about the spirit: they said I'd find
The cutest Visitation in this glum
And barrel-chested church, so, wined and dined,
I'm here and have to laugh—it seems I've come
Full circle to the proving-ground of youth:
I'm bang in front of something I adored
When as a thrusting expert seeking truth
I first encountered it: the Virgin bored,
The Baptist's mother a strange shaft of blue
And two dogs fighting round their feet, the limbs
Half spastic but in everything a hue
Collated from the spectrum's antonyms—
Lorenzo Lotto, my first darling, I
Assigned you half a page in my big book
But more than ten years seeking-out—are we
Then reconciled—you with your beaky look,
Your death's pre-echo and me at the gates
Of terror and oblivion? Your luck

Was to be provincial in the Papal States,
Not smart enough for Venice where they suck
Up gold from mud and splash it on the stars—
You worked a density that fashion loathed
And paid the price of it, your avatars
The quirky poses, matrons overclothed
And cats astounded by angelic draughts.
Old friend, I'm with you now, I've done with fame
If never quite with money—Arts and Crafts
I leave to Night School mumblers and the same
For those grand galleries and owners—let
Them examine sizes, pigments, drapes, x-rays,
I'll give a provenance in a minute
They won't unseat—and Lotto, our last days
Can be the sweetest; you in the warm wind
From the Adriatic fixing the bizarre
With daily habits; me, more sinning than sinned
Against, and princely in a chauffered car,
Doing my lap of honour coast to coast,
Detesting Modern Art, unpenitent
Of theft or fraud, the last admiring ghost
Of Europe's genius, all passion spent.

CARRY HIS WATER TO THE WISE WOMAN

At the age when any pair of us
wonders who will go to the other's funeral,
to write extended poems where dull fact
is milked of its significance
is the terrible temptation.
Your bank card number, why you're snubbed
by taxis with their lights on, a nail-
clipping in a muesli bowl—something
is trying to get in touch, even if it's only
that now-forgotten dream's prognostication.
You might attempt a definition of unease,

a way to misinterpret Ruskin—
good ideas have little conscience
about the minds to which they will
entrust themselves: there is even an oboe phrase
of winsome beauty in the *Purgatorio*
of Liszt—and so since Pandemonium
the Devil's share of tunes has made
soft afternoons in Heaven something more
than La Grande Jatte with bandsmen
brushed by spittle. What's not expected
is any sort of timetable for this
or theory of interpretation.
We know it's better not to know
our hour of death but have a penchant
for the handier reminders: we go
to plays where youthful love is decked in
lavish packs of flesh, and wise retainers
mouth the nasty things they've kept in store
for sulks and spoilsports. Precedence
crowds the table when my granddaughter
says suddenly, 'No carrots!', an un-
equivocal insistence like the sun;
the world becomes more manageable and death
and vanity late versions of an institutional
pastoral. Martha, my gratitude,
you are my brief redeemer. Nothing can
be known beyond the instruments which measure
it and in such proud reports, as well as stuttering
by numbers, the graves and witches of a tortured
West confess. I must be simple—yes, I plan
to live forever, ripe, as they say of plums,
for picking. All those funerals I've kept
my dark suit for, plus the need to wear a tie:
I've promised to take both granddaughters down
to Glyndebourne in the year 2009—
bless me then you omens and you oracles
and keep the postman walking past my door.

DEATH'S DOOR

I'll have to make it harder, is my thought
    Appropriate to this last decade of
    A century which even old Kutusov,
Cunctator of scorched earth and starving fort,
Could hardly dignify by slow retort—
    Despair I think should shade my attic cough.

For I am using Browning's patent stanza,
    But not to tell a story as he did,
    His curious but circumstantial grid
On which he hung a strange extravaganza
Of narrative wide-ranging as a panzer,
    A cross between *King Lear* and *El Cid*.

No, my intent is to dredge memory
    Of those embarrassments I hope will show
    The turbulence pure spirits undergo
When launched against their will on a dead sea
Of circumstance: here childhood entropy
    Joins hands with geriatric afterglow.

We can't believe that life's a pilgrimage
    To nothingness, that moral monsters stand
    Along the dark backwaters of the land
And tempt us like drunks on a window-ledge
To self-destruction as our privilege,
    God's world before us, His hand in our hand.

'There is no God' and 'God is our Defender'
    Are two precise unprovable decrees:
    A supplicant or a campaigner sees
The same hard option and will cry 'Delenda
Est' or 'Love is such a sweet surrender'
    Inside his tank or falling to his knees.

If all paths take us to the grave, then why
    Not choose the path of glory; that at least
    Enjoys some dedication—sage and priest
May be outmoded but you still might try
As tycoon, mediator, super-spy
    To join Top Table for the Final Feast.

And yet our bodies tell us that the *cena*
    Will be the same for everybody—not in
    Its terror or serenity, forgotten
Faith or everlasting love, but vainer
Hopes, a metaphysics stormed by saner
    Fact: the soul is filed away in cotton.

Or rises in a Zoroastrian draught
    Through council chimneys while a little dust
    Put in a box rejoins the earth's soft crust.
Why make a fuss, the swallows ask, their craft
The whiling of the world, an overstaffed
    Theme Park, like Euro–Disney going bust.

The seeming misery is to do without
    A meaning to existence, but the child
    Though born to fear might still not be beguiled
By what his veteran instructors shout—
A system with high precedence and clout
    But showing murder in the way it's styled.

He lacks the will to pit himself against
    A seasoned state with his apprentice No;
    Before him integers and pundits go,
He sees a place that's arrogantly fenced,
Apportioned stupidly, obscurely tensed,
    Its progress A to B, mere to and fro.

Where can he seek the sign who has to die
    Unhallowed by the work he's here to do?
    He cannot own the world he's summoned to
Or rent it at a human rate; he'll try
To lift his aspiration to the sky
    And in the black of dreams discern some blue.

And that is when he's first brought to the door,
    A portage plain enough, no fancy locks
    Or gilded handles, and just as he knocks
A squirt of music fountains up before
The stroke, there's tears and moonlight on the floor;
    He makes no sound tiptoeing in his socks.

He trusts the cunning of his dreams; behind
    This door is everything there is and nothing,
    So it will never open and he's bluffing
When he lifts the knocker—he's resigned
To being something someone else designed,
    A serious doll made comic by its stuffing.

You cannot quarrel with this door: it stands
    As birth-gift to each complicated brain—
    But what you can do rather than explain
Your choked resentment is to watch your hands
As they plan empires, issue hot commands
    And find an alibi for any pain.

Then voices come which give the door a name—
    There's love, invention, curiosity,
    Truth, evolution, God, eternity—
Some tall abstractions keep it in its frame,
Through each allegiance it will seem the same,
    Roads lead to Rome, all vistas show the sea.

As children and as almost ghosts we glare
  Like Bluebeard's wife at what excludes our gaze.
  It might swing open at one magic phrase,
It might show Blake's hydrolysis of air,
A Paradise we make by being there,
  Justification startled by God's ways.

This door, like some crazed Tardis, will appear
  At certain moments when all else seems bright:
  Not just in cold epiphanies of night
But when the flesh is picknicking and fear
Has donned Rossinian motley with the beer—
  A Casa Santa, it moves at speed of light.

Arcane explainers hasten to its side,
  It lights up like a cinema organ's desk
  For *danse macabre* or *graveyard humoresque*:
No matter what philosophers provide
It stays the one impassable divide
  Between the paradisal and grotesque.

Thus given that we need a Paradise,
  To prove it we've proclaimed this ritual door;
  Our minds which live on time can now explore
Pre-emptings of reward and in a trice
Move up to bonding from the merely nice,
  Once having tasted love hunger for more.

And with no evidence say love is real
  Though fear like Fafner keep the iron gate
  (The hour you knock at will be called your fate!)
Love's what you want to do and think you feel,
Love's voice is music but its touch is steel
  And death not Venus may be your blind date.

You wait for her outside; you're carrying flowers,
   Those garden innocents which symbolize
   A world before the watershed of lies,
But these she spurns, she's after other dowers,
The Dance of Company and not of Hours,
   A house this entrance can't epitomize.

I'm trying, as you see, to change the rules,
   Reverse the major symbols of the trade—
   I've posed a door which opens inwards, made
An inner space, a torturer's school of schools,
More Funeral Gondola than Ship of Fools,
   The gravedigger's and not the gardener's spade.

The door leads out of Eden, not back in;
   It only swings one way. How then did we
   Arrive at this auspicious garden, Tree
Of Knowledge waiting for us, Fruit of Sin
Et cetera? Philosophies begin
   As Browning wrote in Natural History.

This happened on an island—Caliban,
   Borrowed from Shakespeare, had a distant God
   He took in with his mother's milk, his quod
Erat demonstrandum, and like Man
Equipped with capitals, Millennial Plan
   And conscience, knew Him by His chastening rod.

As much as Caliban we must accept
   Existence as an axiom; we come
   Out of the dark and go back where we're from—
But where is that? The keeper and the kept
Are both conspirators; the spark that leapt
   The Sistine ceiling struck its watcher dumb.

Which did not stop the myths from piling up.
   The end of life must be triumphalist;
   Transfiguration, yelling, will insist
You taste the garden agony and cup,
Blaspheme like Don Giovanni as you sup
   With fiends to get on God's guest list.

The island and the garden are just two
   Of our grand venues. Take the many wars—
   St Michael and the Dragon, The Rebel Cause,
The Raptors' Ten Year Siege, The War of Cru-
soe's Ear, Marx's Millennia, The Glue-
   Pot of the trenches—famed for opening doors

On death and on its catalogue of stories!
   Who gains the most—the Church with its cold hope
   Of discipline descending from the Pope,
The artists poised to paint and sing the glories
Of their rulers, or crooks, from Whigs and Tories
   To Republicans, modelled in soft soap.

At least beyond this door the imagery
   Will not be taken from the grisly bits
   Of our decay. A paradox—the fits
And starts of terror stop this side—to see
On fresco'd walls ecstatic devilry
   With forks and irons toasting bums and tits

Is hardly frightening today. Our hells
   Are in Old People's Homes and high-rise wards
   With surgeon's scalpels for King Herod's swords,
Our worst incarceration cancer cells—
No reasoned tone or priestly sign dispels
   The loneliness our dying health records.

And our imaginings of Heaven too
   Now need to be updated. The Child's Park
   Where all is play and no one fears the dark,
Cockaigne enskied, The Land of Cloud Cuckoo,
Cold Calvin Hall, predestined to come true—
   We'd swap them all for earthly sounds by Bach.

Perhaps that's it—the door's for listening through!
   Melodia suavissima, a grace
   That's independent of both time and place,
Settles on every Caliban like dew
And whispering love, says 'this is just for you.
   To you alone I show my real face.'

We all must die. After so long a span
   Truisms should be easily understood.
   The world will rail, the evil and the good
Be pictured on the coin of Everyman,
Our Vale of Tears seem just some Five Year Plan,
   Ourselves lost in the heart of a dark wood.

This poem's now as long as Browning's: his
   Courageous spirit's always hovering near
   And in these verbal junketings you hear
(I say immodestly) the worldly fizz
Of his deliberate Anabasis:
   Childe Roland's slughorn sounds out loud and clear.

DRAGONS IN THEIR PLEASANT PALACES

For Bruce Bennett

*And the wild beasts of the islands shall cry in
their desolate houses, and dragons in their
pleasant palaces . . .*

Isaiah, 13:22

KINGS AND MESSENGERS

Someone, leaning out, said Look it's what
We call the Learning Curve and bang the freight
Shifted in the back and whiffs of hot
Macadam wafted in: I saw my chance
And shouted at them all, No need to wait,
A dream's imagination's ambulance.

That's when the Kafka rules took over—we
Ate aphorisms like porcini, wrote
Our paradoxes as love-letters, free
In their compulsive intellect of all
Simplicity, and what we chose to quote
Was backstreet grovelling by a prodigal.

The rushing messengers disowned their kings
But relished livery: they had the Arts
For ukase, scams and heists and stings
To keep them modern, and appraising thoughts
Of sex and synergy, their counterparts
Successive saviours at besieged airports.

A GREAT RECKONING IN A LITTLE ROOM

As I wake from sleep I see
the shape my body makes upon the bed.

It's the on-her-side posture
my cat adopted at the Vet's

when supine from a sedative
she waited the injection in her heart.

It can be stamped as art—Maderno's marble
effigy of Cecilia in the cistern.

Better to see it as the foetus caught
by amniocentesis before birth.

Thus first or last we settle on our side
avoiding Heaven and its avatars.

A summary of life's allusiveness,
out of one dream, attending on another.

HARDY, 1913

When she he mourned had guided him beside
The cliffs and gates of courtship long ago
And ghost-like by the sea which howled below
Her form had surged and eddied with the tide,

When birds whose names both knew still multiplied
In makeshift air around, and counterflow
Of cloud and leaf-light once more set aglow
Her cheeks and nurtured his defensive pride,

He came back to his desk and framed in words
Those elegies in which his world lay wrecked,
His New Year songsters changed to mangled birds,

And still to show him what life cedes to art
Remorse kept house with her safe in his heart,
Her pets all killed or dead from his neglect.

ABOUT AUDEN'S JUVENILIA

He knew he would be great
   And told his tutor so
But lots of second-rate
   Ramshackle lines 'to go'
Like pizzas on a plate
   He ordered up: we know
His Hardy phase, his Yeats.

But as we sort out from
   The country metaphors
(That almanac birdsong,
   Those Edward Thomas spores)
The few bits which belong
   To his mature scores,
We smell death on the Somme.

He didn't write of war
   But just like Isherwood
Saw straight sex as the flaw
   Which cost a decade's blood—
His poems should restore
   A world before the flood,
The cooked renew the raw.

NATIONAL SERVICE

My childhood watchword—what could that be but Duty
Though my uncles made it a pure rhyme for booty?

I appreciate now that our family was unknowingly modern,
Good Australians, though of the line Hastings to Culloden.

But they never gave a thought to the UK as Home.
Three more uncles are buried in France, and all hated Rome.

Their Nationalism was unconscious, more like Red Neckery,
But they were townees, no truck with bush, bull or peccary.

The Poms were funny but you answered their bugle call:
The mills of Manchester and Oldham had my father in thrall.

We had one Yankee in town, an osteopath named Con,
And Oscars and Giulios in the ranks of Doug and Don.

I wasn't told at the time I'd be classified *Empirish*
Since no part of my ancestry was in any way Irish.

Playground language was barefoot, crude and near,
The very tongue which had nurtured Shakespeare.

Variant dialects: in Brisbane the dunny was 'the dub'—
They did The Lambeth Walk at the Peninsular Golf Club.

My grandfather served Davis Gelatine after leaving The Customs
    House.
He looked like Bernard Shaw but was timid as a mouse.

My mother had the guts, the sassiness, the gloom,
She showed me how terror could fill up a room.

Uncles were tight enough, but aunts were closed purses.
Our Protestant family trusted only Catholic nurses.

The Japs came, the Yanks came, eventually Sex came.
The expense of spirit was OK, but not the waste of shame.

They never called me up but I did my National Service.
The myths of a country conceal where its nerve is.

I moved on: I live in London: I'm grown quite mannerly.
But death will put me on the tram to Annerley

And I'll look out for the familiar sign on the shop
Bushells' Blue Label: I'll have got to my stop.

BREAKFASTING WITH COCKATOOS

They go well with baroque flutes,
with charity on a stick
and with the tremor of night-stallions
(to give those bearers of bad dreams
their proper gender)—they incline
a head above their fodder and warn us watchers,
this is not Grace but cantilever greed,
dribbling being nicer far than gratitude.

They defy us to be other than anthrop-
o—is it morphic, ludic, metric?—
cockatooness is unknowable
and consider the only tool we have for an assessment—
wheelbarrow words, rejigged, resprayed
but stationary on the superhighway
whose all roads lead to CD-Rom.
You photograph our souls, they say,
and what you get is quite a pretty plate
fit for The Book of Venerable Beards.

Now, as a gulp of tea goes down my shirt,
I sight a sulphur crest imposed
on Byron's pompous helmet and know
this bird would see no point
in liberating Greece. But wings are shadows
under which a million deaths are waiting
extraterrestrially to be born.

Birds will be Boyds,
beheaders of the worm voyeur
and snatchers of unguarded gristle;
they have platformed, so we think,
Darwinian aeronautics
from where they'll spring to any point
which offers exponential sloth.
They merchandise the proper lines
to front a marble fort embroidered
round the pelvis of a Doge
and when I put my cup down, faced at last
by my long-prevaricated, charismatic toast,
one of my cursory considerers,
non-verbally but colloquially,
pronounces our audience at an end
and offers in exchange a pilgrimage
to decorate a postcard, and I see
the picture in its heart, a true romance,
the embarkation for some special
Cythera of bulging rubbish bins.

OLD GOLDFIELDS, MARYBOROUGH

                              A terror made for midday,
they had walked in galleries beneath our feet
through tinted naves of clays and quartz
five miles and back to Maryborough
and hardby vents and blowholes seen the pulleys
raising ore through Roman arches
and the spacious graveyards fit for those
who never could feel safe in only air.
And now stout Hattie, energy's own dog,
is on the wrong side of the underworld
scouting at the creek's torn barbican
to sniff to life the latest of lost worlds.

Down such a rabbit hole
the Nineteenth Century lured our grandfathers
and great-grandfathers—
                    gold made sense
of leaving home, entitled all who hate themselves
to test the power of fortune: impervious gold
was a gem in destiny, and all along
a parliamentary Nature was on hand
to clean the mess up. For fifty years
the earth lay gashed by hopefulness and built
a sort of easily assembled Babylon
for these new-minted Gods—today
some sixty souls are forum for the trumpet
of its silent Judge.
                    When Hattie's rambles
take her to the mullock heaps, she skirts
a fossicker with detector and soft hat
looking for the fillings in this skull.
                    The landscape now
is featureless as scar tissue
though scrub revives wherever water rides
and ghosts of acid-fingered men
hover as hurt roses or the plums
which fall before the sun has sugared them.

MOBILE POOL CLEANER

This is the nation's capital; its pools
May not be blocked by leaves and drowning bees,
And so all day this driven mouthpiece drools
And tide-like sweeps the city's Inland Seas.

Then citizens in whom the moon has hung
A lamp of fear to keep their passions pent
Look down through chlorinated blue, among
The shifting shadows where the light is bent

And see, like Cardinals with conscience, what
Careers and pensions and a good address
Have wrought, and whisper tensely, 'You forgot
To buy the god that goes with cleanliness.'

DISPLACEMENT

Some would die for a word, some would find
a word only after having planned a death.
John's gospel raked in God, but he came in
number two to his plainsong syllable.
Words are like tonnages, displacement
of existence after settling in a sea
of language. They have their Piltdown grunts,
a history run backwards. A word would give
a party and leave the guests to clean the mess up.

Word me a word says the tyrant, these days likely
to be a Californian behind a cyber-desk;
judge me a word, the judiciary and the press
insist, and press them to death *ex cathedra*;
joke me a word, the communicators in
the nimbussed anarchy joke till the end;
silence me a word or otherwise theory it
assert the reasonable clerks of teaching,
betrayers of their own first love of purpose.

And it was like this when the speculative great
appreciated they could not be absolute,
turning their disappointment on to their own
eclectic brilliance, a Counter Reformation
of conjecture, biting at a Being Beauteous
or a fertile finger. Work and exhaustion
and then metaphor assumed the look of God—
Resto prigion d'un Cavalier armato—
darkness re-forming in the gaudy chapel.

MEN DIE, WOMEN GO MAD

No ideas but in things, but things
aren't words and understanding clings
to limitation's symbols: the caged bird sings.

Sharks would drown if they ceased swimming:
Cities of God and of the Plain, a twinning
as it was in the beginning.

Within the Book of Self called Commonplace
despair writes libels of disgrace
and Judas/Jesus has a Janus face.

The angel with the lily's at the door,
the cat is terrified, the girl just bored—
'Another thing we can't afford.'

To call my true love to the dance
I need the sonnerie of circumstance
and not the damp disclosures of the Manse.

Men die early, women live on, mad—
it didn't happen to my Dad,
a long life has more reason to be sad.

Vermeer and Donne had eleven children each—
that is, their wives did. D. could preach,
V. paint, with sex and death just out of reach.

We never truly learn to count past one
and hope that when we die we will become
the nothing new under the sun.

THE WESTERN CANOE

We are all in it together, paddling downstream
as in that clip from *Sanders of the River*
but with no one around to shout 'Come on Balliol!'

Undoubtedly here's history in the Steiner sense,
so late into creativity that commentary
gets the prizes, the sexy must of lecturing.

And Bloom's great gun booms heartily
making up for all those snubs, and if he seems
a kosher butcher, at least he's not the Theory Fairy.

In truth, this is a well-equipped canoe,
brother to the Gulf War one, and as attrition
weakens Gibbon, the crew is laser-limning history.

Films are shown on board: *Sophocles' National Service*,
Pico and Vico at the Deux Magots,
Alkan the Alien—but what's so terribly difficult

is starting up afresh. How did they do it, Emily
and friends, out there in the sticks, knowing that a gang
of snobs and clerics had turned the signposts round?

Bliss in that dawn! And if our dawns are chemical
some things never change—a Suburban Sports Reporter
enjoys the engine capacity of a Dickens.

As the canoe beats the rapids to enter the vast
waters of the Eco Pool, drums are calling
for a TV war replete with ice and orphans.

Dangers of shoals and drifting debris, reading habits
of electronic shoppers—and for the academically-inclined
dropping buoys off in The Swamp of Likenesses.

It reminds us of Maurice Bowra cruising the Aegean—
Daphnis and Chloe country for the educated—
and what are our lives but a narrative of metaphor?

Approaching us, a war canoe half The Lady Murasaki,
half state-of-the-art modem, and in a dream
the 'Waratah' still on her maiden voyage.

Hot in headphones, brushing off the monkeys,
Mr Kurtz hears what the King of Brobdingnag
told Gulliver. He'll reappear upriver.

TWO CULTURES

Walking with friends along pathways
of a chemically smelly canal
I watch a bright duck break from cover
and then disappear—how banal
its existence, I think, and how apt
for what pastoral Switzerland's about,
a compromise keeping life going
while money sneaks in and sneaks out—
I might as well joke my compliance
and as the duck flaps back in view
let Nature play straight man to Science,
self-consciously say, 'Oh look there,
it's our mallard imaginaire.'

And often in lanes and piazzas
of a village in the Alpi Apuane
I find myself watching and cheering
the local dog Otto, an army
of dogginess summed up in one dog,
a proof to Mankind of its mildness,
of King Stork in league with King Log—

I've little Italian but know that
such lovers of engines and slipstream
are unsentimental and no cat
or dog would be named for an emperor:
beware the Two Cultures debate,
Otto's birthmark's a clear figure eight.

Not far from there in dusty Pisa
where the Campo Santo braves tourists
and art and religion are partners,
I like to check prelates and jurists,
grave notables walled up in stone—
I'm seldom surprised by their calling
though once I was shocked—'Fibonacci,
why you? and why here? What a falling
off for the king of mathematics
to be buried surrounded by all sorts
of fantasists, duds and ecstatics!'
He gloomed at me: 'Series or Ceres,
Death's schooling stops short of world theories.'

DRAGONS IN THEIR PLEASANT PALACES

Where are the Science Students? Gone to Media Studies,
so why not take the Bible down and get a high
from old Isaiah? Half of what we mean by poetry
is still the rhetoric Hebrew makes in English.
Phasing in a little modern jargon—The Internet,
Pacific Rim, bi-polar wiring—and off we go
back to the full portfolio of lamentation,
the Psalmist's barefoot cries in Askalon,
the Voice of Him that cryeth in the Wilderness
and still breaks wind in Wollongong or Widnes.

The hilltop villages are plangent with goat cries
as water-carts ascend past millet-rows—
stop the bus! this coping stone's an uncle to
reluctance, and *Insh'allah*—where sparrows splash
a generation of fine mercers trained to be
the only hosts a prim cénacle knew—
here Tancred and Clorinda made the closing scene
while ravens, Hittites and black scorpions
catered to the Prophets. These stone museum lions
once were hungry mouths for Ashurbanipal.

As God Eternal joined time in his Mother
phenomena persist of dust collecting in
the sealed mechanism of a watch
and teeth come up decayed. Since figs must ripen
as they did a million years ago, eyes in
the Bible Lands dilate at searing jets
and burning rigs are pillars raised by night—
the very air has purged itself of progress—
such dragons not away on a consultancy
are making inventories of our palaces.

FAT AND SALT

Hear the voice of the pub inside the man
Inside the pub. Millenarian rain falls
Perpetually out of doors, but here
A glaucous injury of spirit finds
Paradise in wit and dying. Names now
Are all of soot and fester; light can't reach
Your eyes until it's passed its millionth spill
Of Guinness, or bowels move you on unless
Pork scratchings salt the freeze-up.
Salt ruin is philosophy: roll on
The body in the case—rational

Researchers gain their temple, minds relaxing
By a bar with afternoons as long
As Milton, and it's true, the world is all
Before us and we need advance no further
Than the clock ten minutes fast forever.
Discipline moves past the wiping cloths,
Dares the bar-high dialectic, averts
Its eyes from pain and contumely since we
Are lost to relevance, playacting all
That's left for courtesy. And we have the shock
Of pier-end museums at our touch,
The monsters under glass, the deviances
Of a far-away Creator: we
Can frame them like home videos—'Moab
Is my washpot, over Edom will I
Cast out my shoe.' The light is deepening,
It's five per cent of content and it won't
Reveal the truth of anything—now pass
The orders upwards—this is the only sort
Of isolation humanity has left,
The subtle chit-chat of self-subtraction,
An inverse Eden rimmed with fat and salt
Whose vacillation's a tautology.

ANXIETY'S AIR MILES

Like the wide-flying Puck of interview
Whose girdle is by CNN and whose
Disposable catharsis gets us through
Our daily fear and boredom, memory
Has dropped its old approach, its panelled lights
And revenants dispensing wholesome guilt,
To be obscene and universal. Time
Has winged the ageing close capillaries
Of this one fearful conscience till plain grief

Has lost its way—not what harm was done,
What crystal pain collapsed in hypo-
thermia or where all hope swam out
To death, but dumb impersonality
May compromise the brutal evidence:
This is the stunted world we have to live in
And I who've ringed the globe five times since that
Eclipse now see myself a frequent flyer
Topping up his helplessness with speed.
The personal is now generic and
To fight this off requires the limits of
An earlier age before a change of hem-
isphere might seem some kind of absolute
When air miles were not banked with hope to make
Anxiety the husbander of harm.
But dreams are twice as fast as Boeings
And visit more appalling shores. The years
Have forced the proper name of love to emulate
Its neuter self. Love is the good which died
That Winter night and with its death became
The wide-winged world—love would be settlement
Of all internal scores—so a mirror holds
The unchanged self beneath its surface,
Happy to exhibit an irrelevance
Of worse and further deeds, knowing what lived
Will go on living until once more
The thin December mist enshrouds the room,
The clock eludes the errant heartbeat and
A closure, like a book put down, defeats
Exhaustion, stepping out of time. Look then
To the great Hobbesean plainness of the world
And hoard its miles against a setting-out.

TOO MANY MIRACLES

Honeycomb-tinted, billiard bald, unblinking,
the baby stretches on his raft of lint—
he is the one quite unselfconscious
thing in a plethora of thinking
and will give his parents no least hint
of what their magic's done or yet will do.
His head is huge, his penis a bold dildo—
the prosthetic ends of life already
exaggerated, our scion of all species
prepares to venture far beyond the steady
proposal of a humanistic thesis
into some overworld—the kin in him,
fancying his mother's breath a zephyr,
knows this is miracle, not synonym.

Where clay foot trod and iron claw dispersed
plants and unctuous animals, a fort
of fragrance hides beneath the ruined grass—
two and a half thousand years have done their worst
to a once civil city and open tombs report
their bodies missing and their souls as well.
Leave the car and find if petrol fumes dispel
the ambience of death: fought-over ground
looks no different from the urban waste
littering the road—here the sherdist found
a crinkly stone and an official chased
the village dogs away. Are they chimerical
these glowing figures who return or is
this just another necessary miracle?

We are not ready for any manifestation
of our special case. But the best of us
eschew conjecture and take by nature from
the gifts encoded in our blood a ration

of hope and then the joy of work—a fuss
of ordered sounds, a roping-up of syllables,
morality of colours, chartered skills—
and far from dark Messapian trappings choose
a sun-kind ripa of philosophy,
as if to die were just to not refuse
a visitable hospice by the sea—
a conch-shell or a goat's horn cornucopia
might spill the face of wonder on the sand,
painstaking painting, miraculous sinopia.

And from the start our baby's being there
will not be pedal note of all sustainable
existence, merely the formula he's given
to make accommodation of the air
and every swarming truth imaginable.
Henceforth equipment matters—tooling up
for universal martyrdom, the cup
which never passes, is his mise-en-scène,
and love and patience and the drip of time
are all apprenticeships. Words intervene
to tell him there exists a far sublime
since there's a word for it: he will discuss
with friends the smoothness of the world and say
too many miracles trouble the meniscus.

THE DEATHS OF POETS

> *answered some*
> *Of his long marvellous letters but kept none.*
> —W. H. Auden

It's been a great strain on the words,
they've had to get leave from their journals,
the *Greenpeace* pamphlets, instructions for
setting-up sub-woofers, Satanists' e-mail,
Share Shop panegyrics—

they're on parade
in their smartly-tailored stiff Obituaries:
they like such gear since obliqueness is in order,
euphemism rules and reading between the lines
is just the sort of secret work they trained for.
　　　　　　　　But those who live by words
find words are dry-eyed at the funeral—
there's too much to forgive, the sleight of tongue
which fazed the weak and faxed the managers,
the pity of self-pity as dawn chorus,
imagination's magical deceptions
which kept unfairness grinning like a Tooth
Fairy outed by a child.
　　　　　　　　　Each meant his life to be
an exemplary success story, but somehow
it all went wrong; death couldn't be postponed,
symposia and Festschriften rotted
among the leaves on crematoria lawns,
hoped-for vindications, complete with jokes
and anecdotes, were never written or
were spiked by teenage editors, while the last
humiliation was the naming of
new names, so up-to-date they featured on
no one's list of enemies.
　　　　　　　　Let fashion do its worst,
they said and then it did. Integrity
was no more friendly: when personified
it looked a bully, just the sort who'd say
'I don't like your face' across a bar
or schoolroom, but you knew that really
sniffer glands had found your fear—the fault's
not moral but in talent, and the tunes
which last are driving death from utterance
however tragic its creation: Woodbird sings
and envious good and grieving evil both
are silent.

                              And now the words which must
accustom poetry to its lower place
in Paradise are gathering at the wake.
Poetry was fun to write, its veterans intone,
and to be young was very heaven et
cetera . . . and the owl of self-regard
is spotted on the mourning tree, cantos
freely flowing, academic picnics spread,
the young recruits around the swollen knees
of old condottiere, salt hay whispering . . .
time for another et cetera . . . then a tyro says
'Consider Auden's poem where the hero
is a man of action, not a poet
and his letters to his loved one
cannot guess that in a desk this stay-at-home
keeps coded entries in a book whose gulfs
of language change thought's very synapses
which even now both Poetry and Science
must labour to catch up with.'
                              The Deaths of Poets
require damp days and a lack of public news
and should be heard of over lunch
or driving to the airport, the latest novel packed,
exchange rate of the lira down—
                              Fountains wait, unblocked
of rubbish, cypresses stand to,
and someone's coming with moist hair to bring
you to the house you've always hoped to live in.

JOHN FORD ANSWERS T. S. ELIOT

You knew I was a lawyer, why be surprised
by my distinctive style? Overall, my plays
aren't centred, but what I know of men
tells me centres will form only when

storms erupt to make them. My poetry
is what a lawyer might describe as small
instances growing great occasionally
(that is on sporadic and ingenious
occasions): for this I listened to the manner
men and women, tiring of the means they use
to hide their thoughts or to mislead
their interlocutors, may suddenly,
as philosophers will do, rush into compact
forms of language not malleable
as dialogue—their passions striking them
without advertisement or strategy,
they loop around them such forensic toils
as make pleached gardens out of parkland.
The paradox is poetry, a sort of
versified cascade not requiring metaphor
but like a fountain in a blindfold villa
unmistakably an image of the heart.

Why, three hundred years ahead of me,
you should commend me for belief in love
eludes me. What is there else to write of?
You with the urgings of an impotence
appropriate to your short-breathed age will put
your own adopted crinkle-crankle doubt
into the sort of poetry which won't
assimilate mankind—instead pathetic
Nature and the ramblings of a rhetor God
are called to make your language beautiful.
You are a Psalmist doing without the smell
of burning flesh. Good and evil mixed, you say,
is not the way to justify a knack
with cadencing, and further, I make occasion
fill the cast-list. And here you're wrong
since you resort so often to that arid
concept 'character'. Brutish husbands, vengeful lovers
are simply steeds the words can ride—if every
speaker were the same at each intrusion

on a sentence, then personae might make character—
instead, I write the only poetry
the broken heart has known—not sympathy
for this or that distracted humanoid
but palaces and obelisks and tombs
of diction, and I set before you shapes
with names and callings, sub-contract them to
a place of some malignity and then
I watch. As they come into focus, syntax
stirs and seeks its opportunity:
for this the human race was made, to build
its only lasting Babel, rusticate
the puffed-up feelings and the blemishes
of tragic pity. I have the instrument
to deal with ruined love—to outlast thought
by being before thought what it would say.

BELLINI AND HEINE COME TO DINNER

Did you know that Liszt and his ridiculous woman
read Dante to each other on the shores of Lac Léman
and the consequence is transcendental pianism
and the higher sexuality? Your opinion, Signor Bellini?

I'm afraid, Countess, you have an all too prevalent view
of the Italians, and I cannot properly blame you.
So many of my compatriots are opera factories,
industrious but coarse. I missed your point, Herr Heine.

It is the German genius to make the Devil a conjurer
but beware you Westerners when his scientific,
aromatic tricks are served up by our sorcerer Goethe—
Signor Bellini's mad scenes will all come true.

You are too generous, Countess, when you propose
that I have liberated the caged bird of the soul:
in *Puritani* I see through words to where the eagle
waits behind the sun. You may sneer, Herr Heine.

Why does God waste beauty, whether of limb or visage,
in framing the crooked structure of the mind?
Probably to laugh at their credulity who think
their fortunes fixed. You will die young, Signor Bellini.

The calm before the storm, the calm which follows it,
anyone, Countess, can show us that. It is the calm
within the storm which I compose. As for you, Herr Heine,
you are a Leopardi compelled to bark in German.

The Greeks were here before you, Signor Bellini.
Hubris with its false Icarian wings sets out
to find sublimity, but by a shorter route
Ganymede is roped up to the impatient gods.

One encounters strange philosophers at your table,
Countess, but I will leave the last word with Herr Heine.
Tomorrow I go with my beloved to the country—
no words, no music, only Nature and Love are there.

BROWNING MEETS WAGNER AT THE SCHLESINGERS'

'Once I wrote of Life's C Major; so prophetic!
It was the very time you made your *Mastersingers*.'
'Few poets can read music; none should use such terms.
These wretched key signatures! But we must be neat.'

'Perhaps, but why does German music conquer everywhere?
Professionalism! Technique, not heartwork governs art.'
'Oh, poet, you have never suffered in our theatres—
I long for just one of Bellini's unpedantic tunes.'

'When I look at paintings I behold the Greek
and Jewish worlds in harness. Is this not so?'
'Our Saviour was an Israelite, yet what he brought
about by Jordan was an upsurge of pure blood.'

'But Master, it is only when Euripides
is yoked to Saul that Western eyes are cleansed.'
'They must be baptised, then my loyal Levi
will show the Germans what conducting is.'

'One of our paper hacks has written of your trip:
"The Future of the Theatre meets The Theatre of the Future".'
'Diamonds in the desert! My life has been devoted
to bestowing ritual on Nature's Morning Song.'

'I'm told you read your Shakespeare like so many
breves and semibreves and words become fixed tones.'
'He is the God who rules us all, so when my art
disgusts me I delve instead among his feasting plays.'

'The world as lyric gesture—so many I have known
have ruined love by harping on its ecstasy.'
'Yes, poet, you are right. Even in *Tristan* I
incorporate truthful dialogue, not just as recitative.'

'The Norse Gods die, but good old savage Germany
endures—a slice for each of G Flat Major bliss.'
'But soon the time will come when by a sea or some
wide lake the heart must pause to hear its own lost song.'

COLLATERAL DAMAGE

'Beethoven was an ugly man, short of stature, with a pock-marked face cut by blunt (or clumsily-guided) razors, and in his late years with a body-odour strong enough to empty the largest table at any of his favourite Viennese restaurants.'

—John Deathridge, *TLS*

I see it this way, Mr Beetfield,
you can't do anything that's true pin-point,
there's always one shot goes astray
and some poor thing that got in range
has to be apologised for when damage
is assessed, with all the pictures in.

And minims, liver-spots on God's back-of-hands,
are disappointment's fine embellishment:
the café empties like a concert hall
at such reiteration, and that wretched frame
the pianoforte's a mechanical lyre
for each new Orpheus with attitude.

Exactitude, as I insisted, Mr Beetharvest,
has its price. I mean any farmer knows
breeding is selection and half a herd
can feel the fall-out. That loaves and fishes draught,
well, you couldn't do it if you had to say
No to factory farming. God gives the means.

Music is prosthesis, the jutting-out of truth
beyond performers' fingers.
Because it makes no difference when we're dead
the extraordinary must be fashioned now,
the impossible made sane ambition
and the body a crucifixion of the mind.

It's as if we're in two parts, Mr Beetsugar,
like that guy Montaigne wrote—imagination
puffs us up and reality deflates us.
When the vet said this won't be a healthy calf,
if I'd believed him I'd have lost
a square-eyed runt became my best milk-giver.

The bombardment lingers in the air
as octaves, and the awful pain of deafness
still resonates above the stave.
Looked at another way, a youthful virtuoso
tells his mistress he mustn't marry
having already composed her rejection of his love.

I'm an amateur of ballistics, Mr Beetweevil,
and I don't value megadeath or even
cluster bombs and shrapnel. The point of God
is perfect aiming, something we can't do
on earth. And yet it seems our progress,
as we call it, comes from near-misses.

Darkness visible—perhaps, or
silence audible—or crowding
immeasurability in a phrase.
The silent piano weeps on earth—
time rots in Heaven, ignoring
the *fingerfertigkeit* of angels.

FAFNER'S NEEDLEWORK

I wanted to control the universe
but now I'm buried in a mass of notes
and night by night my dreams are getting worse.

That selfish genius took me from a myth
and kitted me out with steam-age harmonies,
anachronisms I can't be bothered with.

So I'm embroidering the history of mankind:
power corrupts etc., and which came first
the healthy body or the healthy mind?

You might say I'm that peerless Trinity,
Das Ich, Das Es, Das Uber-Ich, and who'd
be master must decapitate all three.

And he'll be stupid, natural and cruel,
hear forests murmur and translate their birds,
then challenge me to fight a bloody duel,

Horns v. Tubas. My enchanted gore
will introduce the simpleton to fear
and start the whole shebang up as before.

Let's call a halt—back to my needlework,
bring up the lights, tell the audience to go home
before the music drives them all beserk.

Bayreuth itself is just Beirut freeze-dried
and all that Early Warning Systems do
is sprinkle holy art on genocide.

THE TENOR IS TOO CLOSE

Our tenor's stumpy, stout and spitting as he sings.
No wonder Doriano, who ran for Italy

at the Olympics, whispers to us softly,
'Il povero, che brutto'. Mozart was small

but rather vain of his good looks. The beautiful
we tend to think does well to stay aloof

and just exist. The actions of the world
deliver up like Fabergé

that ruinous perfection Czars desire,
loving most its pointlessness.

So if you aren't a gracious object
(however subject to time's overlay)

you go down coughing mines or boil your eyes
in lapidary drilling, milled with slaves.

While memory continues there'll be art
but think of Heaven where we had

blank space of everything potential
and revelled in iconic nothingness

which childhood was the first to smirch.
One day we'll be adult and then we'll know

that truth is comparable to Shakespeare,
miraculous for being possible.

But distancing stays difficult, so we duck—
the tenor now is right in front of us

and Mozart's notes survive a hail of spittle.
You need, like Doriano, to know you're loved.

A DANCE OF DEATH

The cows sidle up to the fence
   To eye these impeccable creatures
Parading their bold present tense
   And mark upon such worldly features
     The instinct of herds,
     The display of birds,
     The polish of words,
Disbelief held in willing suspense.

The sheep snatch at tussocks of grass
   While watching bright hampers unpacked,
In the theatre a musical farce
   Shows love going down on its back—
     Black tie out of town
     Where bubbly may drown
     A matronly frown—
Troppo Glyndebourne, alas, O alas!

Beasts and humans aren't built to discern
   A dance which extinction has planned,
That whatever it is that they earn
   They're all to be duly trepanned,
     The wealthy donator,
     The TV debater,
     The tone oscillator,
Each one made redundant in turn.

A few vocal decades from now
   This freshly-cut stone will have warmed
And the glories which rich men endow
   By time will be hugely deformed,
     New verities loom,
     New shapes to a room,
     New rites for a tune
And the orbital cropping of cows.

SKINNING A SKUNK

Now there's a taking title. What
Can I who've only once been on
A horse compose in verse to show
My Nature Wisdom: do I know
The latest Georgics, can I pleat
Our ancient art to modern song,
And is my skunk-lore sound? It's not.

But be a Rocky Mountains bard
At least on paper is the urge
As anthropologists whose belts
Of Aztec silver hang with pelts
Of phones and CDs startle birds
By shouting tropes at ocean's verge—
The sky is high and life is hard.

The Grizzly droppings blaze like gold,
What could a city poet say
Of caymen craft or lizard lurch,
Coyote's spoor and condor's perch,
Or even how a stockman gelds
A horse or what vets do to spay
A cat. Stop! Poems must be sold.

And in Australia now they hymn
The last black queen Van Diemen's Land
Sent into exile, and lags who
Joined tribesmen living on grub stew
And baked galah: a native theme
Has critics eating from your hand.
Parnassian suits an interim.

Today the skunks and foxes meet
In litter-bins while dolphins die
In mile-long trawls—it's poets now
Who roam the woods and gild the bough
And banks which skin the vertebrate.
Life changes, but not poetry:
Skunks stink and poets have to eat.

VERDI'S VILLA, SANTA AGATA

Within a radius of fifty miles
round Reggio and Modena
the landscape smells of shit.
Miracles are never kind
and Emilia-Romagna's cooking
is renowned throughout the world.

The sun turns steadily
over the standing fields,
imported Kiwi fruit
replace the orchard crops
and dry-course rivers sleep
below heraldic bridges.

They farmed their art one time
with the same intensity,
and still you see the turbid
fruits of death and nature
in Dosso's boskiness
and buttocks by Correggio.

Where though to find that grand
ordinariness which marks
the few world-eating geniuses?
Great families shrink at last
to names on famous forts
and visits after lunch.

Verdi's villa has every touch
of provincial stylessness—
cramped rooms, dull views,
the decorations of
a Paymaster-General's widow,
glassed memorabilia.

In the garden a sluggish pond,
a tumulus for ice,
rambling paths leading
to a prairie gate
and a melancholy cat
prescribable as noon.

THE LION OF ANTONELLO DA MESSINA

              My lion tells me
that the word can kill and will do so
without warning. Together we have
house-trained terror till it's fit
to undertake a miracle for Science.
The underworld of things is Paradise,
the sun in stained-glass portholes made
to adore the laws of its dismantling
and all the books which must be studied
if Creation is to stay on course—
witness then the sheer assemblage
of this quiet; has any other sainted cell
so radiant a cross-section?
Without my lion nothing would connect,
he is the way imagination went
while God was still explaining it.
Antonello can't domesticate
my cauldron of a mind and so
he tidies everything and has the lion state

Jerome is king of thinking beasts.
But to get the entire world into
so small a painting is more than skill,
it adds up to theology.
Of all the lions I've had, this beast
of Antonello's is the most complete;
he lays his muzzle in my lap
as if he knows it is a fearful thing
to fall into the hands of the living god.

WHAT BORROMINI SAW

Something appropriate to being Bernini's butler,
An upstart world of feigning ecstasy,
An inflammatory geometry growing ever subtler,
A foothold of angels on the slope of a pea.

The House of Melancholy as a Temple of Reason,
Concavity, in shape as a recessive gene,
The Mass compressed to just Kyrie Eleison,
Earth's curve, Sky's line, Man in between.

From the latin 'caedo', a stonecutter's suicide,
But loved by materials on scaffold or in hod,
Rome's bridegroom ditched by his hard-faced bride,
The Phoenix Basilisk of an Incarnate God.

THE PINES OF ROME

for Katherine & Royston

As ghosts of old legionaries, or the upright
farmers of that unbelievable republic,
the pines entail their roots among the rubble
        of baroque and modern Rome.

Out by the catacombs they essay a contradiction,
clattering their chariot-blade branches to deny
the Christian peace, the tourist's easy frisson,
        a long transfiguration.

Look away from Agnes and the bird-blind martyrs,
the sheep of God's amnesia, the holy city
never built, to the last flag of paganism
        flying in mosaic.

Then say the pines, though we are Papal like the chill
water of the aqueducts, refreshment from a state
divinity, we know that when they tombed the martyrs
        they ambushed them with joy.

Rome is all in bad taste and we are no exception
is their motto. Small wonder that Respighi, 'the last Roman',
adds recorded nightingales to his score *The Pines*
        of the Janiculum.

And the scent of pines as we dine at night
among the tethered goats and the Egyptian waiters
is a promise that everything stays forever foreign
        which settles down in Rome.

Therefore I nominate a Roman pine to
stand above my slab, and order a mosaic
of something small and scaly to represent
        my soul on its last journey.

THE COCKS OF CAMPAGNATICO

The heart grown old can't fake its scholarship
And won't essay that glib insightfulness
Which once it made a moral landscape from:
This village, half its human figures and
Its cats and dogs enthroned in windless sleep.
Law's brutal now—a German bus deep-parked,
A gang of no-ones-in-particular
Kicking to death a pigeon—how may they be mapped?

Only within the self can scales be hung.
Ignore mere detail says the ageing conscience,
Encourage emblems any mind can hail.
And so the roosters of the valley stir
As if to answer such a challenge, though
They're late, their tubs of sun already full,
And beautifully redundant to themselves
Propose and repropose the Resurrection.

THE ROSE GARDEN ON THE AVENTINE

Where may I take my now imploded body
To encompass vanities outside itself
That calming all its spasmic platitude,
Its counting days to dying, miming health
As if it woke each morning in a pot
On a dry balcony and felt the wind with stealth
Approach, it might for once appear at ease?

Only some site where grief has entertained
A lifetime's certainty could host such grace,
A tumulus of constant living, veined
By hope and its humiliations—here

Along the slopes which lead down from the hill
Of Saint Sabina's Wedding Saturdays
Where Aventine internees prosper still.

A great unswervable unfairness of
Well-off with poor, long-life with death, despair
With hope—this is the place Rome handed on
To sequent centuries; the very trees compare
Each person at their feet and measure love
And loneliness as if stalled on a stair
Where saint might doubt or devil cease to tempt.

The Roman Commune on this ground has made
A straggling garden fused with modern roses—
Nearby, the Circus Maximus decayed
To little but a rubbish dump hears cars
Re-echoing its chariots while the bells
Resounding modern couplings can keep faith
With life beyond the silence of monks' cells.

But roses, killed by time, live outside time
And open, fold and blow as if the world
Were just the moment when they come in view,
No different tomorrow, petals whirled
Away by wind but new buds setting fire
To morning when the rim of Rome is pearled
By risen dust encircling milky sun.

Now, in my sixties, I have quarrelled with
My friends, including that old friend, my brain,
And sated with the remedy of myth
Have no resort but using my tired eyes
To reinvent the day—a thousand flowers
Undisciplined but municipal
Vie with St Dominic and the flying hours.

No rose would stammer for a catacomb
Or candle-tinted altar, but repeat
The litany it's rooted in, the round
Of youth, and genuflecting to the seat
I'm on, point at exhausted Rome to prove
Through roar of motorinos time's defeat
Even in this its consecrated heart.

THREE OTRANTOS

The first *Otranto* was my ship.
How yacht-like were those working vessels,
long grey slivers dipping below the waves
through periscopic sights—
born Barrow-in-Furness in the twenties,
ready to carry me docilely
from Hamilton Wharf to Tilbury
in 1951. Down on H Deck
with the hides and green bananas
we rolled in half-light through
seas more imaginary than real—
brandy ten pence a glass,
The Orient Line white jackets of the stewards,
smoked haddock in warm milk,
married women taking off their rings,
a smell perpetually of creosote
and cooking. No more beautiful ship
ever edged the stuffy waters of the Med
or showed the flying-fish
how riding gracefully through waves is done.
Later, among the cabin cruisers of the Thames,
guessing her in the breakers' yards,
I paid my dues: *The Otranto*, I said,
was the true umbilical which linked me to
my never-to-be-known, all-knowing mother.

My second Otranto was all Walpole's,
his gothic castle so unlike
the actual Norman, Angevin
and Aragonese fortress in Apulia.
In my thought it represents the lies
I told and go on telling as a writer.
I traced the progress of the Gothic Novel
in examination papers earning
fulgent marks while never having read
a word of what I praised. Such dubious means
to powerless ends. At least I learned
two things—Horace Walpole was a brave
if over-fastidious man, and Peacock's
Nightmare Abbey, and his *Melincourt*
are more fun than the Gothic modes they mock.

The third Otranto's the real site.
In that side-chapel of the Cattedrale
I wondered at the several cupboards
flanking the plain altar—why store crockery
in such a place? Grey utility cups and saucers
stacked behind glass doors. Up close
they proved so many skulls and pelvises and femurs,
a vile Old Mother Hubbard's hoard
of ghastliness. That murder done in 1480
should look so pointless with its faith
and courage drained away was shocking to
my secular and self-decoding mind.
The decapitating blade, in profile like
the Adriatic, hovered in the air.
The smell of sea-food cooking and the sharp
sting of restorers' lacquer brought
the present back. Otranto stretched its arms
to inventory the day. Almost lunchtime
it declared, enrobing ancient martyrdom
in a blue inclusiveness of sea.

A LAMENT

In valleys where winds meet,
in silences of chambers
untouched by the sun,
in tufa uplands and long strata
of the vanished waters,
we will find them—
our salted ancestors
in households still outflanked
by cat and ibis mummies,
the losing parts of ghostliness
not magicked now by moon or stars—
their eyes would sweep forever
super sydera, but that they have no eyes
nor ears, but only a long nothingness
imagined by the gods.

In dreams they visit us
but it is our lives which are
their prison. They made their tombs
and temples to invigilate our thoughts
and their dementia is our memory.
Though such messages are fading from us
a chemical exchange goes on—
a dynasty of prayers becomes a waterfall,
a warrior's resting place the chair
of some sand-flooded tractor.

When all the lives which ever were or ever will be
are trimmed like stone and share
stone's magical inertness
winds will still lament the strangeness
which was life and silence look to find
its birthplace in an allegoric music.
And the winds say
What did you do in the war, Daddy?
and the reply, I kept my gas mask on.

Nothing is straightforward
and the shortest distance between two points
may be the way to death,
and gravity is bounced about the rocks
by private zephyrs. The only sound now
is a lift ascending to the floors
of non-existence. They wait there for us,
our friends and lovers recognizable
as we shall be by their perfect missingness.

A SHORT BALLAD OF UNBELIEF

It's not a good time for risk-taking
The baleful brain says to itself.
You're not well, you ought to propitiate
The God who ordains failing health.

But he might respect greater defiance,
No whimpering crossing the bar,
The Atheist's Comedy praying,
The invite marked 'come as you are'.

Have they found what they looked for, those faces
Whose names are now washed off their stones?
Do their mounds keep them warm out of Domesday,
A permanent summer of bones?

You might toil up precipitous stairways
To visit high altars and tombs,
Find Maria d'Aracoeli is worth it,
Love shrunk to a handful of rooms,

But nothing can prove your existence
Will keep going after you're dead.
You may think that it's owed you—for instance
That Paradise looms in your head

And millions are born to ensure
Creation should lead on to you
With all the juridical gestures
Which keep the elect very few.

But can Art and Aesthetics survive when
The body is held at discount
By old age, and hope of survival
Is more of a cringe than a flount?

Will you ever convince your intelligence
To accept the intentional breath
Of frescoes and candles and statues,
The paraphernalia of death?

Unbelief has just enough cunning
To be grateful when nailing the lie
Of transcendence that still every steeple
Points nowhere but into the sky.

A REINTERPRETATION

After the Miracle of the Loaves and Fishes
Was sought the Miracle of the Further Wishes,
That the nurturing of ordinary folk
Should count for more than simply to evoke
A loving god, but daily be set forth
(Because Your Father, slow to come to wrath,
Knoweth ye have need of all these things)
In food and drink and love and cherishings—

Yet like the parables, the miracles
Were too exemplary to be much else,
And ants and birds were drawn to gulp the crumbs
And grass regrow beneath ecstatic bums
And scribes and painters muddy up the scene
With praise of what was just a go-between's
Brief granting of unnatural exemption
The while the dutiful indifferent sun
Content that life on earth had come to stay
Lighted the miraculous and the following day.

IL LACERATO SPIRITO

Refreshment of life
is the principle which damns us all

Nature or Nurture? The lamb trots after its mother
up the ramp and into the waiting ship

Death cannot bear its own company,
it destroys life to go on creating it

The peace of nescience is the dream
of plants and stars and parallel lines

Spirit, being God's intake of breath,
constantly admonishes its maker

Such insubstantiality restricts
Paradise to the interface of time

Emerging unsorted in the world
we have to learn to tolerate our shapes

And that is why the spirit's torn
from the body to be eloquence

So let my cry go out and let my fear
inseminate the numbered elements

MUTANT PROVERBS

Nine stitches are a waste of time.
It's the early worm who gets caught by the bird.
A Mossy Stone gathers a Rolls.
Sleight of hand makes many work.
There's no police like Home.
Space for the goose is spice for the gander.
Butter the devil you know and batter the devil you don't.
The child is farther from the man.
When in Rome do the Romans.
An apple a day is not a doctor's pay.
A friend in tweed is a friend in need.
No fuel like a cold fuel.
Vedere Napoli e poi mentire./See Naples and lie.
Pour encourager les auteurs.
Après le déluge, c'est moi.
Blood is quicker than mortar.
Spokes of the Devil.
In drains begins responsibility.
The family that prays together slays together.
From cleanliness to godliness, what next?
Apotheosis of the dons.
A rose by any other name would cost much less.
A diamond is for Eve.
Jam yesterday, jam tomorrow, logjam today.
Life is a dram.
By their frights ye shall know them.

Dying will be a great invention.
Sweet are the uses of advertising.
Virtue is its own regard.
Our hearts were young and grey.

DEATH AND THE MOGGIE

Good Morning, Citizen Cat,
I am Death who's come
To take you from this flat
Back to where you're from.
Are you ready, Comrade Cat?

Don't pester me, Sir Death,
This is my morning rest
When I forget that teeth
Shred flesh from bone with zest.
I'd fillet you, proud Death.

Stay calm, Signore Gatto,
You have to leave but you're
In that anthology from Chatto
On page 174.
Va' ben, amico gatto.

Listen, egregious Hades,
Those only give you power,
Fine Gentlemen and Ladies,
Who recognize their hour.
Don't mix with rough trade, Hades.

The time has come, Herr Katz,
To chew what you have bitten,
This languor is ersatz;
That you can't stay a kitten
Kein Rätsel ist, Mein Schatz.

I'm not, you Modern Hermes,
Quite ready yet to die.
Though this the end of term is,
I'm still as bright of eye,
A beautiful brown Burmese.
Each star helps light the sky.

BOTH ENDS AGAINST THE MIDDLE

For Christine,
words and more than words

Time, like an ever-rolling stream,
  Bears all its sons away;
They fly forgotten, as a dream
  Dies at the opening day.

—Isaac Watts

LEAVING MANTUA

I woke up early as I invariably do
    when I have an early train to catch—
    a dream-master has no need of clocks.

The night before I'd argued in my language
    with two Italian ladies who might have been
    happier in theirs: had I been rude or thoughtless?

One was wrong, undoubtedly, to think Shakespeare's
    works were written by the Earl of Oxford
    but they both resided in Mantua and I

Was in exile from myself, or so I told myself,
    looking at the stallions on the wall
    of the Palazao Te: 'here is for me no biding'.

And wasn't I as grossly opinionated
    about Italian painting as she on Shakespeare?
    My head hurt after a thick wine they'd been happy

To leave to me, and I'd toyed with beetroot-coloured
    strips of meat once more maintaining
    our Northern barbarism—drink ahead of food.

Struggling past the desk (I'd had the sense to settle
    the bill the night before) I pushed my case to the street
    sheeted from eave to cobbles in soup-thick mist.

Where in this Dantesque gloom might the station be?
    I knew Id find it and that in the meantime
    I'd enjoy the sense of apprehension.

Some text-book facts were circling in my mind:
    the lakes formed by the Mincio which made Mantua
    unhealthiest city in all Italy,

The midday gravitas which even bold Mantegna
    found obsessively marmoreal, the grim
    abutting jokes which Giulio proved sexy.

Yet the Gonzaga, as their Estense neighbours,
    lived in the sun and left it up to Shakespeare
    to conjure terror for us from their name.

I'd seen King Charles's pictures bought from
    Mantua's sack, or what we have of them
    after Cromwell sold them off—I'd followed

A troop of noisy children just to view
    the Pisanello frescoes in the Reggia.
    I'd been in Mantua only once before,

And that had been a time I was unhappily in love
    and yet felt hopeful—hope meant now just
    images and archives and a muffled street.

At last in the swirling vapour of a Bogart movie
    I bought my ticket, registering I had
    to change at Fornovo, and ate a warm brioche.

I was leaving Mantua. I was curiously content.
    I thought of James Wright, who in a sense
    I'd wronged, and of his rescue of a bee

Imprisoned in a pear beside the gasworks
    outside Mantua, and of his Virgilian tag,
    'the best days are the first to leave.'

As the train pulled out we entered total mist.
    We choked along an isthmus, so I thought,
    wholly immersed in whiteness like a veil.

'Smooth-sliding Mincius, crowned with vocal reeds,'
    harsh-sliding train carrying one man
    beyond all Lycidases to his Luna Park.

Last to leave! May this be my inscription!
    Light and no vision, such was better than
    a dream, more reassuring than oblivion.

Ahead the Apennines and knowledge that
    the sun would penetrate the mist,
    the soul, that passenger, stand at last

With few regrets on Platform One, changing trains,
    willing to see Mantua again, hoping to make
    the last days best, fleeing fast or slow.

SQUARE HALOES

That the saints should be shown adorned
with the perfect geometrical shape
is not only appropriate, it was designed.
Though cynics have observed that a halo
may look like a noose, we shall prefer
to see it as encircling love, held above the mind.

So the mosaicist cut cheerfully
the whiter pieces of his lapidary stone
to shape this crown without a thorn.
His was the duty of rendering sheep and palms,
the City of God and the hemisphere of Heaven,
but to fashion goodness he could follow a simple form.

The world may not be expelled, of course,
and nobody expects it to be: immanence
is the perfect justification of power.
But distinction goes on being made
between the heavenly and its earthly approaches
and at all times THINE takes precedence of OUR.

Good men are to be honoured, donors prepare
the way, and the present somehow sanctified,
so there by Jordan's waters or at Zion's gates
or ranked below Christ Pantocrator
the living in their squared-up haloes still
anticipate the mad completeness of the saints.

BASTA SANGUE

In the National Gallery of Victoria
Is a nineteenth-century genre painting
Showing a ewe on guard beside the body
Of her dead lamb while all around her sin-
black crows stand silent in the snow. Each time
I pass the picture I find I shudder twice—
Once because good taste is now endemic
And I cannot let the sentimental go
Unsneered at—I have gone to the trouble of
Acquiring words like 'genre' and will call
Them to my aid—but secondly I know
I've been that ewe and soon will be that lamb,
That there's no way to love mankind but on
The improvised coordinates of death,
Death which rules the snow, the crows, the sheep,
The painter and the drifting connoisseur.

Enough of blood, but Abraham's raised knife
Is seldom halted and any place for God
(Even if he didn't give the orders)
Will be outside the frame. A melody
Can gong the executioner's axe awake,
A painting take away our appetite
For lunch, and mother-love still walk all night
To lull a baby quiet. Whatever gathers
Overleaf is murderous: we move
On through the gallery praising Art which keeps
The types of horror constant so that we
May go about our business and forget.

LANDFILL

Where do they go, the dead we've known?
We've seen their bodies variously
Disposed of—in fire, graves, the sea
On hard occasions. Their souls have flown.

That is, the part we now call presence,
The most missed part, is only absence.
A photograph, some words—they're back
To taunt us with their well-aired lack.

Their souls are being used in landfill
At the edge of Heaven, that vent
Notoriously subsident
Needed to house Faith's overspill.

A CHANGE OF SCENE

for Nezil Onur

Between The Gate of Felicity and Aya Sofya
above a flight of steps where vendors offer
woven mittens and a whole saray of scarves
a dog is lying, feet in air, a grimace
set along its jawline, teeth ensnarled.
Asleep or dead? I ask. Dead, I'm told.
Justinian's church is waiting. The dog
looks more itself than other dogs foraying
by the gates. But an occlusion hovers.
What if this were not a case of life departing
but of death arriving? Suppose we live
a negative and die into a positive,
that being born entire but incomplete
we wait for death to come to life in us.
Pallid sky and recurring clouds above the sea,
the midday call to prayer, the Christian
hundredweights well shored against the blue—
I make no gesture but I see the change,
four added minarets, four legs in air.

KEIN VÖGLEIN

While the coffin rests on rollers
a lifetime's words and movements shuffle in
seeded like the muted wood
of crematorium stalls. What used to be a body
stood above the dockside forty years ago
and looked out over slate and martyrdom.
A page not yet written on,
a soul trolleyed out of nothingness
to compass further nothingness—
Absurd to be at an end
but never to have known the start,
no whisper of heavenly death,
no pondering, no pardon,
preposterous assurance that ceasing to be anywhere
will have its resonance.

Those who mourn may hope to hear
how such going brings words to them,
the ridiculous rephrasing of a memory,
parents, schooldays, blind-alley obligations
of the flesh, an adolescent paucity
of inclination. But of the real voice
of love, the catechism of desire
nothing but a stale caesura of the air.

We have heard that solace comes internally,
listening in the dark to our own blood,
knowing the road which everyone will tread,
a chant for unction and forgiveness.
What do we think is being said,
what news of hope for us?
A neap, a nothing,
not a dicky bird.

IF I HAD BOUGHT THAT HOUSE
IN ALEXANDER STREET

If I had bought that house in Alexander Street
I'd have moved into the strange normality
of life on earth. I live on earth hereabouts
but am not properly (i.e. by right of property)
part of life on earth. Yet am I life-in-dream?
(not Coleridge's 'Life in Death'—there are some nightmares
too pure to aspire to, and dream is to earth
as an airbrushed tyrant to a balcony
of red-starred czars)—thus I am waiting
somewhat impatiently for the singularity
to cease. In Science this is the hole whose edges
draw all matter down to non-existence—
in me it's the inescapable web-site
my thinking builds the universe upon,
a hateful egoism whose credulous
insistence undermines all objectivity.
Loping the basket with my cat scratching at its sides
I hurry forward down Alexander Street;
ahead, the vet's light is on; it's early, but it's Winter
and the London darkness settles like the inspissated
black of Conrad's river. There, I say, as if to my
own documentary feature, that's the house
my wife and I so nearly bought in '61—
is it the one where later on I watched
a corpse in zip-up bag brought down by firemen?
The scorching has all gone. My wife has gone, yet she
was palpable and took our cat to see the vet.
A different cat, a different vet, a different wife.
I see us living in the house—we've let the front
run wild, but at the back some roses frown,
an out-of-order gramophone is dumped, a tricycle
squats on a mound of dripping magazines—Stop!
this is the house we never had, it can't be
fantasised to life. We meet, we spend some time together
and we move off to those silences assigned

us in the great star chart of personality—
Schoolboy memories, marching into class,
left, left, I had a good job and I left—
and then the cynic's change—*right, right, I know
what I like and I'm right*—the little glowworms
of our wounded childhood glitter, glitter:
a square piano pounded by an ugly woman,
hair in ringlets, sets the sunlight scalpelling
the grey washed walls. How can tropic brightness
tolerate the smell of piss and eucalypts?
This far-off life has no connection with
the Sunday Readership of Alexander Street;
The Might-Have-been's the land injustice
likes to live in—its slyness even gets to ask
whether the music Mozart wrote is half as good
as what God put him on the earth to write;
he too might need an Alexander Street
to bring the sun out on his patio: but you,
my friends, my glibly juxtaposed inheritors,
my fellow-passengers on the *Lusitania*,
will garden in the endless afternoon of death,
reward attained at last. My cat stays overnight;
thyroid permitting, he'll join me once again
in our occludled exile. We shall plan a globe
to live in out of Rabelais, always good-humoured,
ever stoical, sociologically resourced—
we will not need to walk this way again,
our Alexander Street shall surface everywhere
and if we need to have a house I'll ask
my fate to buy it for me while the price is right.

MYOLA

My father walks his marker down the court
And whitewashes the boundaries line by line.
I'm seasoned to male sweat. The deep sunshine
Of Queensland brings us out for Sunday sport.

The Catholics come after church. We've dined
On charcoaled mutton, knuckles for the dogs.
The ones beneath the roses are his logs
Of loneliness, his bachelordom defined.

Myola is the name above the gate
Of my grandfather's Old Colonial house.
My mother's Sydney certainties arouse
Suspicious feelings in this outlaw state.

Myola we presumes a native name.
Our Anglo–Scottish usurpation seems
To pre-ordain an Eden of our dreams
Waiting in the sun for us to claim.

THE CROSSOVER LIBRARY

for Peter Steele

Because words are poisonous once they're filed
      you must wear protective clothing
when you visit this building for research.
      Its pedigree is poor since it began
with a fire-storm and has declined to just your local,
      but on the other hand such magic stacks
are the fissionable rods of knowledge
      and will not cease to be required
given the *Warspite* circuitings of memory.
      As 'the richest man in Vienna' ordered
the two entertainments will begin together,
      the serious and the popular,
since each is as sentimental as the other,
      though one is loud and long-drawn-out
and the other merely loud. Yes, we will admit it,
      this is not truly a library
but a treffpunkt modelled on the human brain,
      low on storage, high on bias.
It does seem like remembering, but if so
      how do you account for this
quite unfamiliar, utterly regular ascent
      to a not before attempted highest note?
Both sides will swap jerseys when they leave
      the field: you'll see Highbrow
trying not to squirm in Lowbrow's decidedly
      off-colour strip and vice-versa
a sort of thesis-length of greyness deck
      the thorax of a First Division jock.
Doctor Spooner and the *Guardian*'s subs
      are in charge of security—
a Grammarian, shocked by his mobile, snarls
      'You're goddam right, this is
The Return of the Dative', and an Historian sighs
      to his wife, 'No, darling,

we're broke, nothing left but Work and Bills'.
      The oddest of wordings is sacred
and stems from no Gospel: 'Next week, if we're lucky,
      we'll be landing at Athens
where I know I can trust there will be waiting
      the amiable five pound note.!
Has theology anything to offer more rewarding?
      We guard a living Continuum
and this, not the clap of some remote once-offness,
      a challenge boiling in laburnum,
ravens' beaks brimming manna, or that illustrable
      moment when a key change buffs
at Beethoven—this, not National Service, is Life's Drill,
      Once in each career any of us
is promoted to philosophy—that's the moment
      when we recognize that dying
makes us Emperors (*K und K*), and gives us
      importance out of all proportion
to our talent. Swift's wonderment that anyone
      should be so unendowed that he
might envy him for anything applies to God:
      a solemnity we can't prepare for
beckons, as when the angel says you've been elected
      to carry death into adjacence.
The book in your hands now, did you guess
      it would reveal such precedents?
And what did we intend when we warned you
      to avoid a verbal poisoning?
Just to suggest you slip into something
      unclassifiably comfortable,
parry the Adversary with parts of speech,
      fit Carroll's catechisms and
Lichtenberg's non sequiturs on chinos,
      above all, refuse enticements
by Collectors, Archons, Lexicographers,
      and never answer questionnaires
from those devising supplements to dictionaries.
      Babel is twenty/twenty

for accountability in the unreal real world
      and every arcane usage
is crossover from an idiot simplicity.
      Be creative if you must
and stock sonatas up of recitation—
      There came a mortal
but faithless was she and alone dwell forever
      the kings of the sea.
While the mind persists, this will be
      our everlasting rendezvous
and all the shifts of love we've ever known
      may hope that we will find them
as we walk out on the lawn to greet our father.

A HONEYMOON IN 1922

The stars will come out early, and you're tempted
To take them for those proving signs of innocence
A couple close to middle-age might need to risk
Their harmony in a hard conventicle,
And so the frisson when timidity's revoked
Starts on its pilgrimage—a short run into darkness
Or a lifelong limping past emergency.

The Old, the New, the Innocent—labels obscuring
The landscapes straight proposal of inclusion—
In Nineteen Twenty-two you take the chunking train
Up to Caboolture and then by horse and trap
On to Tewantin and its old hotel built round
A tree, and let the river whisper you to sleep
Unscorned by spotter plane, marina, surf or sun.

Buttoned in flannelette up to the neck, the mode
Of gladiators of punt and fishing rod, racquets
Ready for a tennis afternoon, the recruits
Of urban discipline and disappointment
Move out of the sexual silence to a world
Foreshadowed by their dreams, an ancient world
Of simple movement, natural inertness.

At midnight when the bar is closed and the new moon
Shares its darkness with one sleepless phantom,
Stars having fled the scene, it might be possible
To qualify both history and geography
And rearrange the passionless disquiet
Which is Australia, placating its ancestral shapes
Whose harms and clarities bequeath such haunting nights.

Warping the sharpie to a jetty and unloading
A creel half full of whiting, flathead, bream, and one
Lone puffer-fish expiring in the bilge, with parts
Of arms reached by the sun a shade of painful salmon,
The honeymooners tell their fellow-guests they've had
A marvellous day out on the water and retire
To planetary disorder rigmaroled as love.

A PIE FLOATER

It's always a glory day for true specifics
Since this is the way the universe palpates,
That the great theme be amalgamation
And not the many shapes of separation,
Those tiddly cosmoses analysis is left with
After everybody's voice is heard and doubt
Has banged its drum and fallen duly silent.

We are what we swallow and theology proves it.
At this late date the law from vegetarianism
To sustainable growth is so sad a thing—
Judge for yourself, a veritable Benedicite
Howls from the pavement—the trodden gum, the spittle,
The cardboard detritus—and don't you like to think
Liberalism's another form of Natural Selection?

Eat or be eaten/Eat *and* be eaten! Even big lads
Come home from school and report how vilely
They've been bullied. There can't be Socialism, you're told,
Not just because your uncles don't approve it
But by balance of need (you may rename it greed)
And the requirements of love. Living forever might be
A possibility if stem-cells hit on a programme.

Get out on the street and up to the pie-stall:
An island floats in green and gravy, a lung
To breathe through, pastry Laputa happily hovering.
The metaphor is lovely—how could you guess
A world so delicious; what sublimity death
By convulsion bestows on existence, till eyes in
The family portraits-glow with recognition.

The great dream of fairness has vanished forever.
Our shapes are all wrong. However profound
Our notion of God we sprawl on his surface—
A mouth which has just said the word 'hermeneutics'
Bites into crust by light years more real
Than *nouvelle cuisine*—our ancestors sit round a fire
With two reds contending, of light and of blood.

SAILING TO CORMINBOEUF

for Robert Rehder

Listing what stands in my way,
I begin—willpower, passport (which needs renewing)

money, dislike of flying, work outstanding,
the weather, the bus services out of Fribourg—

So it will have to be Istanbul,
(courtesy of the British Council), Queensland,

Ruvo di Puglia (I couldn't get into the Duomo),
Loreto (those frescoes round the Casa Santa)—

But is 'sailing' the right word? Yeats may have gone by ship
but more likely he went overland. One thing,

he was so myopic held never have been able to make out
detail in the mosaics in Sant' Apollinare in Classe.

Some admirers say his 'mackerel-crowded seas'
and later his 'gong-tormented' ones are tributes

to his visionary gift. I prefer to think he injected
tinsel in his veins and went on looking in the mirror.

I don't need to travel to Queensland
as I was brought up there—so I can write about

the old windmills with their corrugated-iron sails,
the dribble of artesian water which they raised

for our school baths, the 'toebiters' living
in the mix of mud and bathers at the bottom,

and, for once, a happy memory, my first cooperative sex,
being seduced in the changing-shed one quiet night.

Yeats went without sex long enough
to see Byzantium—he'd have done better to book

on the Orient Express and visit Sinan's masterpiece,
the Sulimanye Mosque, keeping Holy Wisdom

for his Tower. Yet, like every other poet,
I envy him his confidence his trust in words .

One cannot speak of 'A Byzantium of the Mind'—
everything is in the mind. Corminboeuf is real

but can't belong to me. In poetry it's the fief
of Robert Rehder. It settles contentedly in itself

and wishes nobody to sail to it, not even
if he's borrowed Lawrence's *Ship of Death*.

Literature is snarled with these nail clippings,
phrases which stick in our wool like burrs.

It's true, a wonderful fear is beamed at us,
the gift of dying, but how dishonest it becomes

in Yeatsian splendour. What was he to do
with a lifetime's posturing? He couldn't keep it for the Senate

and poor John Synge was dead. So he sailed and sailed
and ended up as Auden said 'silly like us'.

Time deals with Yeats. But what to do with poetry?
You can stomach-pump the vanity from poets

but not from poetry. Blake on the fool and his folly
simply isn't true. It's wiser not to write at all.

And never to die. As for wish-fulfilment,
today I prefer to admire businessmen-artists,

Palestrina, Rubens, Wallace Stevens. Alas,
I'm not like them, I see myself sailing

to eternal life, but am afraid to go to sleep,
I might dream of Yeats, Byzantium, and Corminboeuf,

I might mistake eternity for somewhere
having no gold or poetry or consciousness.

INITIUM SAPIENTIAE TIMOR DOMINI

All the Latin in the world's inscriptions
will not sweeten the evasions of this little hand.

So wrote the glorious Shakespeare,
'Tex' Shakespeare, that is, teetotal evangelist.

Inside the church geometry prepares
to be as close to heaven as to gravity.

And will its whiteness, brightness, symmetry
yield right of way to the deities of Latin?

Which reminds me I prefer Stravinsky's *Nightingale*
in French (I learned it as *Le Rossignol*.)

And this despite my aversion to that language—
as Death leaves him, the Emperor sings 'Bon Jour à tous!'

Does that include the Lord of this inscription
which I chose because I wanted a Latin title,

One I could translate at sight,
unlike the abbreviations on so many tombs?

Though Borromini killed himself, I feel
he's like Stravinsky's Emperor,

Saying 'Good Morning' genially each morning
to the world at the foot of the bed,

The Angel of Death having just relented.
One morning I shan't be able to write

About Borromini, Stravinsky or myself
and the world will miss some valuable redundancies.

Here in San Ivo I began to feel
the necessity of praising worldly power.

The reason? To leave something behind you
when you go: one good church deserves another.

To know the beginning of wisdom is the need to work
and to endure the rage this knowledge brings.

Everyone is so ambitious—what on earth
were all those massacres and slaughters for?

Was it to add another patch to the great quilt
of authority? The stitches of an envy?

Someone has given me a book of poems,
Schlegel Eats a Bagel, the higher joking.

The shame is overwhelming. Pray for me, Borromini,
on your unhappy craftsman's scaffold,

Tell me that style is all important
and beside the point. Inscribe the truth:

All poetry is language poetry, but
not all language poetry is poetry.

BOTH ENDS AGAINST THE MIDDLE

Deep inside the Imperial War Museum
Where children are surprised by undreamt dreams
        Destruction's most impartial theorem,
The Rolls-Royce Merlin Aircraft Engine, gleams.

It seems just lowered by Donatello's tackle:
He would have known why copper pipes entwine
        So murderous a tabernacle
And where control and fate might share a line.

Would we be right to look for innocence
Or guess that need to kill has shaped such grace?
        Here uncompanionable Science
Is linked to everything that is the case.

In similar mode the sculptor's brilliant carving
Regains in bronze a living massacre.
        Death eats, the vivid world is starving,
Each holocaust become a shepherd's star.

The Spitfire's engine's once kinetic fury
And Donatello's layered appetite
        Are Humanism's judge and jury,
The Alpha and Omega of delight.

A REAL VISIBLE MATERIAL HAPPINESS

The poetry we say makes nothing happen
Is being interrupted in my flat
By Sondheim tapes played loudly just above.
If I were Rilke I'd personify love
As the old Objectivist Geheimrat
To whom all self-admiring hands come cap-in.

That way I'd solve the highly systematic
Problem the modern poet has of how
To fill his poems up with real things
But serve abstraction: so one writes of wings
Alongside sunlight, CDs, a red cow,
The Broadway noises coming from the attic.

You should rely on stuff to keep you happy.
Excitement fades away, you can't take joy
Morning after morning. Sothebys may call,
The cat-scratched sofa look right in the hall,
Dreams be scattered like a lost convoy
And everything improvable stay crappy.

THE DAUGHTERS REMEMBER THE FATHERS

'For my Father on his birthday',
Gift only innocence would make,
Schoolgirl essays' gauche display,
A Notebook garlands for his sake
She wills the hapless words to say
Between ruled lines that hearts will break.

A perfect love cannot exist
But children, put in ideal's pawn,
In homes of dogs and nets and whist,
Are told that by their being born
Lamps are lit, the raised face kissed,
And heaven tented on the lawn.

And afterwards the daughters tread
The same indoctrinating path,
The several uses of a bed,
Untruth's plaster, habit's lath,
The mouths in nests which must be fed,
Agamemnon in his bath.

The world keeps all this in its view.
Daughters turned mothers change their creed
And bottle truths as they accrue.
In hospitals the fathers bleed:
'Daddy, what have they done to you?'
Is all the forgiveness they'll concede,

LE JUGEMENT DES URNES

Were does she sit, casting her vote,
His ordinary and spectacular mother,
Seeing everything in Heaven, afloat
On love of her son, supreme survivor
Of death and disfiguration? Remote
From responsibility, will she wrap
Him in happiness, her many-coloured coat?

And across a divide of fear from her,
His other guardian, still dressed in pain,
Dawn-gazing ever—is she thinking of how
She can help him, or is she dreaming again
Of never existing? And should she try,
A forsaken Ariadne, to explain
Forgiveness to him, because he weeps for her?

His two angels have not yet spoken
And did he but know it are his accusers
As well as his intercessors. Woken
From their dream of blaming, they must listen
To his plea of extenuation—a broken
Will in one and in the other a broken heart,
And from each one's hand the casting token.

RECREATIONAL DRUGS

My scary drug was Reason; I got by
On several priggish antidotes to doom.
Today I watch the gilded young get high
On skunkweed in a downstairs billiard-room,

Whenever someone smokes or sniffs or swallows,
Tries dangerous sex, the end-of-century kick,
It's Dionysus scorning all Apollo's
Actuarial arithmetic.

My contrary manoeuvres when I blacked
My nervous system out in reasoned hope
Were planned to keep the world of sex intact
With love on hand as recreational dope.

NEIGHBOURHOOD WATCH

Out there all virtue passes through a prism
And dissipates, foregrounding selfishness.
White light from God is coloured by the schism,
Mother and Father rant, it's Liberalism.

Amelioration is most hateful. Make better
Leaves the unimproved part narcolept.
We've always been imprisoned, so the fetter
Tends the sore, the law lights up the letter.

There's some relief when I sit down to play—
A singing right hand and a listening left.
Lord God of skilfulness, grant me today
Your true rubato, your profound delay.

Then let my body's hunger be the Watch
Kept in the Garden, spirit's resurrection,
But don't stare so, or not right at my crotch,
And wash away the clawing crab with Scotch.

A SKIN THAT SHRILLS

'In den schönen Feierkleidern
Dir mir meine Mutter gab'
                    —Hofmannsthal

Who may doubt it's criminal to despair,
So many constant minds have faced the facts
And matched great thought to situations where

Only connivance made sense of the acts?
Sam Johnson lanced his dropsy but that's not
The sort of triumph meant. Nor quite those pacts

With Devils, croupier Gods, the Huguenot,
The Catholic, 'the Meeting by the River',
Eternal Youth, Stigmata, dot dot dot

The problem rests: do we regard the giver
As greatly good or are receivers blessed
Being a good man's chance? And should your liver

If stout enough claim virtue in excess
Not wasting to cirrhosis though your days
Be boiled in drink—is this your mystic dress?

Which girl expects a God, his limbs ablaze,
To carry her to Constellation X?
That scarring now, that's just a playground graze?

Our several skins are living's bibliotheques.
We're stitched in metaphor—eyes' cataracts
Pose as Tiresias's pebble specs.

It all ends when it ends; the artefacts
We put in tombs, like masks declare
Eternity comes down to one fixed stare,
A surface art for sensuous didacts.

BRAINS ON YOUR SHOES

In the heyday of Hong Kong, late
Nineteen Sixties, when the fate

Of thousands hung on good results
In examinations and the pulse

Beat faster once a year as mail
Brought judgement with its Pass or Pail,

Old Hands who knew the Colony
Preferred to stay at home than be

Forced to walk about outside
Beneath apartments and high rise.

The cult was Hard Work: Chinese pride
Ran all the way to suicide

And life endured constant stress
At the altar of the God Success.

Tall balconies and a frowning sky
Gave Failure lines to measure by,

And no one in the Month of News
Wanted to get brains on his shoes.

THE SHELLFISH GENE

In theory Evolution's just as open
To altruism as to selfishness
But as the waters lave me I betoken
No abstraction beyond shellfishness.

The problem is our tide-warped mensuration.
We live not long, our scale is planetary;
Just single soldiers of a warrior nation,
Time-truncated, ex-explanatory.

I can't be pictured but in diagram,
Yet this one shell's to me a satrapy—
A trillion more of me and still I am
Like Atreus's House an atrophy.

'The Rocks! The Rocks!' ten thousand voices quicken.
Some self-inspired things from sea have waddled
And others seen their adaptation sicken,
Myself in sheer adjacence safely swaddled.

JUMPING SHIP

Though we shall never travel to the stars
We've put a rover on the face of Mars
And all the troubles which on earth accrue
Will soon apply to the red planet too.

The sun appears above a salmon sky
Lighting the Martian genius loci
And stalking plains, no living creature thriving,
Reveals a solemn sight, of rats arriving.

ALL WE LIKE SHEEP

How blessed we have become of late,
    The offspring of statistics,
A million million share one fate,
    The same for sloths as mystics.

Our scientists catch up with God,
    A hubris of intending—
They sack the goats, give sheep the nod,
    Mark human beings pending.

Caligula foresaw their coup
    By dint of wild surmising,
Proclaimed the people's neck hacked through
    An ethical downsizing.

From ledgers where till now the Lord's
    Bookkeepers scanned their systems
Shall fade all trivial fond records,
    As one life fills existence.

Yes, *Dolly, Polly and the Clones*
    Will top the charts forever,
Their Hit of Hits, 'And shall these bones
    Live?' rate each ram a wether.

It's Transference: the lives of sheep
    Attract our metaphoring,
Our guilty cries reduced by sleep
    To atavistic snoring.

NIJINSKY'S LEAP

This is just one of the ways
of imitating music.

How can we do anything valuable
who are tied to meaning?
I leap, I jump, I stay still
on top of the air. Can a musician do that?
I am working on vibrating at the top,
And not coming down.

The men who interview me
at this hospital don't believe
I am still at the top. They talk to me
only when I come down.
I am definitely here
but I have not come down.
Because I am on top
I will not leap further. They want me
to admit I am a dancer.

Please, I am not a dancer,
I am the man who drives the poleaxe
and kills the animals.

I could exaggerate
and say everything smells of blood.
But if everything did smell of blood
we would eat only vegetables.
We are not hardened,
we are not habituated,
we can love animals.

But it is what we have done to animals
(ourselves included)
which has made me mad—
i.e. in shadow, insane,
when I'm out of the sun.

And I see it, see him,
that mask with its shoebrush moustache,
that penis in astrakhan—

Ever since that day
I have been dancing away from him
though I've always known
he owned all the music.
I've had to learn to dance without music.

Now I dance all the time
without sets, without ballet-master,
without Chopin and Weber,
in my old man's costume,
my fat body and shrunken legs.

To be with God
you must hear no music.

Your beautiful imitations—
believe in them. In the uterus
it is dark, it is a place of pure sound,
of eternal adjacence. Let no light in
and then you can leap.

JAM ON THE PIANO KEYS

1

Had they wiped it off and kept the kids in order
Borodin's Fourth might have graced the air,
But don't leap to the future, view the now—
A Russian family with its children playing,
Sleds in the garden, Mother in fur hat
And happiness a revolution words allow.

How could you match this in the concert hall?
Are the demands of chemistry as mystical
As Rasputin's touch? Didn't Mendelyev
Compose the Periodic Table? Wonders of the mind
Are underpinned by duty (including getting drunk—
Mussorgsky!)—The Queen of the Night's high F

Or Alexander at the bench with tubes!
We'll keep this Nineteenth-Century Primitive
Where measurement goes all the way to God.
Leave it to Rimsky is the cry of all,
Including Balakirev—our composerholic
Battles with chords to build his Novgorod.

2

Skip a century and look out on the lawn,
The kids are playing while the TV rests.
Among the china ducks (the house is hired)
A poet plays at dying hoping for
A shift to seriousness from soft diurnal—
The kids, he thinks, won't come in till they're tired.

Love and the dead are sufficient subject matter.
The little buggers get jam on the piano keys.
Thank Heaven a poet needs only a page
To play the monster. Given or chosen feelings?
Either will work in lights on his keyboard,
His favourite children vanity and rage.

SCHUBERT'S DOG

The ladies are waving their declamatory scarves
To welcome back our darling 'Little Mushroom',
And I'm at my old place behind his chair,
A furry pedal to his wandering feet.

But I have ears to hear what they cannot—
A middle rage composed of poisoned sweets
Inside old revelry, a breakdown of
The very air which carries joy to them.

He won't live long and dogs live shorter still,
But what's proportion got to do with it?
For while he plays a slippered appetite
For life makes living sweetly pleonastic.

A big word for a dog and bigger at still
For angels of the keyboard keyed to God
Whom these respectables have camphored in
Their consciences, like silence after singing.

The ladies' dresses reach right to the floor.
A dog might look at ankles and think breasts.
Franz pounds the pedal, several scented queens
Are being strangled by the shores of Alpine lakes.

Bitter and sweet, the cliché underlined—
We have these old materials, the flesh,
The hearing, logarithms elevated
Like the Host and anchored everywhere.

What wished-for ending nestles in high waists?
He must go on, he says to Kupelwieser,
The storm of life will not blow out, the only
Cure for masterpieces is to die.

TO MY GRANDAUGHTERS
SWEEPING SPELSBURY CHURCH

It's August and hay-fever weather,
We've left the house in Summer's tether—
While you girls scamper hell-for-leather
   And climb the wall
Our adult hopes are all on whether
   We'll find the Earl.

The youthful Earl of Rochester
In this small parish church interred
Proclaims the triumph of the word,
   A true contrition,
For penitence is gravely heard
   In a patrician.

A bully, fiend and alcoholic,
A brilliant Hobbesean melancholic,
A frightened sinner, parabolic,
   Yet first and foremost
A mind which rendered apostolic
   Sad Reason's ghost.

What would we find if we, instead
Of looking pious, raised the lid
Of where he lies encased in lead—
   Memento mori?
I doubt it—when the flesh has fled
   All's nugatory.

His soul which bigotry would save
Is shrunk to copper in the nave,
A mere inscription, Thus the grave
   Keeps all in sight
And wife and son may only have
   A year's respite.

But bouncing through the door, you girls
Pounce on the verger and with skirls
Of laughter, sudden whirls and curls,
　　　　Take up his broom,
Then, like George Herbert, for the Earl's
　　　　Sake sweep the room.

When Martha and Amelia raise
A little dust to rightly praise
The magnitude of other days,
　　　　They're only playing—
It's Grandad's pompous paraphrase
　　　　Which is dismaying.

Life works the other way around:
It's what George Herbert saw which wound
His metaphor into his sound—
　　　　A parish priest,
He'd keep his ear to the ground
　　　　This much at least.

So give the verger back his broom
And let the Earl sleep out his doom,
I must return to London soon
　　　　And you to Rome—
Though you're not Catholic, you assume
　　　　There God's at home.

Is Oxfordshire more savoury
Than the ill-swept Trastevere?
Is Rome all foreign knavery?
　　　　Our cows are mad,
Our people sunk in slavery,
　　　　Our climate bad.

But still we speak a language which
The whole world seems to have an itch
To learn, and this may make you rich—
      England supporters—
And since you don't stray on the pitch,
      Dutiful daughters.

SASSETTA'S EPITAPH

What in this lapdog world may be duly sainted
May also by imagination's hand be painted.

Sassetta's polyptych from Borgo San Sepolcro
In London's National Gallery is still on show.

Or parts of it—and there St Francis lives once more
Along one wall, interrupted by a door.

It isn't picturesque, it may even be chilling
To see what Spirit endures if Flesh is willing.

But paint is the eye's true blood and blood must dry
On man and stone and animal and sky.

MUTANT PROVERBS REVISITED

Live? Our savants will do that for us.
It's never too late to spend.
The king was in his counting-house discounting all his money.
There's a pot of gold at the end of the rainforest.
Pantomime horse, Sibling Cavalry.
The Sermon on the Mint.
And on the Seventh Day he rusted.
She shall have Muzak, Asda and Waitrose.
Room at the tap.
The shortest distance between two pints.
The bigger they are the harder they fall on you.
Is there a doctor in the hearse?
Love at first slight.
A Dame Luck economy.
This Happy Greed.
Once more unto the beach, dear friends.
The road to Hell is paved with good inventions.
Room for one more outside.
Damn relaxes, bless embraces.
Wait till you see the whites of their ties.
La belle dame sans souci.
Tomorrow is another delay.
The courage of his defections.
When did you last see your future?
Anglican indignation—Savlonarola.
Market Forceps.
Promises, premises.
Patriotism is the last refuge of a scandal.
The Gloss of Innocence.
Technique shall inherit the earth.

ECHT DEUTSCH

A short suite of German Lieder managed into English

Wanderers Nachtlied (Goethe)
The Wanderer's Song at Night

Above the mountain peaks
everything's at peace,
no living creature speaks.
You will not hear
among the trees
the least incursion of a breeze.
Birds fall silent in the wood.
O heart oppressed,
only wait, soon
you too will be at rest.

Anakreons Grab (Goethe)
The Grave of Anacreon

Here where roses unfold, where the vine and the laurel entwine,
Where the turtledove calls and the cricket's cry rattles on yet,
Whose grave is this? It is Anacreon's. He, whom the gods
Gave long life and renown to, rests peacefully here.
Spring and Summer and Autumn nurtured the fortunate poet
And now the grave's mound keeps him from Winter's onset.

Epiphanias (Goethe)
Epiphany

Three Kings of Orient, travelling with their star,
Three eating drinking, drinking eating travellers we are,
Eating's fine, drinking's fine, but paying is a bore.

Three Kings of Orient are knocking at your door,
If one more came in with them, there would then be four,
Three Kings on your doorstep, no room for anymore.

I'm the first, the white one, the bright one, the cute,
See me by daylight with my spices and my lute,
Yet girls don't care much for me, despite my great repute.

I, on the other hand, am brown and tall and strong,
All the women know me and listen to my song,
'Brown and gold together, gold and brown belong'.

Now we come to little me; I'm black and minuscule,
Life and soul of the party, the Marquess of Misrule,
I love to eat and drink as well, and never lose my cool.

Three Kings of Orient, with good intentions armed,
Looking for the Mother and the Christ-Child in her arms,
Joseph and the oxen, down on the farm.

We bring you myrrh to cherish, we bring you all our gold,
We bring you fragrant frankincense to make the ladies bold,
And drink your health a dozen times to keep out the cold.

But what see we here: no ox or asses in a stall,
Only ladies and gentlemen and top coats in a hall,
No Manger and no Saviour, so good night to you all!

Die Götter Griechenlands (Schiller)
The Gods of Greece [one stanza of a longer poem]

Shining World, what has become of you?
Return again resplendent Age of Nature.
Song's magic lore alone can now make true
The graceful imprint of your fabled creatures.
The countryside laments its desolation,
The gods have gone away: the ruined scene
Once warm with every touch of animation
Is but a shadow framing what has been.

Der Arme Peter (Heine)
Poor Peter's World

1

Hans and his Grete are dancing for joy
And shouting at friends impolitely.
Poor Peter is hardly that sort of boy,
His chalky face grimaces whitely.

Hans and his Grete are bridegroom and bride
Decked in their wedding clothes brightly.
Poor Peter's chewed fingernails hang by the side
Of his overalls torn and unsightly.

Poor Peter is talking just to himself,
His friends observe him contritely—
'If I weren't so sensible, I'd kill myself,
But I'd be sure to do it quietly.'

2

I have a pain here in my breast
Which splits my heart asunder,
Wherever I go, from east to west,
The only way is under.

It takes me to my darling's side—
Perhaps she has the power
To heal me, but to save my pride
I flee from her and cower.

I clamber to the mountain top
And here where I choose to stop
Where nobody will find me
My falling tears blind me.

3

A figure staggers past the door,
Limping, deathly pale—it's Poor
Peter, and the desperate sight
Stands people stock still in the street.

The young girls hardly dare to wave,
'He must have climbed up from the grave!'
Ah, no, you ladies kind and knowing,
Rather, the grave is where he's going.

He's lost his love—the grave's the place
He'll see her always face to face,
Where true affections don't decay
But sleep on till the Judgment Day.

Mein Wagen rollet langsam (Heine)
My carriage rolls on slowly

My carriage rolls on slowly
through woods of welcoming green,
along flowering valleys—Summer's
magic transformation scene.

I sit and remember and dream
and think of my sweetheart away,
when three vague shadow-shaped figures
enter the coach, heads asway—

They skip and grimace, make faces
so mocking and timid at once,
and swirl with the mist, then together
vanish with sniggers and grunts.

Die Stille (Eichendorff)
Quietness

Nobody knows or can guess at
How contented I am, how content!
I'd tell you but think it's best that
My days are in quietness spent.

Outside lies the snow at its densest,
Such silence and secrecy there!
The stillness which fills all my senses
Is set as the stars in the air.

I wish I were a small bird who
Flies over forest and sea
And never stop till I come to
Wherever Heaven may be.

Hälfte des Lebens (Hölderlin)
Halfway through Life

Hung with burnished pears
And full of wild roses,
The land above the lake—
And gracious swans there
Drunk with kissing
Dip their high heads
In holy sobering water—

Alas, where have they gone,
In Winter time, the flowers, and where
The beaming sun
And shadows on the earth?
The walls still stand
Silent and cold; the wind
Blurs the weather-vanes.

Der Gärtner (Mörike)
The Gardener

Atop her prancing stallion
as white as falling snow
the most exquisite Princess is
riding down the Row.

And where her dazzling mount goes
stepping high and bold
the garden sand I scattered
glistens as if gold.

You little rose-pink hat that
goes bobbing up and down,
Oh drop a single feather
shyly on its own

And if you want a flower
to fill your beauty's rift
take one or take a thousand—
all are in my gift.

Um Mitternacht (Mörike)
At Midnight

And now the night is covering up the land,
The mountains dream beneath its giving hand.
It watches how time, running-on, entails
A golden mean of equally balanced scales,
But yet how -boldly jutting dreams appear
And whisper to the night, their mother's ear,
About today, the day that was today.

The water's old and primal lullaby
She hardly notes, or hears it pass her by;
Far sweeter to her sounds the Heaven's blue,
The fleeting hours unyoked, then lost to view.
But those untiring streams keep murmuring
And in their sleep shall never cease to sing
About today, the day that was today.

Da unten im Tale (Folksong)
Down in the Valley

Down in the valley the drab waters run,
I can't let you know for me you're the one!

You've a big mouth for loving—you'll always be true,
And with fingers crossed, you'll be faithful too,

If I tell you I love you ten times a day
And you stay looking smug, then I'll scarper—OK?

But thanks all the same for the love we once had:
I'll take the good times, leave you the bad.

Klage an das Volk (Schubert)*
Lament Addressed to the People

Youth of our Days, gone like the Days of our Youth!
The People's strength, unnumbered impotence,
The Crowd's gross pressure without consequence,
The Insignificant our only glimpse of Truth.

The Power I wield springs always from my Pain,
That remnant of a preternatural striving.
I cannot act, and Time with its conniving,
Treats all our deeds with infinite disdain.

*Schubert's last poem, not set to music by him.

The Nation lets its Sickness make it old,
Youth's works are dreams which every dawn disperses—
So soon forgotten are those sacred Verses
That Faith would once have written out in gold.

To Art alone, that noble calling, falls
The task of leavening a world of Action
And give relief in time of brawling Faction
To those whom Fate has huddled within walls.

ACKNOWLEDGEMENTS

Acknowledgements are due to the editors of the following periodicals and newspapers in which some of the poems included in *Both Ends Against the Middle* first appeared: *Adelaide Review*, *The Age*, *Ambit*, *Antipodes*, *Eureka Street*, *Heat*, *Interchange*, *London Magazine*, *Meanjin*, *Salt*, *The Sunday Times*, *The Times Literary Supplement*, *Ulitarra*, *Westerly*. A considerable number were written while I was receiving a Fellowship from The Literature Board of the Australia Council. I am especially grateful to the Board for its help at such a crucial stage in my career as a writer.

OXFORD POETS

Fleur Adcock
Moniza Alvi
Joseph Brodsky
Basil Bunting
Tessa Rose Chester
Daniela Crăsnaru
Greg Delanty
Michael Donaghy
Keith Douglas
Antony Dunn
D. J. Enright
Roy Fisher
Ida Affleck Graves
Ivor Gurney
Gwen Harwood
Anthony Hecht
Zbigniew Herbert
Tobias Hill
Thomas Kinsella
Brad Leithauser
Jamie McKendrick

Sean O'Brien
Alice Oswald
Peter Porter
Craig Raine
Zsuzsa Rakovszky
Christopher Reid
Stephen Romer
Eva Salzman
Carole Satyamurti
Peter Scupham
Jo Shapcott
Penelope Shuttle
Goran Simić
Anne Stevenson
George Szirtes
Grete Tartler
Edward Thomas
Charles Tomlinson
Marina Tsvetaeva
Chris Wallace-Crabbe
Hugo Williams